Deweyan Transactionalism in Education

Also Available from Bloomsbury

Cherishing and the Good Life of Learning: Ethics, Education, Upbringing, Ruth Cigman
Children, Religion and the Ethics of Influence, John Tillson
Hannah Arendt on Educational Thinking and Practice in Dark Times: Education for a World in Crisis, edited by Wayne Veck and Helen M. Gunter
Friedrich Froebel: A Critical Introduction to Key Themes and Debates, Tina Bruce
Lacan and Education Policy: The Other Side of Education, Matthew Clarke
Paulo Freire: A Philosophical Biography, Walter Omar Kohan
Politics and Pedagogy in the "Post-Truth" Era: Insurgent Philosophy and Praxis, Derek R. Ford
Wonder and Education: On the Educational Importance of Contemplative Wonder, Anders Schinkel

Deweyan Transactionalism in Education

Beyond Self-action and Inter-action

Edited by
Jim Garrison, Johan Öhman and Leif Östman

BLOOMSBURY ACADEMIC
LONDON • NEW YORK • OXFORD • NEW DELHI • SYDNEY

BLOOMSBURY ACADEMIC
Bloomsbury Publishing Plc
50 Bedford Square, London, WC1B 3DP, UK
1385 Broadway, New York, NY 10018, USA
29 Earlsfort Terrace, Dublin 2, Ireland

BLOOMSBURY, BLOOMSBURY ACADEMIC and the Diana logo
are trademarks of Bloomsbury Publishing Plc

First published in Great Britain, 2022
This paperback edition published in 2023

Copyright © Jim Garrison, Johan Öhman, Leif Östman and Bloomsbury, 2022

Jim Garrison, Johan Öhman, Leif Östman and Bloomsbury have asserted their right under the Copyright, Designs and Patents Act, 1988, to be identified as Author of this work.

For legal purposes the Acknowledgements on p. xiv constitute
an extension of this copyright page.

Cover design by Charlotte James
Cover image © shulz/Getty Images

All rights reserved. No part of this publication may be reproduced or transmitted in any form or by any means, electronic or mechanical, including photocopying, recording, or any information storage or retrieval system, without prior permission in writing from the publishers.

Bloomsbury Publishing Plc does not have any control over, or responsibility for, any third-party websites referred to or in this book. All internet addresses given in this book were correct at the time of going to press. The author and publisher regret any inconvenience caused if addresses have changed or sites have ceased to exist, but can accept no responsibility for any such changes.

A catalogue record for this book is available from the British Library.

Library of Congress Cataloging-in-Publication Data
Names: Garrison, James W., 1949- editor. | Öhman, Johan, editor. |
Östman, Leif, editor.
Title: Deweyan transactionalism in education: beyond self-action and
inter-action / edited by Jim Garrison, Johan Öhman and Leif Östman.
Description: London; New York: Bloomsbury Academic, 2022. |
Includes bibliographical references and index.
Identifiers: LCCN 2021035353 (print) | LCCN 2021035354 (ebook) |
ISBN 9781350233317 (hardback) | ISBN 9781350233324 (pdf) |
ISBN 9781350233331 (ebook)
Subjects: LCSH: Action research in education. | Dewey, John, 1859-1952.
Classification: LCC LB1028.24.D48 2022 (print) |
LCC LB1028.24 (ebook) | DDC 370.72–dc23
LC record available at https://lccn.loc.gov/2021035353
LC ebook record available at https://lccn.loc.gov/2021035354

ISBN: HB: 978-1-3502-3331-7
PB: 978-1-3502-3335-5
ePDF: 978-1-3502-3332-4
eBook: 978-1-3502-3333-1

Typeset by Integra Software Services Pvt. Ltd.

To find out more about our authors and books visit www.bloomsbury.com
and sign up for our newsletters.

Contents

List of Illustrations		vii
List of Contributors		ix
Acknowledgements		xiv

1	Introduction *Jim Garrison, Johan Öhman and Leif Östman*	1
2	Philosophers' Problems: Transaction in Philosophy and Life *Frank X. Ryan*	17
3	Transactional Perspectivalism: The Emergence of Language, Minds, Selves, and Temporal Sequences *Jim Garrison*	39
4	Transactional Systems of Exploration and Learning *William J. Clancey*	51
5	Democracy, Education, and Transaction: The Importance of Play in Dewey's Thought *Andrea Fiore*	75
6	Applications of Transactional Methodologies for Analysis of Teaching and Learning Processes *Pernilla Andersson and Johan Öhman*	87
7	Analyzing Teachers' Functional Coordination of Teaching Habits in the Encounter with Policy Reforms *Malena Lidar and Eva Lundqvist*	99
8	Learning through Encounters with the Physical Environment *Susanne Klaar and Johan Öhman*	111
9	The Dramaturgy of Facilitating Learning Processes: A Transactional Theory and Analytical Approach *Katrien Van Poeck and Leif Östman*	123
10	Transactants in Action—Examples from a Craft Remake School Project *Hanna Hofverberg*	137
11	Sensing Together: Transaction in Handicraft Education *Jonas Risberg and Joacim Andersson*	149
12	The Museum as Exploration *Petra Hansson and Johan Öhman*	165
13	Aesthetic Experiences and Artistic Creation: A Transactional Analysis of Learning in Computer Programming *Michael Håkansson, Lennart Rolandsson and Leif Östman*	179

14 A Transactional Perspective on Ethics and Morals *Louise Sund and Johan Öhman*   193
15 Transactional Analyses of the Entanglement of the Aesthetical, Moral and Political in Learning Processes *Michael Håkansson and Leif Östman*   207
16 Links between Pandemics, Politics, and People *Ninitha Maivorsdotter and Joacim Andersson*   221

Notes   233
References   236
Index   250

Illustrations

Figures

2.1	The Containment Predicament	18
2.2	Mind-Dependence and Mind-Independence	19
2.3	Mind-Dependence	20
2.4	The Circuit Inquiry	22
2.5	Containment within Inference	24
2.6	Existence and Experience in Interactional and Transactional Pragmatism	31
2.7	The Reciprocity of "How" and "What"	35
4.1	*Okeanos* exploration system—telepresence-enabled ocean exploration	53
4.2	Examples of images publicly available during a dive, illustrating (clockwise from upper left) varied geology, control room onboard *Okeanos Explorer*, animal life, and using temperature probe with ROV robotic arm	54
4.3	*Okeanos* exploration system dependent hierarchy	57
4.4	*Okeanos Explorer* Control Room, showing morning deployment of Seirios (top middle), ROV (top right), inset of Bridge Deck Officer (top left), ROV engineers, and scientists sitting in the back	61
4.5	Lines of communication during a dive	62
4.6	Robotically mediated work system design	64
4.7	Imaginary oppositions shown as dependent hierarchies, most generally showing a designed or natural system/organism in an environment. (Concept adapted from Wilden, 1987: 82)	69
4.8	Broader view of the dependent hierarchy of the *Okeanos* exploration system	71
12.1	Whipped Peter	172
12.2	Black Students Integrate Little Rock's Central High School	174
13.1	The trajectory of learning with four phases	181
14.1	The circle of moral doubt-belief (adapted from Ryan 2011: 21)	201

Table

15.1 A Model of Transactional Learning Moral and Political Concerns *for*   209

Contributors

Joacim Andersson is Senior Lecturer in Sport Sciences at Malmö University, Sweden. Andersson seeks to clarify philosophical and sociological concepts in order to empirically explore transactional specificities of embodied learning. He has pioneered the development of important methodological and theoretical innovations in the research group SMED (Studies of Meaning-Making in Educational Discourses). He is the lead author of two book chapters on the topic of transactional and artistic learning in the book *Learning Movements: New Perspectives of Movement Education* (2020). His publications have recently appeared in *Qualitative Health Research, Physical Education and Sport Pedagogy*, and *Qualitative Research in Sport, Exercise and Health*.

Pernilla Andersson is Senior Lecturer in Social Sciences Education at Stockholm University, Sweden, and Researcher in Educational Sciences at Uppsala University, Sweden, where she focuses on sustainability, economic, and social sciences education. She is a member of the research environment SMED and has used a transactional methodology in combination with "logics of critical explanation" for studies of teaching and learning processes. Her most recent publication is a book chapter entitled "Embodied Experiences of 'Decision-Making' in the Face of Uncertain and Complex Sustainability Issues" in *Sustainable Development Teaching: Ethical and Political Challenges* (eds. Van Poeck, Östman and Öhman, 2019).

Michael Håkansson is Senior Lecturer in the Department of Education at Stockholm University, Sweden. His research explores how political conflicts can be educative in teaching activities such as citizenship education and education for sustainable development. Among his recent publications are Wildemeersch, D., Læssøe, J. and Håkansson, M. (2021), "Young Sustainability Activists as Public Educators: An Aesthetic Approach," *European Educational Research Journal*, and Håkansson. M & Östman, L (2019), "The Political Dimension in ESE: The Construction of a Political Moment Model for Analyzing Bodily Anchored Political Emotions in Teaching and Learning of the Political Dimension," *Environmental Education Research*, 25:4, 585–600.

Jim Garrison is Professor of Philosophy of Education at Virginia Tech University, USA. He was Chancellors Visiting Professor at Uppsala University, Sweden (2014–18). He is past-president of the Philosophy of Education Society and the John Dewey Society. He has books and papers published in ten languages other than English. Garrison's most recent book is *Empirical Philosophical Investigations in Education and Embodied Experience* (2018), co-authored with Joacim Andersson and Leif Östman.

Bill Clancey is Senior Research Scientist at the Florida Institute for Human and Machine Cognition, Florida, USA. He earned a Computer Science PhD from Stanford University, USA, in 1979 and Mathematical Sciences BA from Rice University, USA, in 1974. He developed artificial intelligence applications for medicine, education, finance, robotics, and spaceflight systems, including ethnographic methods for modeling work systems (Institute for Research on Learning, 1987–97) and agent systems (NASA Ames Research Center, Chief Scientist of Human-Centered Computing, Intelligent Systems Division, 1998–2013). He is Fellow of the American College of Medical Informatics, Association for Psychological Science, Association for Advancement of AI, and the National Academy of Inventors.

Andrea Fiore is Assistant Professor of Contemporary History at the Pontifical Salesian University, Rome, Italy. He was awarded his PhD in 2018 with a dissertation on the emotions, connecting J.S. Mill, William James and John Dewey. He published "Il valore pedagogico del gioco in John Dewey" (2019) in *Per la filosofia. Filosofia e insegnamento*, a journal that deals with issues of philosophy and education. He also published (2020) the chapter "Storia e memoria per un'educazione alla vita politica: riflessioni sulla proposta di Martha Nussbaum," in the book Butera R. – Caneva C. (eds.), *La vita si fa storia. Narrare, ricordare, costruire.*

Petra Hansson has a PhD in Education and works as Senior Lecturer at Uppsala University, Sweden. Her research interests concern relations between aesthetics, literary studies, and meaning-making within the context of Environmental and Sustainability Education and Museum Education. Her research combines empirical discourse analyses with conceptual and methodological development. Her most recent publication is, "Teaching as a Matter of Staging Encounters with Literary Texts in Environmental and Sustainability Education," in *Sustainable Development Teaching: Ethical and Political Challenges* (eds. Van Poeck, K., Östman, L. and Öhman, J., 2019).

Hanna Hofverberg is Associate Senior Lecturer in the Department of Natural Science, Mathematics and Society at Malmö University, Sweden. She has a PhD in Educational Science with a specialization in Environmental and Sustainability Education (ESE) and Arts and Crafts Education. Her research interest focuses on teaching and learning, sustainability, remaking activities, reverse engineering, post-fossil pedagogy, learning environments, aesthetics, and new materialism. She has published in *Environmental Education Research* and in the *Nordic STS Journal*. Her latest papers have been submitted to the *International Journal of Art and Design Education* and *Techne – research in Sloyd Education and Craft Science*.

Malena Lidar is Senior Lecturer in Education in the Department of Education, Uppsala University, Sweden. Her research focuses on various aspects of teaching and learning; for example, how science teaching and science teachers' views of science can change as a result of educational reforms; how knowledge, values, and power relations are linked in the classroom; and how teaching-developing research can be conducted. A recent publication is Lidar, M., Lundqvist, E., Ryder, J., and Östman, L. (2020), "The Transformation of Teaching Habits in Relation to the Introduction of Grading and National Testing in Science Education in Sweden," *Research in Science Education*.

Eva Lundqvist is Senior Lecturer in Curriculum Studies in the Department of Education, Uppsala University, Sweden. She mainly conducts research on learning and socialization in Science Education. Besides the research interest in sociocultural studies of classroom interaction, her research focuses on educational reforms and the potential impact on teachers' practices. In her current research, she is focusing on research-based development of teaching, a work that is done in close collaboration with teachers. She publishes in such journals as *Science Education* and *Cultural Studies in Science Education*.

Ninitha Maivorsdotter is Associate Professor in Public Health at University of Skövde, Sweden. Her research interests include the study of meaning-making and learning in different educational contexts. She has explored and developed the concepts "gender habits" and "bodying." Lately, her research interest has been directed toward using the concept "environing" in a public health context, combining the works of John Dewey and Aaron Antonovsky.

Johan Öhman is Professor of Education in the School of Humanities, Education, and Social Sciences at Örebro University, Sweden. He is one of the founders of the research group SMED (Studies of Meaning-making in Educational Discourses), and a leader of the research group ESERGO (Environmental and Sustainability Education Research Group Örebro). He is part of the International Advisory Board of the journals Environmental Education Research and Adventure Education and Outdoor Learning. His works include numerous international research papers, book chapters, and books. Among his recent books is *Sustainable Development Teaching*, written in collaboration with Leif Östman and Katrien Van Poeck (2019).

Leif Östman is Professor of Curriculum Studies ("didactics" in Swedish) at Uppsala University, Sweden. He is one of the founders of the research group SMED and the current director of SMED and the research school GRESD (Graduate School for Education and Sustainable Development). He is also a member of the Swedish National Commission for UNESCO and reviewer of the network Environmental and Sustainability Education Research at the ECER conference. Among his recent books is *Sustainable Development Teaching*, written in collaboration with Johan Öhman and Katrien Van Poeck (2019).

Jonas Risberg is Senior Lecturer in the Department of Education at Uppsala University, Sweden. He conducts research on social interaction in workplace settings and has a specific interest in everyday learning and instruction in collegial and informal encounters. Risberg also conducts research with a focus on embodiment and movement in formal educational settings. His work is grounded in the empirical enterprise of ethnomethodology as well as in the field of transactionalism and is frequently accomplished through video-ethnographic approaches. He has recently published in *Discourse Analysis, Interchange,* and *Physical Education and Sport Pedagogy*.

Lennart Rolandsson is Senior Lecturer of Didactics of Technology at Uppsala University, Sweden. With a Master of Physics degree, he taught Mathematics and Physics for many years. As a researcher, he studies how computational aspects involving machines are introduced into schools as well as teachers' development of new competencies in mathematics using digital technology. In 2017 and 2018, he was one of the leading speakers in a seminar series arranged by the Swedish National Agency of Education for thousands of teachers regarding the history of programming in education. He publishes on programming and computational thinking in schools.

Frank X. Ryan is Associate Professor of Philosophy at Kent State University, USA. His research focuses on knowledge and objectivity from the lens of American pragmatism. Ryan advocates a transactional perspective that "sees together" distinctions of internal–external, subject–object, and mind–body prevalent in traditional realisms and idealisms. Known internationally for his work on Dewey's transactional philosophy, he is currently working on a book-length critique of philosophical realism from a transactional perspective. His most recent book is *The Real Metaphysical Club: The Philosophers, the Arguments, and the Writings, 1868–1883*, co-edited with James A. Good and Brian E. Butler, 2019.

Katrien Van Poeck is Research Professor in the Centre for Sustainable Development at Ghent University, Belgium, where she coordinates the Centre for Sustainable Development's research line on sustainability education. She is currently also affiliated half-time with Uppsala University, Sweden, research group SMED, as a Marie Skłodowska-Curie Fellow (2020–3). Her research focuses on the role of education in the pursuit of building a more sustainable world. In 2020 she received a Starting Grant from the European Research Council. Her most recent book is *Sustainable Development Teaching: Ethical and Political Challenges*, edited with Leif Östman and Johan Öhman, 2019.

Susanne Klaar is Senior Lecturer at the University of Borås, Sweden, where she works with preschool and primary teacher education at the Faculty of Librarianship, Information, Education, and IT. Her research concerns methodological questions about how to investigate and evaluate teaching and learning in preschool practices based on John Dewey's concept of transaction. Susanne is a member of the research group ECE (Early Childhood Education) at the University of Borås, Sweden, and recently she has been involved in a research program about inclusive learning environments in preschools. Her work has been published in numerous international research journals.

Louise Sund is Associate Professor at Mälardalen University, Sweden, and Researcher in Education at Örebro University, Sweden. She is a member of the Environmental and Sustainability Education Research Group at Örebro University, Sweden. She is a founding member of EERA's Environmental and Sustainability Education Research network and a member of the convening group. Recent publications include a book chapter in *The Bloomsbury Handbook for Global Education and Learning* and an article in *Journal of Environmental Education* on delinking global issues in northern Europe classrooms.

Acknowledgements

We would like to thank Uppsala University for their support in funding the 5th Swedish Pragmatism Colloquium on Education & Transaction where the papers in the present volume were originally presented before they were selected for refinement and publication.

1

Introduction

Jim Garrison, Johan Öhman and Leif Östman

What is different about this book than almost any other in philosophy of education is only three of the contributors are philosophers. All the rest are empirical educational researchers. They are, however, philosophically sophisticated researchers. They are unique in that they rely on philosophy, not the social sciences, to provide their theoretical frameworks and inform their methods of empirical investigation. These chapters may be read as a contribution to what is sometimes called "applied philosophy" by those who do not realize that a philosophy that cannot be applied is nonsense.

While the contributors draw on other philosophers, here the focus is on the transactional philosophy of John Dewey. Philosophers, including educational philosophers, as well as educators of all kinds ignore Dewey's (1949/1989a) last book *Knowing and the Known*, co-authored with Arthur F. Bentley. It is the only place Dewey's transactional philosophy is explicitly thematized.

As the title *Knowing and the Known* suggests, it is primarily an epistemological and methodological work, although it has much broader implications. By examining Dewey's earlier work, it is possible to expand the range of transactional ideas as they are informed by his last book. Dewey and Bentley (1949/1989a) themselves identify two places where Dewey was already thinking transactionally. First, the reader is told, "The beginnings of this attitude may be found in his famous paper 'The Reflex Arc Concept in Psychology' (1896/1972)" (101 fn. 8). H. S. and V. T. Thayer (1985) comment that the "theory of 'transaction' was developed by Dewey as early as 1896 in the article on 'The Reflex Arc Concept in Psychology' and is basic to his position in virtually all of his educational writings" (xxv).

In his reflex arc paper, Dewey rejects the idea that living creatures are passive organisms that must be prodded to action by an external stimulus. Living beings act by virtue of being alive. All a stimulus can ever do is redirect action. For Dewey (1896/1972), we always begin with an organism–environment transaction;

therefore, "We begin not with a sensory stimulus, but with a sensorimotor co-ordination" (97). Like organism *and* environment, stimulus *and* response are merely useful analytic distinctions. Nothing is a stimulus without a response, nor, transactionally, is anything a response without a stimulus. Instead of a reflex arc, what we have is a circle, and "The circle is a co-ordination" (Dewey 1896/1972: 109). Stimulus-response is an ongoing functional "co-ordination" of an organism–environment transaction. Coordination replaces *mediated* correspondence in Dewey's transactionalism.

Dewey and Bentley (1949/1989a) also ask the reader to compare the idea of "trans-action" with the "use of 'integration' in Dewey's *Logic: The Theory of Inquiry*" (101 fn. 8). There Dewey (1938/1986) makes such transactional statements as "the processes of living are enacted by the environment as truly as by the organism; for they *are* an integration" (32).[1] Since Dewey was already thinking transactionally in texts dating back decades, one may use earlier texts if they can be understood transactionally.

Here is Dewey's statement of transactionalism in his *Logic*: "But all changes occur through interactions of conditions. What exists coexists, and no change can either occur or be determined in inquiry in isolation from the connection of an existence with coexisting conditions" (220). Elsewhere Dewey (1925/1981) states: "The stablest thing we can speak of is not free from conditions set to it by other things" (63). Dewey (1931/1985) also avers "every occurrence is a *con*currence" (9). Whatever exists is the emergent consequence of integrated coexisting conditions. This is Deweyan transactionalism's most important insight.

Dewey and Bentley (1949/1989a) distinguish three ways of understanding action; they are:

> Self-action: where things are viewed as acting under their own powers.
> Inter-action: where thing is balanced against thing in causal interconnection.
> Trans-action: where systems of description and naming are employed to deal with aspects and phases of action, without attribution to "elements" or other presumptively detachable or independent "entities," "essences," or "realities," and without isolation of presumptively detachable "relations" from such detachable "elements." (101–102)

In "Self-Action," one finds "pre-scientific presentation in terms of presumptively independent 'actors,' 'souls,' 'minds,' 'selves,' 'powers' or 'forces' taken as acting events" (71). Self-action assumes independent self-caused objects with intrinsic powers and essences. Meanwhile, "Interaction" is: "Presentation of particles or other objects organized as operating upon one another" (71). Interaction presupposes independent separate objects and elements having connections *between* them *mediated* by detachable external relations. Trans-actions assume a total situation. For instance, instead of understanding organism and environment as two independent "things," they are understood as a single integrated system: organism–environment. Understood transactionally, organism–environment is a unity such that coexistent, co-dependent relations are as primordial as the relata. Transactions are unmediated.

Dewey and Bentley state, "Our own procedure is the *transactional*, in which is asserted the right to see together, extensionally and durationally, much that is talked about conventionally as if it were composed of irreconcilable separates" (67). Organism–environment is a transactional unity separable only for analytic convenience. Another example of seeing together involves how the coexisting conditions of the carbon cycle give rise to consequences for human functioning, and, transactionally, human functioning is a condition having consequences for all other functions of the cycle. Circularity is a transactional trait going as far back as Dewey's reflex arc paper. Dewey and Bentley adopt "procedure in a circle— openly, explicitly, emphatically" (62). Traversing circles carefully contributes to seeing things together, including one's distributed self, in the grander scheme of transactional coexistences.

Researchers must first strive to see coexistences together. Later, for analytic convenience, they may simplify and think in terms of interaction or even self-action. As Frank X. Ryan (2011) points out, "Transaction is a tool for science, not the tool. It is not the business of philosophers to tell scientists when and where to use it" (40). The contributors to this collection wield the transactional tool deftly, but they do not let it stand in the way of appropriate methodological simplifications that allow them to more carefully examine segments of the circumference when needed as they chart a path around expanding transactional circles.

For Dewey and Bentley, "Behavior" (activity, conduct, and such) is durational and extensional; it is not simply located in space or time. It takes space and time enough for the empirical investigator to see together what belongs together. A "Behavior" is "always to be taken transactionally: i.e., never as *of* the organism alone, any more than *of* the environment alone, but always as of the organic-environmental situation, with organisms and environmental objects taken as equally its aspects" (Dewey and Bentley, 1949/1989a, 260). It is never to be taken in the sense of reductionistic behaviorism associated with John Watson (79 fn. 17). "Action" and "activity" are "characterizations of durational-extensional subject matters" (259). "Regarding behaviors as events of organism-environment in action," Dewey and Bentley write, "we shall find the differentiation of behavioral processes (including the purposive) from physical or physiological to rest upon types of action that are observable directly and easily in the full organic-environmental locus" (136). This means that *human physical, physiological, and cognitive states characterized by purpose and intentionality, including learning, may be inferred from the transactional unity of organism-environment. This fact is appreciated by all the contributors to this book and explored in one way or another by all of the educational researchers.*

Among scholars of Dewey's philosophy, **Frank X. Ryan** is the name most associated with transactionalism. Although not his primary purpose, chapter 2 nonetheless serves as an introduction to many of the most important ideas of Deweyan transactionalism. The primary goal of Ryan's chapter is to further develop his distinction of "containment" from "inference" in defense of his "transactional interpretation of classical pragmatism" (this volume). The containment paradigm cannot be maintained in a durational–extensional world where nothing is simply located. As Ryan states, the world of transactionalism is "a world without withins or withouts" (this volume).

Once we break the containment paradigm, learning can be intelligently inferred from observable activity (conduct, behavior, and such). As Ryan observes, "Dewey advises us that the 'cultivated naivety' of a directly accessible world is achieved only by the 'severe discipline' of philosophic thought that replaces containment with inference as the paradigm of objectivity" (this volume). Ryan explores Dewey's (1903/1977) The Postulate of Immediate Empiricism wherein everything is what it is experienced *as*. We cannot be mistaken about having an experience, but it is easy to make false logical inferences about it. Experience—whether while awake, dreaming, or using psychoactive drugs—is an immediate experience of reality. However, the immediate experience is not the same experience as one that is the product of intelligent inquiry. Most of the contributors to the present book explicitly cultivate the naivety of Dewey's realism using the sort of "severe discipline" of the methods described in the paper by Andersson and Öhman in Chapter 6.

In the inference paradigm, *what* is known is not separable from *how* the inquirer comes to know it. Methods are usually thought of as detachable from the objects of knowledge they discover, which is a mistake. For Dewey (1938/1986), knowledge is a product of the process of inquiry wherein "objects are the objectives of inquiry" (122). Dewey gets his ontology from his methods, not his methods from ontology. Dewey (1925/1981) uses the phrase "*the* philosophic fallacy" to identify what is perhaps the greatest error in philosophical thought: The "conversion of eventual functions into antecedent existence" (35). In the circle of transaction, methods of inquiry are often modified along with the knowledge of objects they produce.

Ryan's chapter demands that we recognize the difference in having an experience and knowing an experience. While reality (existence) is given, knowledge of reality is not (see Garrison 2019). Dewey (1925/1981) used the phrase "arbitrary 'intellectualism'" to characterize the "great vice of philosophy," which is assuming that "all experiencing is a mode of knowing" (28). Arbitrary intellectualism is also the great vice of educational research. A great deal of experience is merely of immediate anoetic quality. It is what William James (1912/1976) calls "pure experience," by which he means, "the immediate flux of life which furnishes the material to our later reflection" (46).

In Chapter 3, **Jim Garrison** examines the transactional perspectival emergence of language, the mind, the self, and the very idea of temporal sequences. He highlights the essay "The Inclusive Philosophic Idea" wherein Dewey (1928/1984) declares, "conjoint behavior is a universal characteristic of all existences" (41). Everything that exists coexists. Dewey also states, "The social affords us an observable instance of a 'realm of mind' objective to an individual, by entering into which as a participating member organic activities are transformed into acts having a mental" function (50). For Dewey, minds emerge by taking the perspective of others in sociolinguistic transactions.

Garrison connects Dewey to the sociological writings of his colleague George Herbert Mead and then both of them to the empirical work of Michael Tomasello, showing that the fundamental condition for acquiring language involves two organisms taking the perspective of the other regarding a third thing. It is a durational–extensional process of ongoing coordination wherein the minds and selves of the participants as well as the shared object emerge and undergo transformation.

The most unique contribution of Garrison's chapter is the demonstration of how the construction of temporal sequences, as opposed to the immediate anoetic qualitative sense of temporal passage, requires the ability to coordinate perspectives. The past, present, and future are constructions of judgment. Ultimately, such claims can only be adjudicated by the community of inquiry. For instance, conflicting claims regarding a sequence of events require adjusting perspectival attitudes involving the determination and use of inference from selected data. Judgments in courts of law provide dramatic examples.

In Chapter 4, **William J. Clancey** conducts a transactional ethnographic study. It is an extension of his (2012) book *Working on Mars*. Indeed, he was invited to carry out the present study because of the similarities of the remote

Mars exploration system to remote systems used for deep-sea exploration. His transactional studies of remote exploration and learning have many implications for education and could be readily extended to online teaching and learning environments.

Clancey's transactional ethnography encompasses "[f]unctional observation" of the "full" Okeanos "exploration system," including a "durationally and extensionally" distributed international scientific collaboration (*op. cit.*). The collaboration is carried out across many time zones using the internet, high-definition video, robotic devices, social media, and graphic interfaces entangled with an array of different institutional practices involving different roles, activities, technologies, procedures, training, and funding (i.e., the how); all are functionally coordinated with *what* is found by exploring deep ocean environments. The "activities among the subsystems (both the how and the what) are transactional because the constraints flow in both directions and pervade the entire exploration system" whereas "viewing subsystems as distinct, independently existing entities is purely an imaginary concept" (this volume). Subsystems of the full functional system are only convenient analytical simplifications. Like stimulus and response, *how* and *what* "always occur together in coordinated form" and must be seen together "extensionally and durationally" to be understood (*op. cit.*). Nonetheless, Dewey and Bentley (1949/1989a) explicitly acknowledge that transactional observation is "actively necessary to inquiry at some stages, held in reserve at other stages" (71). Clancey is sage in holding transaction in reserve in some analytic stages. Self-action and inter-action can be useful analytical simplifications as long as one avoids reifying the results.

Andrea Fiore identifies and draws out the transactionalism already present in *Democracy and Education* by concentrating on chapter 15, "Play and Work in the Curriculum." Fiore identifies play as a fundamental "transactional activity/category" of behavior, which means it is a durational–extensional event (this volume). Fiore cleverly links play with the Deweyan circuit of inquiry, a connection few ever make.

Taken as a transactional activity/category, Fiore identifies two fundamental elements of play that are helpful for developing democratic social intelligence: imagination and emotion. High-quality inquiry involves creative imagination. As a function of social intelligence, creative inquiry allows citizens to perceive the possible in the actual. As Fiore observes, imagination also facilitates empathetic understanding of others who are different from ourselves.

Fiore recognizes that for Dewey, imagination involves emotions. For instance, in his essay "Affective Thought," Dewey (1926/1984) remarks, "Art also explicitly recognizes what it has taken so long to discover in science; the control exercised by emotion in re-shaping natural conditions, and the place of the imagination, under the influence of desire, in re-creating the world into a more orderly place" (106–7). Although Fiore does not cite this passage, he does draw out the social-political implications implicit within it.

In Chapter 6, **Pernilla Andersson and Johan Öhman** introduce the reader to the transactionally inspired methodological frameworks employed in the chapters to follow. They also discuss the role of the German and Scandinavian *didaktik*-tradition with its emphasis on educational content, encompassing learning of knowledge as well as socialization and person-formation in these transactional frameworks. The chapter chronicles some of the earlier groundbreaking work done by many of the contributors to this volume. Although some of the papers in the present volume extend and further develop this framework, readers will find these refinements easy to follow given Andersson and Öhman's clear and concise contribution. Their ensemble of philosophically informed empirical methods is designed to empirically capture the complexity of learning, including micro-analysis of critical moments in the learning process that evade less-discerning approaches. These methods do the same for subtle but significant actions undertaken by teachers to promote learning. Many readers will never think about or research teaching and learning in quite the same way again: They will instead begin to transactionally think and see together things they have previously overlooked or considered disconnected.

The next two chapters explore embodied habits as transactional subfunctions of a single, unified organism–environment transaction. The first investigates teaching habits in the context of policy reform. Education policies restructure teachers' environments and thereby disrupt the co-dependent relations of organism–environment integration. Following the requirements of policy reform will almost always transform teachers' habits. The second paper examines how young children are transactionally integrated into their physical environment.

Like stimulus and response, Dewey (1922/1983) began thinking of habits transactionally quite early; for example, Dewey begins *Human Nature and Conduct* by remarking that "habits may be profitably compared to physiological functions ....[H]abits are like functions in many respects, and especially in requiring the cooperation of organism and environment" (15). He further remarks that "habits incorporate an environment within themselves. They are adjustments *of* the environment, not merely *to* it" (38). Habits are not simply located under the skin; rather, they are located wherever they are active in a world without a within or a without. Habits-environments, including the social environment, are co-dependent, integrated systems. They emerge and are transformed together in a single ongoing transactional becoming.

Malena Lidar and Eva Lundqvist report a case study of a teacher re-learning transactions and incorporating the social environment of educational policy into their habits of action. The teacher must learn to reinhabit their world. Dewey insists "habits are arts" that "involve skill of sensory and motor organs, cunning or craft, and objective materials" (15). They provide skilled "know how" even in the absence of propositional "knowing that." According to Dewey (1938/1986), "Habits are the basis of organic learning" (38). Dewey (1922/1983) also declares, "Customs persist because individuals form their personal habits under conditions set by prior customs" (43). Cultural customs establish norms of correct conduct that are embodied in habits. Accordingly, these habits serve to transactionally preserve the custom across longer and shorter durational expanses. Established policies are norms of cultural practice. Hence, a change in policy can greatly disrupt one's habits, thereby creating a problematic situation. Such changes require inquiry and modification of one's habits (as well as norms) of practice that may perpetuate across the course of a career or, should it become a deeply entrenched custom, many generations of teaching careers.

Lidar and Lundqvist's four-year case study follows how the continuity and change in a teacher's habits of functional coordination with the teaching environment occur as a result of dramatic policy changes involving the implementation of new national tests. Dewey asserts, "All habits are demands for certain kinds of activity; and they constitute the self" (21). Lidar and Lundqvist study how one's teaching self may change over time. In his *Ethics*, Dewey (1932/1985) bluntly states that "the key to a correct theory of morality is recognition of the *essential unity of the self and its acts*" (288). It is not possible to separate who we are from what we do; this is especially so in teaching as a moral practice. The result is a transactional integration of the self, its actions, and the policy environment. Dewey's transactional circle gives both self and consequences indispensable roles. It is a circle where "the [teaching] self is not a mere means to producing consequences because the consequences, when of a moral kind, enter into the formation of the self and the self enters into them" (286). When teachers act, they express the present self while forming the future self. Lidar and Lundqvist's conclusion combines the transactional circle of the self with the unity of the act to provide the following astute observation about policy implementation: "We do not want to claim that following state mandated prescriptions to the letter is what makes you a better teacher. Rather, the claim is that in order to make reforms functional, or to successfully implement reforms, presupposes that teachers get time to make the reform continuous with their teaching habits" (this volume).

While Lidar and Lundqvist examine teachers re-learning transactions that involve incorporating the social environment into habits of action, **Susanne Klaar and Johan Öhman** study children's learning transactions that incorporate their physical environment into their habits. In Chapter 8, they explore how to understand learning as an active process that "intertwine[s] earlier experiences and previous knowledge with present and future unknown, but not unexpected, experiences" (this volume). They strive to see episodes of past and present learning as well as the capacity for future learning together on broad durational expanses. While they emphasize learning that involves the learner and physical environment transaction, they are fully aware of the importance of the social environment. Among other significant findings, their chapter provides empirical evidence for Dewey and Bentley's claim cited earlier that action is "observable directly and easily in the full organic-environmental locus" (*op. cit.*). For Klaar and Öhman, young children (toddlers) are the "organisms." They specifically concentrate on how these children learn "in and through bodily and non-verbal experiences" (this volume).

Klaar and Öhman emphasize the learners' practical and emotional learning along with cognitive modes of human experience exceed the cognitive limits of mere intellectualism. Thinking, feeling, and acting are inseparable on a transactional account. Klaar and Öhman particularly emphasize the role of embodied habits in functionally coordinating with the learning environment in the ways discussed above. The careful reader will note several instances of embodied, transactional inferences in this chapter. Understanding the transfer of learning to other contexts has been a major concern of educational researchers for many decades. Klaar and Öhman fully exploit Dewey's solution to the problem while providing abundant empirical examples of embodied learning.

In a variety of ways, Chapters 9 through 15 accentuate the artistic and/or creative along with aesthetic perception and appreciation. Dewey (1934/1987) asserts, "Art denotes a process of doing or making. This is true of fine as well of technological art" (53). The artistic work of production is transactionally integrated with aesthetic perception. Dewey regrets that there is not one word combining both because artistic creativity and aesthetic perception are inseparable. To create a work of art, an artist must continuously perceive and critically appreciate what they are making. Simultaneously, to appreciate a work of art, one must creatively carry out the work of art for themselves. Dewey asserts, "A work of art ... is actually, not just potentially, a work of art only when it lives in some individualized experience" (113). Therefore, a work of art "is recreated every time it is esthetically experienced" (113). Like organism and environment, the *artistic* production of art as an environmental object combined with the *aesthetic* appreciation of the environmental object produced is a transactional integration.

Katrien Van Poeck and Leif Östman amalgamate transactionalism with sociologically inspired dramaturgical frameworks for the didactical purpose of developing a transactional theory about, and an analytical approach to, investigating the practice of facilitating learning. Dramaturgical studies focus on how human interactions are affected by the context and how humans have developed a lexicon (scripting, staging, performance, etc.), the vocabulary of which the authors use and extend in order to include a transactional perspective. They highlight and illustrate that the planning of facilitation needs to incorporate the transactional character of any performance; that is, it is an important didactic tool to be able to take the perspective of others who make imaginary anticipations of transactional receptions. Scrutinizing its durational-extensional dimensions, Van Poeck and Östman argue and illustrate that transaction constitutes a crucial didactical element—*"didactical timing"*—in any facilitating (and teaching) activity.

There are interesting connections here. First, a primary source for dramaturgical approaches is the work of Erving Goffman, who attended the University of Chicago where he was influenced by George Herbert Mead's student Herbert Blumer. Therefore, some of the ideas in Garrison's paper are applicable to this chapter and to dramaturgical sociology, especially the idea of taking the perspective of others, and vice versa, in ongoing meaning-making transactions. Second, in his introduction to Dewey's *The Quest for Certainty*, Stephen Toulmin (1984) discusses the many similarities between Wittgenstein's thinking about "forms of life" and "language games" and Dewey's thinking about "action" (xiv), therein mentioning the "micro-sociological analysis of Erving Goffman and his successors" and referring explicitly to his "dramaturgical model for the analysis of human conduct" (xiii–xiv). Toulmin also suggests ways Wittgenstein advances Dewey. Likewise, Van Poeck and Östman show possibilities for advancing Wittgenstein by moving from "action" to "transaction" and by providing precisely the kind of empirical "micro-sociological empirical analysis" mentioned above.

Among Dewey and Bentley's (1949/1989a) "firm" trial group of names near the end of *Knowing and the Known*, there is one that reads, "*Transactor*: See *Actor*" (272). When the reader follows the reference, they find: "*Actor*: A confused and confusing word; offering a primitive and usually deceptive organization for the complex behavioral transactions the organism is engaged in. Under present postulation Actor should always be taken as postulationally transactional, and thus as a Trans-actor" (260–1). Unfortunately, Dewey and Bentley say little about "Trans-actor." However, in Chapter 10 **Hanna Hofverberg** has a great deal to say about an original concept she calls the "transactant" that is drawn from her reading of Dewey, Bruno Latour, Frank X. Ryan, and others. "Transactant" is meant to "acknowledge both human and non-human participation in transactional activities" (this volume).[2] The concept is an important extension of transactional philosophy, which Hofverberg employs to conduct empirical educational research on craft learning in the sloyd (*slöjd*) classroom. Sloyd is a system of handicraft-oriented education that is a compulsory subject in Swedish and Norwegian schools. Dewey himself was well aware of it and even wanted to invite its founder to speak at the University of Chicago.[3]

When Hofverberg states that "neither a student nor a material *is* but rather *becomes* in the transaction," she expresses an instance of what is perhaps transactionalism's most profound insight (this volume). Dewey preferred verbs and adverbs of action over static nouns. Larry A. Hickman, director emeritus of the Center for Dewey Studies, Carbondale, argues that Dewey's understanding of "nature" was functional and emphasized gerunds (verbs that function as a noun and end with *-ing* in English). To clarify his point, he turns to Wolfgang Schadewaldt who reminds us that the Latin word for nature (*natura*) derives from *nasci*: "to be born" (think of emergence).[4]

In an inspired move, Hofverberg links Deweyan transactionalism to what is sometimes called "the new materialism," which emphasizes the dynamic nature of nonhuman materials as active participants in natural events. She makes particularly good use of Latour's notion of "actant" while carefully distinguishing it from her somewhat more constrained, Deweyan inspired idea of a "transactant." She also keenly observes, "It is not possible to know beforehand what will become a transactant. One must conduct an empirical study to see what actually causes the activity to turn in a specific direction" (this volume).

In Chapter 11, **Joacim Andersson and Jonas Risberg** also study school sloyd by developing a valuable construct for carrying out empirical transactional research. They foreground "sensing together" as an important aspect of "seeing together." Recall that "the great vice of philosophy is an arbitrary 'intellectualism'" (*op. cit.*). Dewey (1925/1981) insists there are "things *had* before there are things cognized" (28). Andersson and Risberg challenge intellectualism by invoking James's nonreflective, immediate, emotional "pure experience" as "sensed qualities of the world (here and now)" while connecting such qualities with "sensed *directions in the world*" (this volume). They explore sensing together in two ways. The first involves literally sharing a common tactile exploration; the second emphasizes that as one acquires practical knowledge, they can sense together what they previously could not.

Andersson and Risberg are concerned with "the student-teacher-body-material-tools transactions" (this volume). The teacher quite literally works with the student, trying to help them get a feel for the material. It is a wonderful example of the following transactional statement from chapter 11, "Experience and Thinking," in Dewey's (1916/1980) famous *Democracy and Education*:

> To "learn from experience" is to make a backward and forward connection between what we do to things and what we enjoy or suffer from things in consequence. Under such conditions, doing becomes a trying; an experiment with the world to find out what it is like; the undergoing becomes instruction—discovery of the connection of things.
>
> (147)

Dewey derives two conclusions from this transactional claim: "(1) Experience is primarily an active-passive affair; it is not primarily cognitive. But (2) the *measure of the value* of an experience lies in the perception of relationships or continuities to which it leads up" (147). The metaphor, "getting a feeling for something," ceases being metaphorical. One can "see" the emergent transactional unity of doing and undergoing in their video frames and accompanying transcriptions of student–teacher dialogue. Andersson and Risberg provide a micro-analysis identifying and drawing out the transactional details of Dewey's educational theory.

Reading pedagogy and language learning are the only domains in the entire field of education that are significantly influenced by Dewey's transactionalism. This influence is entirely due to Louise M. Rosenblatt's (1978/1994) highly influential *The Reader, The Text, The Poem*, which draws very explicitly from *Knowing and the Known*.[5] Rosenblatt traces Dewey's transactionalism back to Dewey's 1896 "The Reflex Arc Concept" (17). Rosenblatt's definition of transaction is discerning: "'Transaction' designates, then, an ongoing process [a becoming] in which the elements or facts are, one might say, aspects of a total situation, each conditioned by and conditioning the other" (17). Organism and environment emerge together transactionally. Likewise, "A person becomes a reader by virtue of his activity in relationship to a text" (18).

In Chapter 12, **Petra Hansson and Johan Öhman** extend Louise Rosenblatt's (1938/1995) thinking about readers (e.g., students), applying the experience of texts as works of art in her "Literature as Exploration" to students exploring a museum as a work of art. Remarkably, Hansson and Öhman are able to use empirical data drawn from students' documented experiences in the museum context to understand meaning-making from a transactional perspective. Their empirical data show how meaning is constituted in transactions among the museum visitors, exhibited museum objects, and the specific situation of the museum visit. Thus, meaning is not inherent in exhibitions: museum objects need to be encountered and evoked to become transformed into what they call "object work." When this evocation takes place, the museum objects are meshed with whatever occupies the "reader" of the object at the time of the encounter. Considering evocation from a pedagogical point of view, they claim that it is important to stage encounters between exhibited objects and visitors in order to encourage visitors to explore both the objects and their selves.

According to Rosenblatt, the meaning of a text emerges transactionally in a given context wherein the reader (organism) and the text (environment) are inseparable. The word "Poem" in her title can be read in terms of the classical Greek *poiesis*, which means making, creating, or calling into existence. In Plato's *Symposium*, Socrates learns that "there is more than one kind of poetry in the true sense of the word—that is to say, calling something into existence that was not there before, so that every kind of artistic creation [*poiesis*] is poetry, and every artist is a poet" (205b). In *Art as Experience*, Dewey (1934/1987) writes:

> A new poem is created by every one who reads poetically—not that its raw material is original for, after all, we live in the same old world, but that every individual brings with him, when he exercises his individuality, a way of seeing and feeling that in its interaction with old material creates something new, something previously not existing in experience.
>
> (113)

"Poem" can be read as referring to any act of creation. Recall that "a work of art" is "recreated every time it is esthetically experienced" (*op. cit.*). Transactionalism is profoundly creative and reciprocally transformative for all participants.

Michael Håkansson, Leif Östman, and Lennart Rolandsson examine three students in computer programming in order to present and illustrate a transactional methodology of value to researchers interested in creating systematic empirical knowledge regarding artistic teaching and learning and its consequences: When student engagement in the subject-matter becomes personal (instead of being passively uncaring), an intimate connection is created between learning and personal formation. As Dewey (1939/1991) observes, "There are occasions when for the proper conduct of knowing as the controlling interest, the problem becomes that of reconstruction of the *self* engaged in inquiry" (70). Meanwhile, "The problem of reconstructing the self cannot be solved unless inquiry takes into account reconstitution of existing conditions, a matter which poses a problem in which scientific knowledge is indispensable for effecting an outcome satisfying the needs of the situation" (71). In creating something artistically, we also create ourselves as persons due to the transactional integration of the self that is engaged in inquiry with the subject matter.

Many might think programming cannot be a source of creative, artistic expression. However, remember, "Art denotes a process of doing or making. This is true of fine as well of technological art" (*op. cit.*). That programming can be an art is reinforced by the fact that poetry in its fullest sense is any kind of production. Indeed, for the Greeks, *poiesis* is the goal of *techne* (art, skill, craft). Any technological art, say creating a computer program, is as poetic as literature. Thinking the humanities and the sciences are entirely different things is a catastrophic mistake.

Håkansson, Östman, and Rolandsson design their methodology by combining the analytical method of PEA (practical epistemology analysis) with Dewey's work on transaction, inquiry, artistic production, and aesthetic experience. The empirical analysis shows in detail how the students turn the transaction of creating beautiful code into something artistic by collectively setting up their own imaginary quality for their inquiry. This process leads them to experimentally engage each other and use their experiences with the material and medium of programming to reach a specific consummation: a program that solves the task, which is the institutional requirement, yet is at the same time beautiful and personally expressive.

In Chapter 7, Lidar and Lundqvist insightfully discuss the importance of reflection in the problematic situation of policy reform that transactionally modifies one's ethical and moral habits. However, they lacked adequate space to explore it more comprehensively. The chapter by **Louise Sund and Johan Öhman** deepens the transactional perspective on morality as situated practice. Just as organism and environment are constantly co-evolving, "morality can be continuously evolving as we are constantly exposed to situations of insecurity and conflict where we are forced to reflect on our choices" (this volume). Morality can thus be seen as an ongoing learning process. They illustrate this process by detailing an instance when a teacher experiences a situation that makes her reconsider her moral habits.

They explicitly refer to *"the essential unity of the self and its acts"* and the importance of continuity and change in the formation of moral habits (*op. cit.*). To better capture the specifics of ethical inquiry, Sund and Öhman modify Frank Ryan's doubt-belief circuit of inquiry (Figure 2.4 of Ryan, this volume). They are especially attentive to Dewey's distinction between surroundings and environment by pointing out that the only "those things" with which one transactionally "varies" are the "genuine environment" (this volume). Mere surroundings are not integrated into organic functioning. One of the most common and serious errors of teaching is to assume that what surrounds a student is part of their environment.

Michael Håkansson and Leif Östman (Chapter 15) offer a transactional model and an analytical approach for creating empirically grounded knowledge regarding the importance of aesthetical experiences and for developing subsequent inquiry for a (re)discovery and learning of ethical–moral and ethical–political "caring for," which can be seen as crucial for developing moral and political commitments. They use Dewey's view of aesthetic as expressed by the Greek term *Aisthetikos*—sentient, feeling, sensitivity, etc.—and the insight that transaction occurs at the level of existence as well as that of essence. The model starts with the disruption of our habits, which becomes obvious for us bodily as a poignant, immediate anoetic affect, such as an aesthetical experience of the "qualitativeness" and intensity of the whole disturbance-situation (Dewey 1925/1981: 82). This experience has no reference. It is something had, but not known. Aesthetical experience makes up the background from whence the foreground arises in the inquiry. First, the experience is transformed into a feeling—a bodily affect with a reference—and a desire to understand and solve. Afterward, "caring for" the subject-matter leads to explicit cognition. The background poignant aesthetical experience is an experience of the unexpected, an intense disruption of our harmonious functioning: it concerns our existence, in this case, as moral and political persons. There are three distinct empirical examples detailed in this chapter that illustrate how to infer this type of learning with the help of the model.

Ninitha Maivorsdotter and Joacim Andersson provide a transactional analysis of pandemics, emphasizing that they are social as well as biological events. They examine the differences between the responses of two neighboring countries, Denmark and Sweden, to the Covid-19 pandemic. The account is historical (i.e., durational) as well as extensional in its connection between public narratives and "a group or communities' past experiences of traumatization to health over time" (this volume). The history of a people's trauma helps one to understand present political events of all kinds and enables future predictions. In Dewey and Bentley's sense, this history is an "event," and events have eventuations; furthermore, events can themselves transact in ways that are often only known after the transaction.

As Maivorsdotter and Andersson say, "Narratives are stories that string events together to construct meaning and establish discourse," which often express an individual's or a nation's identity and shape collective memory (this volume). Their paper compares and contrasts narrative differences regarding the Covid-19 crisis between two nations with a common "Nordic" history as expressed by the respective leaders. They connect these national narratives expressing different cultural customs to differences in individual habits of action. Following instructions requiring social distancing, frequent hand washing, and limiting social contact requires people to learn new habits. By calling on the resources of body pedagogics and the body politics of political discourse, they advance Dewey's transactional thinking about habits, which they then integrate into Aaron Antonovsky's salutogenic approach to health. The field of education itself is often pathological; it would profit from more salutogenic thinking.

2

Philosophers' Problems: Transaction in Philosophy and Life

Frank X. Ryan

Introduction

A few years back I distinguished "containment" from "inference" in defending a *transactional* interpretation of classical pragmatism (Ryan 2016). In taking perceptions to be mental entities set apart from their physical counterparts in the mind-independent world, the venerable *containment paradigm* has long been easy prey for external world skepticism. As such, I followed John Dewey's lead of ditching the epistemological precedent that initially distinguishes "within" from "without." Dewey opts for an *inference paradigm* wherein mind is differentiated from object as a function of the minding or managing of problems to objects/objectives showcased in a transactional circuit of inquiry.

In this chapter I extend the critique of containment from overt realism and externalism to *interactional* forms of pragmatism. The first two sections rehearse skeptical challenges to containment avoided by an inference paradigm and introduce a pragmatic phenomenology suggestive of a modest Deweyan "system." The section "Transaction without Hedges" advances our main argument by identifying containment variants still widely (if unwittingly) embraced by "interactional" pragmatists, and proposes a transactional makeover of problematic concepts such as experience and existence, sign-behavior, and embodied consciousness. I ultimately hope to show that a transactional approach to "philosophers' problems" yields a "cultivated naïve realism" capable of "seeing together" theoretical and empirical connections that otherwise remain hopelessly disconnected or opposed.

Dewey's Philosophical "System": Containment, Inference, and Objectivity

Skepticism and the Containment Paradigm

Dewey famously invites us to turn from "philosophers' problems" to the real-life problems we face collectively as humans (1917/1980: 46). Following his lead, most pragmatists scoff at both the "epistemological industry" bent upon showing how subjective minds can access mind-independent reality and skeptical challenges that declare such access impossible.

Though such dismissive responses generally satisfy pragmatists, they've impressed few others. John Greco notes that skeptical challenges resist refutation, and the doubts they raise about knowledge and evidence are genuine (2008: 109). More significantly, faulty epistemological commitments exposed by skeptical doubts invite constructive pragmatist alternatives we can't advance if the challenge isn't taken seriously.

Though it seems far-fetched to suggest we may be brains-in-vats or deluded by an evil genius, external world skepticism has a credible response: the primary challenge to the veracity of perceptual experience is not about what's likely or probable, but one of *cognitive access*—a predicament of *location* inherent in what we'll dub the *containment paradigm*. Presuming that what we experience

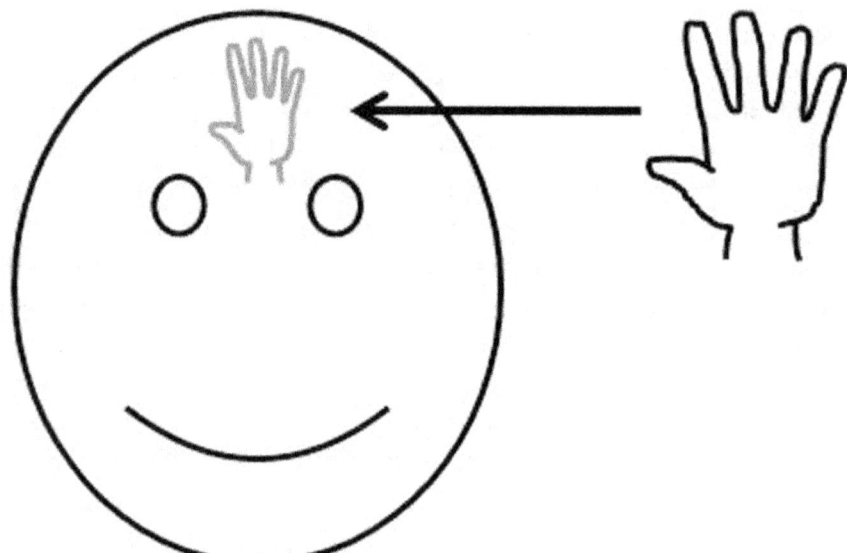

Figure 2.1 The Containment Predicament.

is limited to or *contained within* the perceiver (the percept or neural event on the left), how does one get *beyond* this to the mind-independent existence (the "real" hand on the right) it purportedly represents?

In David Hume's famous analysis, regularities among percepts warrant no inferences to external existences as their likely causes. Good inferences of this sort, he notes, are from *like* to *like*. Sufficiently repeated, my perception of a hand allows me to infer future hand-percepts; inferring mind-independent counterparts, to the contrary, is a radical case of *like* to *unlike*: "The mind has never anything present to it but the perceptions, and cannot possibly reach any experience of their connexion with objects. The supposition of such a connexion is, therefore, without any foundation in reasoning" (Hume 1748/1977: 105). To be sure, pragmatists have eagerly joined heavyweight realists in contesting Hume's conclusion. Why, they ask, must we assume that experience is *confined* to perceptual content? We see *hands*, not hand-percepts! Experience *reaches* beyond itself to *access* objects in the external world.

Let's visualize this rejoinder by converting the "head and hand" illustration into a simple Venn diagram of mind-dependence and mind-independence:

The overlapping area (x) marks the interactive confluence of mind-independent things with what is we can access cognitively. But, replies our skeptic, in granting that we have no cognitive access to mind-independence per se, but only to the confluence, it is ipso facto limited to that realm.

With access to what is exclusively mind-dependent, what *evidence* can be summoned on behalf of mind-independence? How shall we suppose it is "reached," "interacted with," or "accessed" from the experienced sensory content? In fact, how can we claim that the lightly shaded area in Figure 2.3 *is* an overlap or intersection? Again, the problem is not about bizarre scenarios or mere logical possibilities—but strictly one of *location*. The barrier between

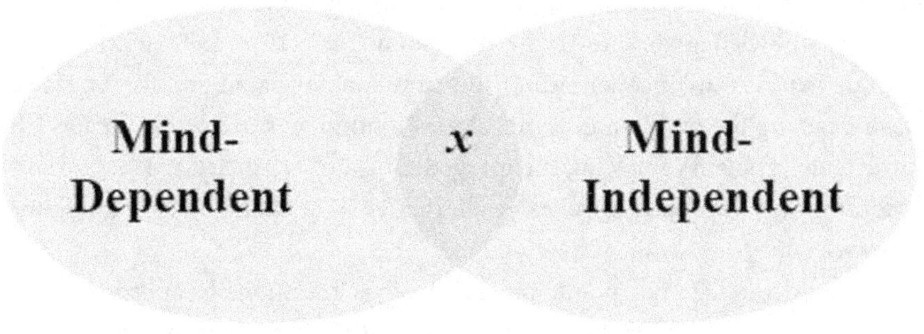

Figure 2.2 Mind-Dependence and Mind-Independence.

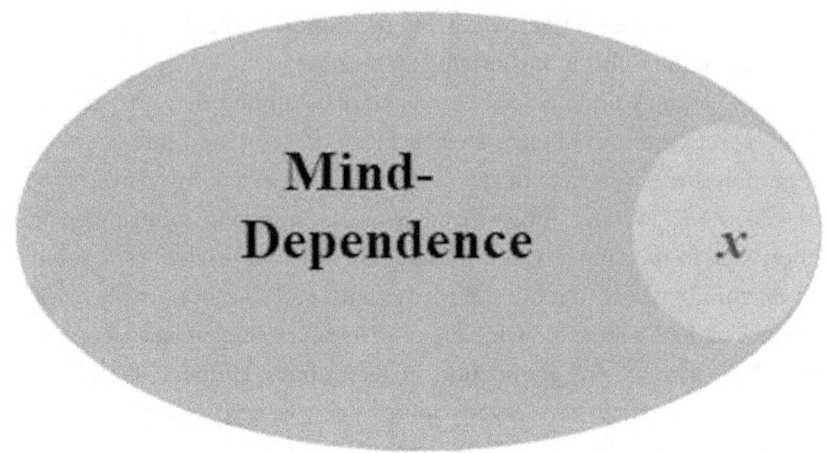

Figure 2.3 Mind-Dependence.

mind-dependence and mind independence seems absolute, precluding not just all claims about what's "out there," but the intelligibility of "out there" itself!

Inference and Ontology

Despite his disdain for it, Dewey never settled for dismissing the "epistemology industry." He exchanged multiple essays with realists Edward Gleason Spaulding, Bertrand Russell, George Santayana, and Arthur O. Lovejoy—warning them of the skeptical consequences of any *salto mortale* (to cite William James's apt expression) from "mind" to "world."

Heeding Dewey's diligence is important. In Barry Stroud's shrewd observation, if you assume you're situated in the world "in certain natural but subtly distorted ways, you will leave human beings as you describe them incapable of the very knowledge you are trying to account for" (1994/1999: 292). Hume's critique exposes the incoherence of the containment paradigm, for, as Dewey warns, casting the problem in terms of how a mind gets to a world creates "the intractable problem of piecing them together again" (1925/1981: 19). Our aim, accordingly, is to propose a cohesive alternative to containment: a paradigm of *inference*.

To build on Dewey's point, philosophy has traditionally approached the question of existence by trying to determine *what* there is: in the containment paradigm, we strive to leap beyond perceptions to grasp what *really* exists in the mind-independent world. In the inference paradigm, however, we insist that any account of *what* is real requires a coordinate explanation of *how* it is accessed. We retain "real" and "mind," but recast these actively as what is real*ized* in the mind*ing* or managing of problems-to-solutions.

Building upon Kant's suggestion that any metaphysics of *what* there is presupposes discerning *how* objective knowledge is possible, Dewey's *how* of objectivity becomes his wholly experimental and scientific "circuit of inquiry" (1938/1986: 105–21). Though not a system-builder tasked with forging an "ontology of existence," his stated aim is "to *convert* all the *ontological*, as prior to inquiry, into the logical as occupied wholly and solely with what takes place in the conduct of inquiry" (Dewey & Bentley 1949/1989a: 316).

A Phenomenology of Objectivity

Dewey's naturalism suggests to some that science is the best way to redress epistemological woes. As we'll see, contemporary neurophysiology powerfully reinforces a transactional theory of situated consciousness. However, insofar as they presuppose conditions beyond consciousness, extended cognition theories cannot resolve the containment predicament without begging the question. Whether consciousness, however far extended, is best conceived in terms of containment or inference is part of the general problem of objectivity—a distinctly philosophical problem whose solution, we suggest, begins with a pragmatist phenomenology.

Let's first distinguish "phenomenology" in classical pragmatism from Husserl's project of mapping the "structure of consciousness." Preserving Peirce's sense of phenomenology as fidelity to what's actually experienced, Dewey simply invites us to "go to experience" and see what it is "experienced *as*" (1903/1977b: 158).

So how is experience experienced? Perhaps the single most valuable revision of modern philosophy asserts just this: in its default mode, experience is predominantly *nonreflective* rather than *reflective.* In Dewey's phrase, *having* is at least as significant as *knowing.* The mind is not a spotlight continuously picking out discrete properties. Instead, when all is familiar, governed by "assurance or control," experience presents itself as an unanalyzed totality, a *gestalt* or fit (159).

Try this yourself: in reading the previous sentence, were you consciously aware of either the individual letters f-i-t or their blackness? Or were they simply *had* and *used* in service to an actual challenge—coming to terms with having versus knowing? And if they stand out now, isn't it because I've posed them as a conceptual challenge—a *problem*?

Further, doesn't this apply equally to *you* as reader? Were you consciously aware of yourself reading the letters? If not, it's clear that the subject–object relation is not inherent in nonreflective experience, but marks a cognitive discrimination *from* such experience in response to a specific problem, need, or purpose: in *response* to the shock that disrupts the gestalt or unity, *I* step forth to deal with *it*. A phenomenology faithful to actual experience rejects the containment paradigm at the outset. The occult metaphysical question "*what* is the *reality* experienced" thus becomes the tractable phenomenological question "*how* is this *really* experienced" (159).

This fidelity to experience is certified as Dewey's *postulate of immediate experience*: What *is* is what it is experienced *as* (158). This doesn't mean that everything is just as I happen to experience it, such that if I experience myself as Napoleon, I am Napoleon! Instead, Dewey is saying that the phenomenological characteristic if each phase of experience is *really* that experience—that (1) nonreflective having, the shock of doubt, and the ultimate cognitive outcome are equally *real* in the conduct of inquiry, and (2) nothing is beyond these that's *more* or *really real*.

To conclude our quick look at Dewey's inferential alternative to containment, let's see these phases of activity at work in his *circuit of inquiry*. At the outset nonreflective experience is restful, dominated by habituated familiarity. The *shock* of the onset of a *problematic situation* disrupts this comfortable state with the realization that something is awry requiring attention. When habit supplies a solution, nonreflective experience is quickly restored. But when the problem persists without a ready solution, *inquiry* is necessary.

With the onset of a problematic situation, inquiry plays the double role of (1) diagnosing the problem and (2) framing a hypothesis or idea of a solution

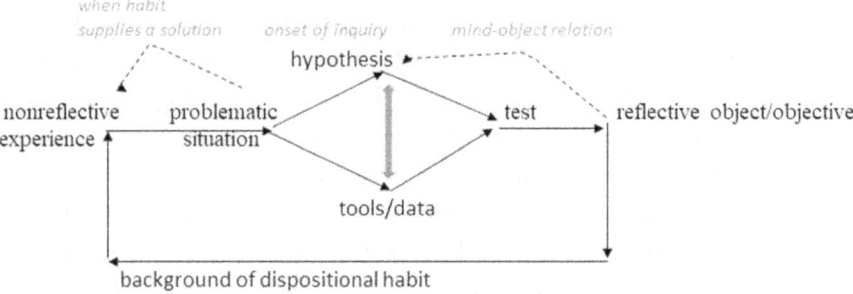

Figure 2.4 The Circuit Inquiry.

to be achieved by directed action. Both steps typically require the skilled use of empirical data and tools.

Once successfully tested, a projected hypothesis achieves its object/object*ive*—the dual terms enforcing the inseparability of *what* is confirmed from *how* it is confirmed. Moreover, for Dewey, "mind" is not subjectively "between the ears," but the *minding* or managing of problems to solutions. The mind–object relation is no longer the dilemma of subjective percept versus objective thing, but of a projected idea/hypothesis and its concrete realization *in* experience. Our world *is* the world of such ongoing constructive discovery—the infant's "stick" becomes the child's "pencil"; further inquiry discloses a graphite cylinder with a carbon core, then their molecular or atomic properties. No single disclosure is "ultimately real," let alone the phantom "thing-in-itself." Instead, inquiry conjures an unbounded fund of potential *reals* suited to various purposes and contexts of use.

Having sketched inquiry's reflective function, we note its seminal return to the nonreflective realm. Inquiry is not an arc, but a self-enriching *circuit*. Once attained, cognitive objectives of inquiry return to and reconfigure the dispositional background of nonreflective experience. They dig the trenches of habit, of the tried and true, that help us cope without the continuous intervention of reflection.

A "Cultivated" Naïve Realism

In summary, nonreflective experience is the focal point of our situatedness in the world because it undercuts the initial presumption of "subjective mind" versus "mind-independent reality" that keeps Hume's skeptic in business. As Dewey notes, we can always doubt what we *know*, but "skepticism as to things we *have* ... is impossible" (1925/1981: 379).

But is desirable or even possible to eliminate containment? Doesn't common sense and science alike acknowledge perceiving organisms *in* a physical, external world? And though inexorably bound up with bodily and social environments, isn't consciousness, strictly speaking, mostly "in the head?"

Each of these questions may be answered affirmatively. Look, the problem has never been about questioning the fact of perceptual events, external objects, or even the belief that the former are in the latter. Instead, it's in supposing that the *philosophical* problem of objectivity is about getting from subjective mind to objective world. Hume's challenge shows us that the containment paradigm fails to get the human condition right. Our phenomenological diagnosis attributes this to not reporting what's actually experienced. The circuit of inquiry aspires to set things right.

To fully achieve this, however, the inference paradigm must overthrow the containment predicament while accommodating the intuitions of common sense and science—specifically, by showing how containment looks *within* inference:

The containment paradox saddles us with getting from [1] mind-independent reality to [2] perceptual content. The inference paradigm, however, tells a different tale—that of two *objects-objectives,* **both** *achieved outcomes of the circuit of inquiry.* One of these, [1] the flesh and blood hand, we mastered early in life in learning to manipulate things in our environment. The other, [2] a complex neural event, is something science still struggles to fully understand. Nonetheless, in terms of cognitive access, both are equally "open and above board" in the encountered world, both are attained *objectives* of inquiry—as is [3] the neuro-physiological question about how brains perceive hands.

In all such cases, empirical questions beget empirical answers, and we may speak of "correspondence" and "cause" as we see fit. But these are different questions, with different objectives, than the philosophical question of objectivity. In vanquishing the epistemological problem of getting from subject to object, we find ourselves at home in a world of hands, heads, and brains—a realism justifiably dubbed "commonsense" or even "naïve." Yet, Dewey reminds us, this is not the direct philosophical realism of things perceived as they are in themselves, but a "cultivated naivety" achieved from the "severe discipline" of philosophic thought (1938/1986: 40, 309).

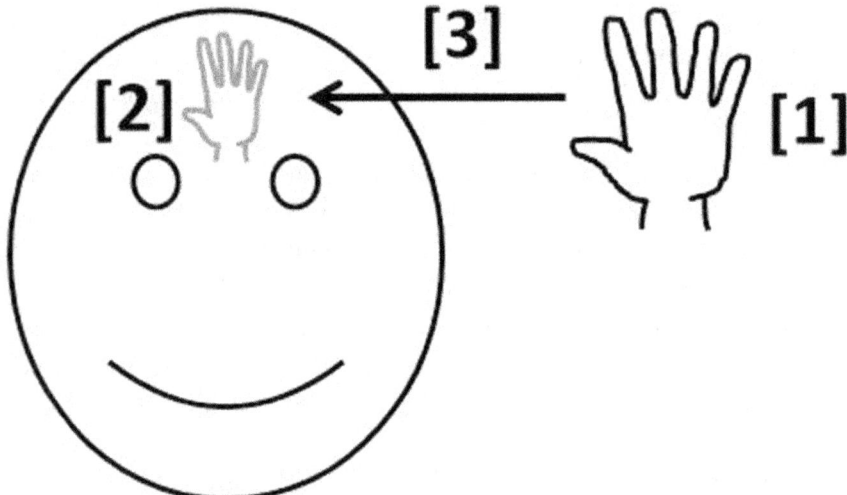

Figure 2.5 Containment within Inference.

Interaction and Transaction

Self-Action, Interaction, and Transaction

With Arthur F. Bentley, in 1943 Dewey set out to "fix a set of leading words" to address misconceptions about his legacy. (1949/1989a: 137). Over a six-year period they published fifteen essays collected in *Knowing and the Known*.

Fearing "experience" was unsalvageable from subjective interpretations Dewey had never intended, he and Bentley settled upon *transaction* as a suitable replacement. In a nutshell, transaction is "the right to see together, extensionally and durationally, much that is talked about conventionally is if it were composed of irreconcilable separates" (120). In *Knowing and the Known*'s seminal chapter, Dewey and Bentley distinguish *transaction* from *self-action* and *interaction*:

> *Self-Action.* Self-action views things as "acting under their own powers." Unmoved movers, animal spirits, *entelechy*, and the *élan vital* all explain behavior in terms of inherent essences or powers. Eradicated from natural science, self-action still haunts philosophy and psychology in the guise of an autonomous "knower" imbued with a soul, ego, id, or psyche (107).

> *Interaction.* Galileo, Copernicus, Kepler, and Newton ushered in science's modern age, with forces and particles in causal interaction supplanting self-actional motion. Interaction equally transformed commerce and industry, from standardized currency to the specialization of labor. Though vastly superior to self-actional potency, interaction suffered a theoretical blow with the discovery that statistical prediction in fields, rather than an aggregate of particles, better predicts outcomes in chemistry and physics (112). Despite regressing in science, interaction still dominates Western philosophy—not just among avowed realists but also, as we'll see, some pragmatists as well.

> *Transaction.* In our intended sense, transaction promotes the inference paradigm while exposing the defects of self-actional and interactional alternatives. First and foremost, transaction rejects the "cosmic pattern" consisting of (1) human organisms, (2) things in a surrounding environment, and (3) dynamic activity by which the former comes to know the latter (9). Where interaction regards organisms and objects as distinct existences, "*transaction* requires their primary acceptance in a common system" (114).

As we've seen, this "common system" is the circuit of inquiry, where (1) *ontological* decrees are converted into *logical* phases of inquiry, (2) subjects emerge as agencies of corrective action, and (3) objects are *objectives of inquiry*. Without a scintilla of subjectivism, Dewey and Bentley declare:

> A "real world" that has no knower to know it has, so far as human inquiry is concerned ... Just about the same "reality" that has the palace that in Xanadu Kubla Kahn decreed ... A knower without anything to know has even perhaps less claim to reality than that.
>
> (128)

Firm Words and Hedges

Perhaps the boldest declaration of Dewey's transactional *weltanschauung* is his insistence that there's no problem of getting to "external" reality because the very move from "internal" to "external" is senseless. We must stop "trying to construe knowledge as an attempted approximation to a reproduction of reality under conditions that condemn it in advance to failure; a revision ... should start frankly from the fact of thinking as inquiring, and purely external realities as terms in inquiries" (Dewey 1903/1977a: 93–4).

Here Dewey both (1) acknowledges the skeptical challenge that dooms the containment paradigm and (2) converts the ontological into the logical by insisting that we speak not of realities "*in* terms *of* inquiries," but "*as* terms *in* inquiries"—the far bolder claim that inquiry is not merely *revelatory* of reality, but functionally *constitutive* of it.

Even more amazingly, this claim was made in 1906—forty-three years prior to *Knowing and the Known!* Dewey and Bentley insist their views haven't changed—they're only correcting previous incautious language about terms such as "reality," "experience," and "existence." Problematic phrases are not hard to locate. Dewey had often depicted experience as a natural product of the interaction of an organism and its environment (1929/1984: 138; 1930/1984: 220) that "reaches down" into nature, "penetrating its secrets" (1925/1981: 11). Accordingly, he adds, we must distinguish the "rhythmic order" of natural *events* from *objects of experience* that interpret events (245).

The dissonance between such statements and the transactional stance as we've sketched it is so stark as to suggest something more than careless phrasing. Indeed, even a sympathetic reader like Richard Bernstein (1961) can't help but report a "deep crack" between "phenomenological and metaphysical strains" in Dewey's thought. In the phenomenological strain, *experience* looms large; we focus upon nonreflective immediacy and the role of inference in attaining objectivity. The metaphysical strain, to the contrary, acknowledges the *existence* of a vast and impersonal universe beyond experience we organisms learn about via interaction. Either option seems disastrous for Dewey. If *nothing* is allowed beyond experience, isn't he confessing to idealism or panpsychism? But if existence extends beyond experience he's snared by the trap of having to explain how beings limited to experience can know or talk about anything *beyond* experience—and thus as vulnerable to the foibles of the containment paradigm as the realists he's claimed to usurp (5–6).

Clearly this is no verbal dispute. Must we, then, concur with Richard Gale's somber assessment that "the reason why no one ever understood what Dewey meant by 'experience' is not because he was a poor writer, as is commonly claimed, but rather because he was formulating a mystical doctrine" (2010:62). I think not. In an effort to "firm" Dewey's previous appeals to "organism-environment interaction," Bentley writes in 1942: "You put the organism and environment in nature, and rest there ... After a while, you use phrasings that seem to imply that 'knowings' are processes of the organism, as opposed to the objects in nature ... phrasings to imply all the old evils you have thrown out" (Dewey & Bentley 1964:116). The main problem, chides Bentley, is that although you "always 'see' existence transactionally ... you do not get it safely so used" (1964: 483). Clearly something more serious than incautious terminology is afoot here. Both realize that Dewey's genial nature inclines him to appease traditional realists and naturalists, when in fact, as Dewey admits, "the position we take so bucks the ways of looking at the world" as to constitute a "heresy ... so extreme as not to be recognized for what it is" (1964: 636–7). According to Bentley, appeasement has caused Dewey nothing but trouble: In rejecting in-itself reality "you at once fear ... you will be subject to attack as idealistic. You, therefore, hedge. Hedging has brought no fruit. I am against any more of it" (1964: 205). In retrospect, Dewey observes that "largely due to him [Bentley], I've finally got the nerve inside of me to do what I should have done years ago" (1949/1989b: 489)—heralding a "radical heresy" for the "very few" capable of grasping that "existential events" unfold *in* "general procedures of inquiry" (1950/1964: 635).

Interactional Pragmatism

I invite the "very few" of sufficient nerve to advance *transaction* as the "firm" name Dewey and Bentley affix to pragmatism-without-hedging. This is no easy sell. Many still contend he's a naturalistic realist (of some stripe) who grants mind-independent existence while deploying organism–environment interaction against the passive "spectator theory" of knowledge. They think Dewey hedges not to appease realists, but to assuage that "permanent Hegelian deposit" of idealism that sadly beckons him in those late transactional years. Let's explore the wages of their *interactional* pragmatism.

In Dewey's heyday, his fiercest competitor for the heart and soul of pragmatism was Arthur O. Lovejoy. Lovejoy's ardent tutorial to "convert some pragmatists to pragmatism" insists that knowledge is the product of a vigorous "commerce" with nature, "a trafficking with lands in which the traffickers do not live" (1920/1983: 477). Since we cannot directly access reality, such commerce requires a "certain venture of belief … that the characters which as present they bear [are] the same characters which they bear as absent" (474). Lovejoy concedes that Dewey's emphasis on hypothesis and experiment tracks this view to an extent. However, Dewey admits only reals *of* experience, and not a *reality* and various surrogates and approximations of it (448). In curbing such idealistic impulses, concludes Lovejoy, we attain a true pragmatism "of man as agent, and as reflective agent, in a physical and social environment" where knowledge is always mediate and achieved (479).

In reply, Dewey agrees that no *knowledge* is immediate. What is immediately *had*, however, is not a "surrogate" of external reality, but a nonreflective starting point *from* which knowledge is the mediate outcome of directed action. For all the talk about "interaction" and "commerce," Lovejoy is actually the immediatist inasmuch as his surrogates point to "some entity immediate and complete in itself" (Dewey 1920/1983:52). What we subjectively experience as "present-as-absent" somehow—magically or mysteriously, but transcendent of experience itself—"hooks up" with "ready-made" existences (Dewey 1924/1988:45).

Contemporary interactional pragmatists include Ralph Sleeper, Raymond Boisvert, Sandra Rosenthal, and J. E. Tiles. For Sleeper, pragmatism signifies "a radical form of realism—a transactional realism in which … thinking entails active involvement with independent reality, an involvement that is causally efficacious" (1986: 3). Boisvert adds that the experienced object "should in no way be confused with" the existing thing (86). To bridge this gap, (1) "immediate givens received by the individual" combine with (2) *intentionality*—the notion that the idea is the "mental inexistence of an object" that nonetheless "includes something as object within itself" (Boisvert 1988: 85). Rosenthal's speculative pragmatism proclaims that the "brute" interface of independent reality with experience (1985: 68) prompts us to picture "the structure of reality as it exists independently of our variously contextually set inquiries" (2001: 43). Though we never *know* the independent otherness, we can "live through" this "ontologically thick" reality via "a rich, ongoing, interactional or transactional unity between organism and environment" (45–8). For Tiles, nothing so arduous is involved once we forsake the idea that perception is mostly "in the head." Rather than thinking of percepts as effects of external things, we "*see through* the events in our retinas" to the things (Tiles 1989: 19).

Though a full discussion and reply awaits another occasion,[1] Dewey's response to Lovejoy applies to each of these views as well. The causal accounts of Sleeper and Rosenthal approximate Lovejoy's vigorous trafficking, though in claiming that reality per se can only be lived through rather than known, Rosenthal's boundary is more opaque. And though Boisvert and Tiles reverse the direction of causality to reflect the intentionality of the agent, the problem of mind-dependence illustrated in Figure 2.3 is as inescapable in an inside-out causality as it is in the outside-in epiphenomenalism of traditional empiricism. Parenthetically we note, with concern, that Sleeper's and Rosenthal's appeal to "transaction" in an overtly *interactional* sense is common among pragmatists who pay lip service to transaction while still operating within the paradigm of containment.

Transaction without Hedges

For several decades Jim Garrison, Tom Burke, Matthew J. Brown, and others have returned to Dewey's logical methodology to balance the naturalistic metaphysics emphasized by earlier successors, such as John Herman Randall, Jr., Sidney Hook, and Ernest Nagel. Discussion of Dewey's aesthetics and moral/social philosophy also thrives. By comparison, transaction has remained in eclipse, mainly promoted by Garrison, his associates in the philosophy of education including Joacim Andersson, Leif Östman, and Jim Henderson, philosophers Jules Altman, Sidney Ratner, Stephen Toulmin, John Stuhr, Shane Ralston, and myself. The project Bentley predicted would take "generations to complete" has barely broken ground.

It's possible, of course, to apply transactional strategies to educational, moral, and social ends without messing with ontology and epistemology. But here are three suggestions for anyone curious about Dewey's transactional quest to "see together."

Configure Existence in Experience

Earlier we recast reality as the real*ization* of hypotheses in objective outcomes. The relationship between existence and experience is even more precarious. As we've seen, a "deep crack" opens in trying to decide whether Dewey "makes everything experience" or acknowledges existence beyond it. Appeasements like "nothing is beyond the *reach* of experience" are unhelpful, since whatever is "reached" becomes experience, and thus reveals nothing about "existence itself" (Figure 2.3). Interactional pragmatists insist—on pain of idealism—that "objects of experience" be distinguished from "independent reality," and even Garrison, our leading transactionist, distinguishes Dewey's use of "existence, the topic of metaphysics, from essence, the topic of logic" (2001: 279; 2006: 26). Instead of Lovejoy's "foreign commerce," he likens existence to grapes pressed by linguistic meaning into the distilled wine of logical essence. But this invites the perhaps shopworn rejoinder—if cognitive recognition is found in the wine, how do we get to the grapes?

Garrison's analogy is benign if, as I suspect, he's talking about existences in a descriptive sense permissible *after* a phenomenology of objectivity has rendered things "open and above board"—Dewey's cultivated naïve realism. But the important difference between describing "things out there" and a *philosophical* commitment to existence beyond experience is worth examining.

There would be no perceived "deep crack," of course, if Dewey's pronouncements about existence and experience were clear and univocal. In the first chapter of *Experience and Nature*, shortly after stating that experience "penetrates" nature, he tells us it is

> double-barrelled in that it recognizes in its primary integrity no division between act and material, subject and object, but contains them both in an unanalyzed totality. "'Thing' and 'thought,' as James says in the same connection, are single-barrelled; they refer to products discriminated by reflection out of primary experience".
>
> (Dewey 1925/1981:18–19)

In the inference paradigm, existence is not something antecedently "out there" that either intrudes upon or is "reached" by experience. Instead, existence *is* the shock of transition *in* experience that sparks awareness of something awry *out there* that *I* must work to resolve.

Let's make this explicit. Figure 2.6 A depicts the relationship between existence and experience in interactional pragmatism; Figure 2.6 B illustrates the transactional alternative:

A. Interaction

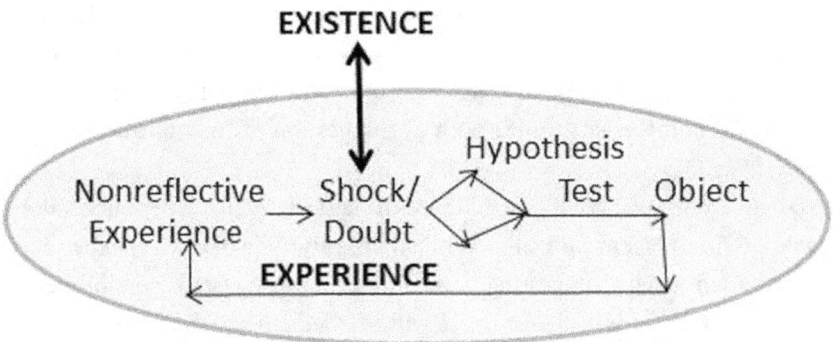

B. Transaction

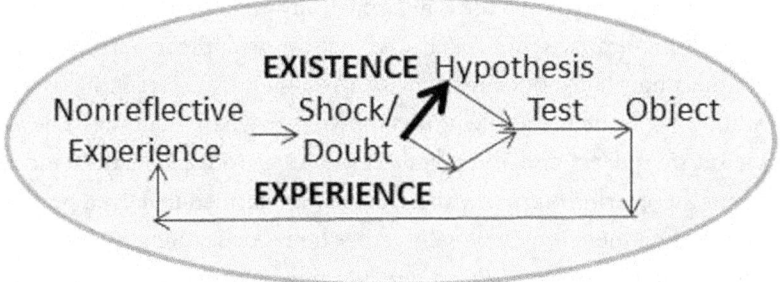

Figure 2.6 Existence and Experience in Interactional and Transactional Pragmatism.

In the interactional model, the "existential event" is outside of and intrudes upon experience—a "knock of the noumenal" that's unknowable, known by surrogates, intentionally "reached," or merely lived through. In the transactional alternative, existence is *what it is experienced as*—the experience *of* intrusion, shock, doubt. It signals a *challenge to thought*—a transition from nonreflective immediacy to the reflective activity of hypothesis, test, and attained objective. The relevant distinction is not between existential events and experienced objects, but rather "events which are challenges to thought and events which have met the challenge and hence possess meaning" (Dewey 1929/1984:246).

If both "thought" and "thing" are in experience, how many things are included? The short answer is *everything!* In the famous paean from *Experience and Nature,* Dewey hails "the planted field, the sowed seeds ... " (1925/1981:18).

A quarter century later, he expands this to "include the environing world." But the "firm" word Dewey and Bentley eventually settle upon to replace "experience" is "cosmos of fact," the entire "system or field of factual inquiry" (1949/1989a: 72). "My use of 'Experience,'" confides Dewey, "was to attempt a name that covers the whole range of transactions ... from the brute to the scientific." "Cosmos of fact" conveys this comprehensiveness with no suggestion of "mentalistic" overtones (1944/1964: 331).

If, with Dewey, we grant that all these things are equally experienced, doesn't Figure 2.6 A now seem a bit silly? While there's always a beyond *of* experience— each attained object suggesting a wealth of undiscovered possibilities—we literally go to the ends of the universe without being *beyond* experience!

Construe Signs Transactionally: The Battle for the Interpretant

Ever since Peirce, *signs* as *sign use* is integral to any pragmatist theory of meaning, with broad implications for social and educational theory. Though Dewey stresses the importance of sign-behavior throughout his career, no systematic exposition appears before *Knowing and the Known*, where "namings-known" are specified as *sign, object,* and *interpretant* (1949/1989a: 68–82). Understanding the relation of these terms is crucial, and Dewey was alarmed that even pragmatists tend to interpret them interactionally rather than transactionally.

Sign-behavior cast as *sign, object, and interpretant* originates in Peirce, though his intended meaning is disputed. Especially noisome is the interpretant, which Peirce vaguely alludes to as "a Third," a sign's "proper significate outcome," and an elucidation of meaning as habit. (1960: 274, 473–5).

Charles W. Morris advanced what's now accepted as the consensus view in the late 1930s. Morris, who studied under George Herbert Mead and regarded his views as "compatible with the framework of Dewey's thought" (1946: 273), offers this straightforward interpretation: (1) *Sign* is sign vehicle—the identifying word or symbol, 2) *Object* is its *designatum*—what the sign refers to, and 3) *Interpretant*, initially the sign's effect on an interpreter (1938:81), later becomes "the *interpreter* itself—the organism for which something is a sign" (1946:17).

Given Morris's pedigree and definitions so seemingly innocuous that even transactionists employ it,[2] the reaction from the normally genial Dewey is jolting. Publicly, he complains that "'users' of Peirce's writings should either stick to his basic pattern or leave him alone" (1949/1989a: 152). Privately, he calls Morris's account a "complete fabrication" and suggests "nailing him to the cross" (Dewey & Bentley 1964: 457).

Morris, complains Dewey, "is controlled by the epistemological heritage of a knowing subject, person, self, or what have you, set over against the world" (1964: 145). But sign, object, and interpretant are not distinct entities that merely interact. Instead, their relation is ascertained *within* constructive activity as directives about what to *do* (1944/1964: 289–90).

According to Dewey, the correct, transactional relation of *object*, *sign*, and *interpretant* is illustrated by Peirce's own example of a drill sergeant commanding his squad to "ground arms." Here the *object* is the desired *objective*—that the rifle butts be placed on the ground, the *sign* is the command, and the *interpretant* is the shared background of experience by which the recruits successfully interpret the meaning of the *sign* and respond so as to attain the objective. The command to "ground arms," as a sign, is meaningful only insofar as the interpretant supplies an appropriate context of understanding (Dewey 1946/1989: 144).

Dewey's ire reveals his adamancy for replacing outmoded interactional views with a transactional alternative grounded in the problem-solving paradigm of inference. Descriptively or empirically, we may get away with talk about interacting objects, signs, and interpreters. But only the "full system" of sign-behavior, transactionally interpreted, illuminates Peirce's insight that communicated meaning is "our glassy essence."

A World without Withins and Withouts Supersedes Embodiment

It's remarkable that nowadays the heavy lifting in transactional theory is undertaken, not in epistemology or pragmatism, but in cognitive science, psychology, and the philosophy of education. These professions optimize sign-*behavior*, and as such are constitutionally suspicious of "percepts" copying "external realities." Andersson, Garrison, and Östman press this even further: "if we had a rich theory of embodied learning, we might not need epistemology as traditionally practiced" (2018: vi).

Embodied cognition insists that experience is "trans-dermal": In Mark Johnson's phrase, "meaning grows from our visceral connections to life and the bodily conditions of life" (2007, ix). Conditions such as sunlight, oxygen, food, and a community of language-users are, as Andersson, Garrison, and Östman observe, "external to individual human existence, but internal to its functioning. Functional transactions dissolve the dualisms of internal versus external, nature versus culture, and body versus mind. The result is a functional world without a within" (2018: 59). If, as these authors assert, "a world without a within" is intended in a practical and empirical sense, "embodied cognition" aptly depicts it. Dewey himself, they note, believes that the epidermis is but a superficial boundary between organism and environment (Dewey 1934/1987: 64).

My concern arises, unsurprisingly, with any surreptitious shift from empirical description to the philosophical problem of objectivity in general—of our basic situatedness in the world. Here "embodiment" flirts with the quagmire of containment—a problem not alleviated by conjuring bigger containers that include air, food, or even a linguistic community.³ Insofar as they assume access to air, food, and a linguistic community, neurological accounts beg the philosophical question of how objective experience is possible. A pragmatist phenomenology of inference is needed to both (1) enforce the futility of the containment paradigm and (2) propose a constructive alternative wherein aesthetic "having" is the "alpha and omega." Andersson, Garrison, and Östman seem to endorse this. But if so, the double-barrelledness of thought–thing, subject–object, inside–outside, suggests not just a primal exclusion of withins, but both withins and withouts!

A Short List of Firmer Names

In *Knowing and the Known*, Dewey and Bentley transactionally "firm" nearly one hundred self-actional and interactional terms. So in addition to our three suggestions—(1) configure existence in experience, (2) construe signs transactionally, and (3) recast embodied consciousness as situated cognition within the inference paradigm—here are five additional tips for thinking and expressing ourselves transactionally:

Looser Interactional Phrase	*Firmer Transactional Restatement*
"Existence beyond experience."	The "beyond *of* experience," or, if Dewey's meaning of "experience" is unrecoverable, "fact."
"Transacts *with*."	Never acceptable, since it superimposes interaction upon transaction.
"Interpretant" as "interpreter."	"A context of shared understanding facilitating an objective."
"Organism–environment interaction."	Acceptable for limited descriptive purposes, stated as such; unacceptable as a philosophical ground of cognition.
"Embodied cognition."	Acceptable for limited descriptive purposes, stated as such; unacceptable as a philosophical ground of cognition. In either application, "situated cognition" is preferable.

Uniting the Philosophical and the Empirical

The Continuity of How and What

In everyday life, appeals to self-action, interaction, or transaction are decided not by ontological fiat but by contexts of use. Mustering fortitude as an inner resource might ease a trip to the dentist; interactional calculations are ideal for sinking a putt. Philosophers' problems about existence, reality, and objectivity compel the transactional paradigm of inference, but elsewhere appeals to self-action and interaction are often appropriate. Consider modern physics: the foundational paradigm of quantum mechanics is transactional—reality is manifest in the function of an entire field rather than an aggregate of interacting particles. Nonetheless, in everyday affairs, from measuring torque to designing bridges, Newtonian interaction remains desirable for its applicability and simplicity.

Perhaps, then, we might plausibly suppose that even if a phenomenological account of cognition is ineluctably transactional, that's no reason to discourage theorists in neuroscience, psychology, or educational theory from preferring "sign-interpreter," "organism–environment interaction," and "embodiment" to their transactional counterparts.

But here's a reason: Dewey always sought *continuities* in events that otherwise seem disconnected or oppositional. And if the inference paradigm of *how* things are experienced is always integral to *what* is experienced, it would be incongruous not to look for this in reverse empirical applications from *what* there is to *how* we experience it:

In our pragmatist phenomenology (left), objects are uniformly *objectives* of inquiry: *what* is objectively knowable is fully constrained by the *how* of minding or managing of problems to solutions. But this philosophical outcome yields a cultivated naïveté where things are "open and above board" to empirical description. In such accounts (right), the *how* consists of tool-users discovering *what* we can learn about the facts of the world, many of which persist independently of human affairs.

The ultimate aim of a fully transactional view, I submit, is seeing together this double-movement of the *how* and *what*. A phenomenology of objectivity

Figure 2.7 The Reciprocity of "How" and "What"

promises to rejuvenate philosophy by undoing centuries of misconceptions about existence, reality, and cognition perpetuated by the containment paradigm. We don't abandon epistemology or the quest for truth; we reimagine it in the real*ization* of attainable objectives. This philosophical renaissance is concurrent with the evolution of transactional approaches in the natural and social sciences that began 150 years ago.

Transactional Bridges

Unlike Kant, Dewey does not separate epistemology from moral philosophy. What we empirically describe as facts or objects are, in different contexts, constructed goods or values. Transaction seamlessly extends epistemological concerns about truth and knowledge to significant ethical, social, and educational aspirations.

From an empirical perspective, this continuity alerts us to the transactional revolution that transformed the natural and social sciences. First manifest in chemistry and physics, anthropology and sociology soon overthrew Western paternalism for a pluralistic perspective embracing every culture is an experiment in the art of living. Economics witnessed the evolution of the business model from self-actional sole proprietor and interactional executive-shareholder to that of transactional stakeholder where the interests of all affected are taken into account. Indeed, science itself is now regarded as social phenomena driven by what works rather than what is presumed to be ultimately real.

The advance of transaction has been slower in cognitive science, psychology, and education. Dynamics systems theory and situated cognition are only now seriously challenging clunky structural and computational schemas of the mind. Psychology is still haunted by self-actional *ids* and *egos*—even if by other names. In education, as Andersson, Garrison, and Östman report, "The traditional modernist notion of the mind dominates educational research decades after Dewey's death while educational researchers still strive to complete the impossible quest for certainty" (2018:11).

Though the challenges are formidable, the prospects are encouraging. I offer those "firmer names" in hope that one day philosophy and empirical practice will unite in regarding transactional alternatives as generally more insightful and empowering. There's no such thing as doing science, psychology, or educational theory without a governing world view. And if the containment paradigm is obsolete, it just makes sense to rethink interactional description from a broader transactional perspective.

Conclusion and Summary

Here's a quick overview of the reasons why a transactional overhaul of "philosophers' problems" is justified and important:

> Transaction allows us to "see together" theoretical and empirical commitments that otherwise remain opposed or disconnected.
> The avoidance of epistemological analysis is a missed opportunity to replace faulty epistemological commitments with constructive pragmatist alternatives.
> Dewey himself vigorously engaged the "cottage industry" of epistemology by warning of the skeptical consequences of trying to leap from "mind" to "world."
> For Dewey, the "cultivated naivety" of a directly accessible world requires the "severe discipline" of philosophic thought that replaces containment with inference as the paradigm of objectivity.

3

Transactional Perspectivalism: The Emergence of Language, Minds, Selves, and Temporal Sequences

Jim Garrison

Introduction

This chapter examines John Dewey's transactional realism as we find it not only in his collaboration late in life with Arthur F. Bentley, *Knowing and the Known*, but also in earlier work. Among the ideas examined in this chapter are the transactional emergence of linguistic meaning, mental functioning, and the self. All these involve taking the perspective of others in linguistic transactions. Another idea that surprisingly also involves taking the perspective of others is the construction of temporal sequences. To expand the transactional circle this chapter turns to Dewey's colleague George Herbert Mead. They initially worked out many of the ideas mentioned above together. Mead later extended and refined Dewey's thinking about time. Here the durational aspects of durational-extensional transactions are emphasized, although the extensional aspect is always there.

Some Fundamental Aspects of Transactionalism

If we are careful, we can identify instances of transactional thinking in Dewey's earlier work. For instance, in his "Introduction" to the Dewey and Bentley correspondence Sydney Ratner (1964: 44) remarks: "Dewey's *Logic* served as the basis upon which the theoretical structure of *Knowing and the Known* was built." It is easy to find such remarkably transactional statements in Dewey *Logic* as "the processes of living are enacted by the environment as truly as by the organism; for they *are* an integration" (1938/1986: 32). In the second chapter, "The Existential Matrix of Inquiry: Biological," Dewey states the core idea of transactionalism: "Whatever else organic life is or is not, it is a process of activity that involves an environment. It is a transaction extending beyond the spatial limits of the organism" (32). Further, "What exists co-exists" (220). Elsewhere, Dewey asserts, "A living organism and its life processes involve a world or nature temporally [durationally] and spatially [extensionally] 'external' to itself but 'internal' to its functions" (1925/1981: 212). Transactionalism recognizes that one's body, mind, and self are not simply located. Rather, they are distributed in a world without withins (see Garrison 2001). In Frank X. Ryan's terms, it breaks "the containment paradigm."[1]

The organism maintains homeostasis through constant transactional adjustment. Among organisms like human beings there is "modification" that "constitutes what is termed habit" (1938/1986: 38). Biological habits of action emerge in organism–environment transactions. The forgoing remarks about embodiment help us better understand why Dewey and Bentley insist upon "transactional observation of the 'organism-in-environment-as-a-whole'" (1949/1989a: 103). There is no need to synthesize seemingly discrete interacting observations if we can see them together in a single integrated transactional unity.

Dewey titles the third chapter of his *Logic* "The Existential Matrix of Inquiry: Cultural." Everything just said regarding organism–environmental transactions holds for human–organism–sociocultural–environmental transactions. While other people, cultural institutions, tools, and artifacts are external to the skin of our bodies, they are internal to our functional existence. Think what happens when you lose your pocketbook or wallet.

The Acquisition of Language, Meaning, and the Mind

Consider the transactional acquisition of linguistic meaning. In linguistic communication physical existences like gestures and sounds directed at other physical things "do not operate or function as mere physical things …. They operate in virtue of their *representative* capacity or *meaning*" (1938/1986: 52). The physical sound or mark gets its "meaning in and by conjoint community of functional use" (52). This is important since "mind denotes the whole system of meanings as they are embodied in the workings of organic life" (1925/1981: 230). Furthermore, "Mind is seen to be a function of social interactions, and to be a genuine character of natural events when these attain the stage of widest and most complex interaction with one another" (7–8).

Dewey begins his essay, "The Inclusive Philosophic Idea" by noting: "Conjoint behavior is a universal characteristic of all existences" (1928/1984: 41). "What exists co-exists" (*op. cit.*). He argues that the more complex the conjoint behavior "the more fully are potentialities released for observation" (41). Life on earth is the consequence of a vast array of transactionally co-dependent physical, chemical, and biological conditions. Biological transactions emerge out of physical transactions much as water (H_2O), which extinguishes class A fires, emerges out of hydrogen, which is highly combustible, and oxygen, which sustains combustion. Likewise, social communication emerges from biological functioning without breach of continuity when animal gestures (e.g., vocalization) acquire abstract symbolic meaning including words, images, ideas, and such. For Dewey, to have a mind is to possess meanings that, as we are about to see, are acquired by participating in socio-linguistic practices. Therefore, with the emergence of language, "The social affords us an observable instance of a 'realm of mind' objective to an individual, by entering into which as a participating member organic activities are transformed into acts having a mental quality" (50). With language, the physical, chemical, and biological acquire meaning. In this sense, the social is the most inclusive philosophic idea. Dewey concludes, "I do not say that the social as we know it *is* the whole, but I do emphatically suggest that it is the widest and richest manifestation of the whole accessible to our observation" (53).

Like the later Wittgenstein, Dewey has a "use" approach to understanding language and meaning that emphasizes the primacy of sociocultural practice (Quine 1969; Medina 2004). However, few recognize that for both philosophers the acquisition of linguistic meanings is emergent, transactional, and not simply located. Here is Dewey's version:

> Language is specifically a mode of interaction of at least two beings, a speaker and a hearer; it presupposes an organized group [e.g., a culture] to which these creatures belong, and from whom they have acquired their habits of speech. It is therefore a relationship, not a particularity …. The meaning of signs moreover always includes something common as between persons and an object.
> (1925/1981: 145)

Dewey depicts a three-term transaction involving A and B coordinating their behavior regarding a common object O in a cooperative social practice, a form of life. To comprehend language acquisition, we must exercise "the right to see" A, B, and O "extensionally and durationally" together as one (Dewey and Bentley, 1949/1989a, 67).

A hen (A), to use Dewey's (1925/1981) example, may respond to a farmer's (B) behavior by "habit, by conditioned reflex" (145). However:

> [A] human infant learns to discount such movements; to become interested in them as events preparatory to a desired consummation; he learns to treat them as signs of an ulterior event so that his response is to their meaning. He treats them as means to consequences. The hen's activity is ego-centric; that of the human being is participative. The latter puts himself at the standpoint of a situation in which two parties share. This is the essential peculiarity of language, or signs.
>
> (145)

A and B must coordinate each other's *perspective* with their own regarding O in a complex durational–extensional transactional process wherein linguistic meanings with objective references emerge.

Linguistic meanings, the use of abstract signs (i.e., symbols) such as words, emerge in the transaction along with the mental functioning of A and B regarding the referent, the object O. Perspective taking is a potentially endless course of recursion. For example, A may know that B knows that A knows B's perspective on O. When they do not agree regarding O the transaction continues. Because A and B cannot instantaneously take each other's perspective regarding O it is always a durational–extensional process requiring A and B to see each other and O together. A, B, and O emerge concurrently in the ongoing transaction. Meaning for Dewey and Bentley is a three-term not a two-term relation distributed wherever it occurs. Behavior is never simply located in a world without withins.

Wittgenstein (1953) says, "To imagine a language means to imagine a form of life" (§19). A form of life, exemplified by Wittgenstein's language games, is a cultural practice. Now imagine A saying to B, "Bring me a slab [O]" (§19). What is a slab? A slab of butter, a slab of beef, or a brick? In Houston Texas, a slab is a large, customized car with high-gloss paint, a high-volume sound system, a fifth wheel, and "swanga" wheel covers. It is considered an urban art form.[2] Imagine saying, "Bring me a slab" on a Houston car lot. The point is that meaning emerges in ongoing linguistic transactions along with the mental functioning of A and B as they strive to negotiate and re-negotiate the shared referent O. Has our linguistic transaction just now changed your thinking about the meaning of O ("slab")?

Distinctively human mental functioning is an emergent organism–sociocultural-environment behavioral transaction. In a typescript titled, "What Is It to Be a Linguistic Sign or Name?" found in the Arthur F. Bentley Collection and reprinted in the Carbondale edition of *Knowledge and the Known*, we find an explicitly transactional statement of the origin of linguistic signs: "Specifiable behavioral operations, *doings and makings* [of O] which involve the body, things and other human beings [A and B], determine certain things, like gestures, sounds, etc., to be signs" (1949/1989a: 304). First, note that meaning, and hence mentality, is a matter of doing and making. Second, note the role of other human beings. Third, linguistic meaning and mentality are durationally (i.e., temporally) distributed functions analytically comprised of at least three transactional terms A, B, and O. Fourth, "Sign and thing designated are constituents of one inclusive undivided set of operations; any distinction drawn between them is the result of post or reflective operations" (304–5). The separation of signifier and signified is only a useful analytic distinction of inquiry that must not harden into a false dualism.

It is worth saying something about the behavioral operations of reflective inquiry. One example is the behavioral operations comprising a controlled experiment. Another is the purely symbolic behavioral operations of a mathematical or logical proof. In both cases the goal (i.e., "the end-in-view") is to render the referent O stable and repeatable among two or more participants in the transaction, A and B. Empirical researchers anywhere or anywhen must be able to reproduce the same behavioral conditions with the same empirical consequences to secure acceptance within the scientific community. Likewise, for mathematical or logical proofs.

The Primacy of Social Perspectives

Michael Tomasello (1999, 2008, 2019) provides extensive empirical evidence for the correctness of Dewey and Wittgenstein's approach to language. Tomasello's (2019) "key claim" is:

> [C]hildren's skills of perspective-taking originate in social interactions structured by joint attention. With joint attention we may say that we are attending to the same thing, only differently; we are triangulating on it, each with our own viewing angle. Without joint attention, there is no common object on which the two of us may have different viewing angles, and no sense of perspective.
> (64)

What Tomasello calls "joint attention" is social perspective taking. Unfortunately, Tomasello is thinking in terms of simple interaction. What he calls "triangulating" is in fact a three-term durationally–extensionally distributed transaction involving A, B, and O. Tomasello argues that while the higher primates can track conspecific mental states regarding objects, they cannot consider their own perspective on the object and then triangulate to the perspective of the conspecific. In Dewey's terms, they cannot place themselves "at the standpoint of a situation in which two parties share" (*op. cit.*).

To further explore perspectivalism, it is helpful to turn to George Herbert Mead, especially his *The Philosophy of the Present*. He emphasizes that "the appearance of mind is only the culmination of that sociality which is found throughout the universe" (1932/1959: 86). Sociality functions for Mead much as transaction functions for Dewey, which is not surprising given Dewey thinks sociality the inclusive philosophic idea.

Like Dewey, Mead recognizes "the objectivity of perspectives" (162). In contrast to physical or biological perspectives human–organism–sociocultural–environmental perspectives also include "other selves with minds" that involve "the individual entering into the perspective of others" (166). A human perspective is much more than Tomasello's "different viewing angles" (*op. cit.*). Different human perspectives (e.g., A and B) involve embodied needs, desires, selective attention, habits, meanings, valuing, knowing, personal history, and more.

Further, human A's and B's have species-typical phylogenetic response patterns as well as an individual's genetic inheritances that are part of their perspective. They also have distinct developmental histories that include different enculturated beliefs, values, and ways of knowing. Finally, epigenetics implies phylogeny and ontogeny are sometimes transactional. Initially, A and B take extraordinarily complex, sometimes seemingly incommensurable, perspectival attitudes toward O that must be mutually adjusted to achieve a shared understanding and regularly readjusted to maintain cooperation. Co-constructing a shared perspective is not a passive spectator activity of simply located organisms. Rather, it is an active durationally–extensionally distributed process conducted in a world without withins involving "specifiable behavioral operations, *doings and makings*" (*op. cit.*).

For Mead, "Sociality is the capacity of being several things at once" (49). Hence, a human "mind as it appears in the mechanism of social conduct is the organization of perspectives in nature and at least a phase of the creative advance of nature" (172). Linguistic "behavior" in a human–organism–sociocultural–

environment situation comprises A and B coordinating perspectives in a transaction involving durationally–extensionally emergent objects (event, idea, goal, *etc.*) O. It is a distributed function integrating, in Dewey and Bentley's (1949/1989a) terms, "characterizations of durational-extensional subject matters" where "Behavior" is "of the organic-environmental situation, with organisms and environmental objects taken as equally its aspects" (261).

Mead thought it possible to be in different perspectives simultaneously only when participating in transitional situations involving a "process of readjustment" (1932/1959: 47). Such situations resemble what Dewey calls an indeterminate situation requiring reconstructive inquiry to coordinate (1938/1986: 109 ff.). These situations involve temporal passages varying in duration depending on how long the period of reconstruction endures. A and B are involved in a "process of readjustment" when they strive to coordinate, or re-coordinate, their transactions regarding some object O. The remainder of this chapter emphasizes the emergence of socially transactional durational (i.e., temporal) perspectives somewhat at the expense of the extensional.

The Perspectival Emergence of Past, Present, and Future

The temporal present is an emergent durational transactional process: "The social nature of the present arises out of its emergence. I am referring to the process of readjustment that emergence involves …. There is an adjustment to this new situation" (Mead 1932/1959: 47). Human mental functioning, norm-governed social behavior, self-consciousness, and self-regulation emerge from sociocultural linguistic adjustment within a durational temporal present.

Mead states that "reality exists in a present" and while accepting that the present "implies a past and future" nonetheless "to both of these we deny existence" (1). The critical idea here involves distinguishing metaphysical existence from logical essence. Dewey does it this way: "Essence is never existence, and yet it is the essence, the distilled import of existence: the significant thing about it, its intellectual voucher" (1925/1981: 144). There is "a natural bridge that joins the gap between existence and essence; namely communication, language, discourse" (133). Thus far, this chapter has examined the construction of the linguistic bridge. The next section examines the construction of temporal sequences as logical essences involving past–present–future.

Dewey states, "Time as empty does not exist; time as an entity does not exist. What exists are things acting and changing, and a constant quality of their behavior is temporal" (1934/1987: 214). He distinguishes existential temporal quality from temporal sequence. Accordingly, "Quality is quality, direct, immediate and undefinable" (1925/1981: 92). Temporal quality "has movement from and towards *within* it" (385). Temporal quality characterizes anoetic durational existence. There is a vast difference between the temporal quality of an evening in the arms of your lover and that of a boring committee meeting. Meanwhile, temporal sequence "is a matter of relation, of definition, dating, placing and describing. It is discovered in reflection, not directly had and denoted as is temporal quality" (92). Sequences of past–present–future are constructions of judgment in inquiry not existential givens.

We often think in terms of an instantaneous punctual, knife-edged present, which is why we spatialize the present as if it was an infinitesimal point on a line. However, this is an abstract construction of analytic reflection. Temporal quality resembles William James's "the specious present" or Bergson's "*la durée*" which is opposed to physical time modeled on spatial movement. However, James and Bergson assume a subjective structuring of time within the temporal stream of consciousness that is then objectified. Mead and Dewey reject this implicit subject versus object dualism in favor of structuring time based on practical durational–extensional, organism–environment transactions involving the objective reality of perspectives.[3]

Regarding "the Biologic Individual" (i.e., the organism), in *Mind, Self, and Society* Mead remarks: "From the point of view of instinctive behavior in the lower animals or the immediate human response to a perceptual world ... past and future are not there: and yet they are represented in the situation" (1934/1967: 350). In instinctive behavior, past and future are "represented by facility of adjustment" to the situation wherein, "[t]he surrogate of the past is the actual adjustment of the impulse [and habits] to the object as stimulus. The surrogate of the future is the control which the changing field of experience during the act maintains over its execution" (351). It is one thing to have something, another to know it, still another to be able to reflect on it and inquire about it.

Immediate, noncognitive, anoetic behavior is confined to the specious present: "The flow of experience is not differentiated into a past and future over against an immediate now until reflection affects certain parts of experience" (351). Mead concludes: "The biologic individual lives in an undifferentiated now; the social reflective individual takes this up into a flow of experience a fixed past and a more or less uncertain future" (351). Later, in *The Philosophy of the Present*, Mead came to understand that the past is as uncertain as the future.

The "biologic individual" has a past and future, but only the linguistic "social reflective individual" with meanings and a mind acquired by durationally–extensionally taking and retaining the perspective of others knows it and can think about what it means (*op. cit.*). The "biologic individual" becomes a "social reflective individual" with a past and future in "social interactions structured by joint attention" (*op. cit.*). The social reflective individual emerges in a human–organism–sociocultural environment.

Eventually, the transactional durational-extensional coordination of perspectival attitudes with others is abstracted and generalized into objective norms of social transaction: "Our thinking is an inner conversation in which we may be taking the roles of specific acquaintances over against ourselves, but usually it is with what I have termed the 'generalized other' that we converse, and so attain to the levels of abstract thinking, and that impersonality, that so-called objectivity that we cherish" (1932/1959: 243). There is a conscious self that humans share with many other organisms. Mead stresses, "[a]s a mere organization of habit the [conscious] self is not self-conscious" (1913/1964: 147). However, the social individual conversing with the generalized other eventually becomes self-aware: "The self arises in conduct, when the individual becomes a social object in experience to himself .... He acts toward himself in a manner analogous to that in which he acts toward others. Especially he talks to himself as he talks to others" (Mead 1922/1964: 243). Self-consciousness emerges as one begins recursively taking the perspectival attitudes of others not only toward objects but, reflexively, also toward the actions of their own empirical self.

As the behavior of socially aware and reflective individuals begins conforming to the norms of the abstract perspective of the "generalized other" individuals begin justifying their actions in accordance with the moral and logical norms of the community. Action becomes more abstract and impersonal. In an important sense, objectivity involves intersubjectivity in transactionally coordinating perspectives. When perspectives do not converge individuals and societies undergo transitions involving "being several things at once" (*op. cit.*). In existentially indeterminate situations the most logical approach involves exchanging reasons and evidence, although sometimes re-coordinating perspectives require a change in social norms regarding what counts as a good reason, which may result in political or scientific revolutions. From whose perspective do you perceive the past, present, and future of recent immigrants to your country?

A self-conscious, self-regulating, reflective being is capable of deliberately engaging in extremely durationally extended behavior: "The stretch of the present within which this self-consciousness finds itself is delimited by the particular social act in which we are engaged. But since this usually stretches beyond the immediate perceptual horizon we fill it out with memories and imagination" (Mead 1932/1959: 87). The past and future emerges in the reflective filling out in temporally extended "functional presents," which are always "wider than the specious present, and may take in long stretches of an undertaking which absorbs unbroken concentrated attention" (88). However, one "can accomplish this only by using symbolic imagery" (88).

Temporal Sequences: The Punctual, Specious, and Functional Present

Only social individuals capable of coordinating with the perspectives of others can acquire the "symbolic imagery," that is, the linguistic capacity necessary to explicitly state the surrogates of the past and future within a durationally extended functional present. These statements may then be placed into a sequential order within the larger context of inquiry. Mead concludes, "The functional boundaries of the present are those of its undertaking—of what we are doing. The pasts and futures indicated by such activity belong to the present" (88). The "functional boundaries" with their unique temporal quality expand and contract according to the duration required for inquiry to reconstruct the coordination of perspectives.

For Dewey, the most intelligent form of reflection is found in his *Logic: The Theory of Inquiry*. Consider the formation of judgment in historical inquiry. The function of constructing a logical judgment "is transformation of an antecedent existentially indeterminate or unsettled situation into a determinate one" (1938/1986: 220). Recall that immediate anoetic quality "has movement from and towards *within* it" (*op. cit.*). Recall too that language is the bridge from existence to essence. Anoetic existential existences do not enter inquiry until they are given a temporal narration or a spatial description.[4] Hence, "Existential subject-matter as transformed has a temporal phase. Linguistically, this phase is expressed in narration" (1938/1986: 220).

The determination of a temporal sequence is a logical function of judgment involving logical inference. Here we may add a small, albeit significant, addendum to Mead. Dewey writes, "To recall a specific past event or to foresee or predict a future specific event requires inference, but in the same sense it demands inference to make a determinately specific judgment about anything said to be present" (1926/1984: 66). The specious present as anything more than a noncognitive anoetic felt qualitative duration is a matter of reflective inquiry as much as is the past or the future. In a temporal sequence there is no present without a past and a future. The qualitative from and toward of the durational present is existentially given, but it is not given as meaning or knowledge. The distinction between immediate anoetic temporal existence and a temporal sequence as a logical essence is crucial.

Dewey marks the difference between "existential change as barely existential" (i.e., existence) and "as subject-matter of judgment" (i.e., essence). Therefore, "Event is a term of judgment, not of existence apart from judgment" (1938/1986: 222). Whatever the temporal quality of existential change, in reflective inquiry, "There is reference to limit *ab quo* [the earliest possible date] and *ad quem* [the latest possible date]" (221). Without "this limitation, a change is not characterized …. No mere flux can be noted, appraised or estimated" (221). Dewey argues, "Absolute origins and absolute closes and termini are mythical. Each beginning and each ending is a delimitation of a cycle or round of qualitative change" (221). The determination of the limits of an event is an analytical function of inquiry structuring qualitative existential change by and for human purposes.

In their final, "A Trial Group of Names," Dewey and Bentley provide the following definition: "*Event:* That range of differentiation of the named which is better specified than situation, but less well specified than object" (1949/1989a: 262). Dewey and Bentley's events resemble Mead's "functional presents" (*op. cit.*). A "Situation" is indeterminate whereas an "Object" is the "firmest specification and is thus distinguished from situation and event" (267). As Dewey says in the *Logic*, "Objects are the objectives of inquiry" (1938/1986: 122). Objects are among the products of the processes of inquiry; so too are temporal sequences.

The details of the construction of a temporal sequence involves all the interrelated functions of inquiry. Here, is a simple example from Dewey's discussion of "Judgments of Recollection":

> Dating, moreover, is nothing absolute. It depends upon connecting a particular occurrence with other events coming before and after in such a way that taken together they constitute a temporal series or history. If I say that "I was at home at five o'clock yesterday," I am in fact constructing as an object of grounded belief a sequential course of events. "Yesterday" has no significance save in connection with today, the day-before-yesterday and a series of tomorrows. (224)[5]

Temporal sequences such as "clock time" are always constructed. Remember, "objects [e.g., dates] are the objectives of inquiry".

Mead states, "The past (or the meaningful structure of the past) is as hypothetical as the future" (1932/1959: 12). The meaningful present is also a hypothesis subject to verification. Should a memory be questioned by another we are back to the situation between A, B, and O where O is the memory being constructed or reconstructed as A and B adjust to each other's perspectival attitudes, which involve behavioral operations such as the determination and use of evidential data, habits of inference, hypothetical if-then universal propositions, and much more as the inquiry proceeds and the essence of the memory is, perhaps, reconstructed. In the reconstruction of personal memory as much as the reconstruction of a scientific or mathematical concept, prediction is important to confirmation. If a construction of the past accurately predicts the future, or some previously unknown past occurrence, it becomes a warrantable assertion.

Conclusion

By emphasizing the objective reality of perspectives, this chapter integrates a robust perspectivalism into Dewey's transactional realism by showing that linguistic meaning, mental functioning, the self, and even temporal sequences emerge transactionally through co-constituting perspectival transactions. The perspectives as well as the meaning, mental functioning, self, and sequences can only be comprehended by seeing them together durationally and extensionally rather than as "irreconcilable separates" (1949/1989a: 67). Because perspectives are embodied, humans to not passively experience time; their development *is* time. This insight helps educators better understand human development.

4

Transactional Systems of Exploration and Learning

The *Okeanos Explorer*

William J. Clancey

Background: An Ethnographic Study of a Sociotechnical System

In 2017, I had the opportunity to observe operations onboard the *Okeanos Explorer* (*OE*), a National Oceanographic and Atmospheric Administration (NOAA) ship that uses a robotic vehicle to explore new regions of the ocean. The *OE*'s multiple-week expeditions are a form of exploratory science, influenced by the interests of the United States Department of Commerce, in which NOAA resides. My study began with Shirley Pomponi, a renowned oceanographer at Florida's Harbor Branch Oceanographic Institute, who became concerned that NOAA was shifting research funding from HBOI's submersibles and ships to shared robotic systems that would transmit video back to scientists at home. The agency believed that telepresence would be more productive and cost effective. Pomponi wondered, "How can oceanographers explore without going to sea?" (indeed, without going to see).

On learning about my studies of the scientists using the Mars Exploration Rover (Clancey 2012), Pomponi realized there might be a parallel, given that, as I explain in *Working on Mars*, we can do field science on Mars without being there. And not being able to go into space isn't discouraging students from becoming planetary scientists. Consequently, Pomponi secured funding to conduct ethnographic studies of this new work practice at HBOI's Exploration Command Center (ECC). Our investigation asked, "What are the limitations or even advantages of the *Okeanos Explorer* system, compared to not being on a ship or undersea in person?"

In this chapter, I provide an overview of the *Okeanos* exploration system, characterizing it as a transactional system constituted by activities of different groups (ship crew, engineers, scientists) having different focal concerns and employed by different organizations with their own ranks, roles, tools, schedules, and responsibilities. Working together, a new exploration capability resulted, ameliorating the scientists' original concerns conceived in interactional terms: the distancing of observer from observed in "robotic mediation." To characterize the success of the *Okeanos* exploration system, we shift stance, viewing expedition operations as "an organism-in-environment-as-a-whole" (Dewey & Bentley 1949: 133). This perspective fits our observations that diverse commercial, political, technical, and scientific interests and capacities constitute a coherent practice, with intricate cooperative actions at various times and places onboard: "no one of its constituents can be adequately specified as fact apart from the specification of other constituents of the full subject matter" (137). This transactional notion is familiar in ethnographic studies (e.g., Hutchins 1991; Clancey 2006; Mindell 2015).

The design of the exploration system is of special interest in how it facilitates learning among the scientists, students, and the public, who are together studying the sea floor with a robotic system. In this broader view, I show how the layout of the control room onboard fits the transactional character of the work. The scientific and educational aspects are not related as producer and consumer, but one exploration activity, reified by a professional cinematographer sitting alongside the engineers: "Act and product belong broadly together, with product, as proceeds, always in action, and with action always process" (Dewey & Bentley 1949: 155).

The *Okeanos* Exploration System

Figure 4.1 provides an overview of the *Okeanos* exploration system, which NOAA refers to as telepresence-enabled ocean exploration. Only two scientists are onboard the ship, a biologist and geologist. They communicate with scientists onshore via an open telephone line and chat room; this remote team may work at university offices, home, or one of NOAA's seven ECCs.

Engineers onboard the *OE* operate two robotic systems. The Seirios camera sled essentially hangs from the ship on a steel cable, rated for operations nearly four miles (6 km) deep. The robotic system, Deep Discoverer, also D2 or just "the ROV" is connected to Seirios on a 30 m soft tether. The scientists onboard

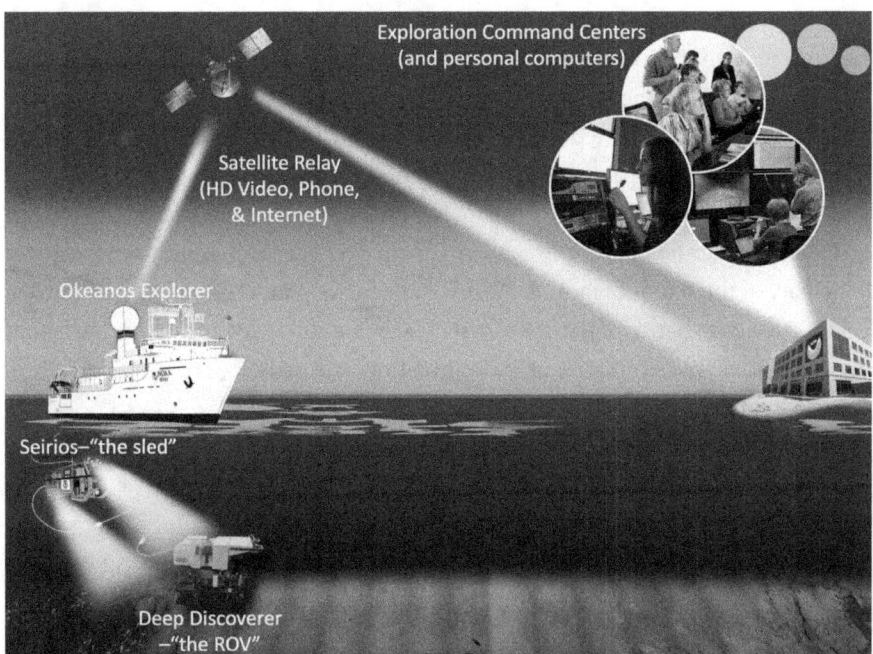

Figure 4.1 *Okeanos* exploration system—telepresence-enabled ocean exploration. Adapted from image courtesy of the NOAA Office of Ocean Exploration and Research.

interact with the remote science team by telecon and a chat room. Everyone is viewing the high-definition video from D2 and Seirios.

The ECCs are outfitted with multiple high-resolution displays depicting the two camera views and a quadrant display showing the dive status (e.g., depth and orientation of the ROV, bathymetric map, the control room). The public website, available on a personal computer, provides somewhat lower resolution camera views, with about a 30 second delay.

The *Okeanos* exploration system is a second-generation version of a design by Robert Ballard (perhaps best known for his collaboration with James Cameron in finding and exploring the Titanic with an ROV). D2 weighs about 4,000 kg, with dimensions of approximately 3 m length x 2 m width x 2.5 m height. It incorporates over 900 m of electrical wiring, twenty LED lights, and nine video cameras (Rogers 2016). The system is maneuverable by remote control of hydraulic motors at pressures almost 600 times sea level. Using robotic arms, geological and biological samples can be cached in boxes and returned to the surface.

The zoom lens provides almost microscopic imagery, which is often the most exciting part of a dive. Seirios's lights and cameras are controlled to keep the ROV in continuous view. Both Seirios and D2 are deployed daily on roughly an 8:00 a.m. to 5:00 p.m. schedule, called a "dive," during which D2 is dropped and "flown" to the lowest part of the path planned for the day, called a "traverse." A dive traverses hundreds of meters moving up from the lowest point.

Dives are planned several weeks in advance by oceanographers who register to be part of the science team. A more detailed dive plan is often laid out the day before, based on bathymetric maps which are essentially topographic charts that the *OE* creates in each region as the expedition proceeds.

Public Views of the Scientific Work

In June 2016 I worked for several weeks with Chris Kelley at the University of Hawaii's ECC in Manoa (Honolulu, Oahu). Kelley was then the science lead for a three-year NOAA investigation of US marine-protected areas in the Pacific. We watched D2's video on a magnificent high-definition wall display. We were often alone in the room but were communicating with the scientists onboard and several dozen others in the chat room and via an open teleconference.

Figure 4.2 Examples of images publicly available during a dive, illustrating (clockwise from upper left) varied geology, control room onboard *Okeanos Explorer*, animal life, and using temperature probe with ROV robotic arm.

After several years working this way, the scientists in different countries have gotten to know each other and their expertise. They exchange personal greetings, prompt each other with questions, and document the animal life they encounter. Figure 4.2 shows some examples of what remote scientists and the public can see.

I was surprised by the varied geology and that everything we saw alive was an animal—there are no plants below several hundred meters (photosynthesis requires light). Besides retrieving rocks and biological samples, the robotic arm can be used to deploy a temperature probe as shown in Figure 4.2.

I was especially intrigued by the video shown periodically of the control center onboard. I could see the two scientists sitting behind three engineers controlling the ROV and Seirios. I could sometimes hear them talking in the public broadcast, but what was really going on behind the scenes? How did the engineers operate the robotic systems? Were the scientists onboard working closely with them? I had to get onboard to find out.

I had the opportunity to visit NOAA's Headquarters near Washington D.C. in 2016 and presented my proposal to do an ethnographic study of the work onboard, formulated around these questions:

- What accounts for the quality of the scientific work using the telepresence-enabled exploration system—including people, roles, computer and robotic systems, procedures, schedules, facilities, etc.?
- What are the work practices in the ECCs and onboard the *OE* during expeditions involving the D2 remotely operated vehicle?
- In particular, how does the exploration system affect the remote scientists' participation and collaboration in collecting data, making interpretations, and ongoing engagement in the exploration process?

These study objectives adopted a perspective similar to my study of the Mars Exploration Rovers, focusing on how the quality of scientific field work is affected by the dramatic change in historical practices, namely, working remotely through robotic surrogates in large teams.

In actuality, these new collaborations, plus the advent of high-definition close-up cinematography on an ROV operated far below where submersibles can go, have turned out to be highly successful for NOAA, increasing the regions of the sea floor that can be explored and bringing to bear international expertise during every dive.

The *Okeanos Explorer* American Samoa Expedition

The story of the ship and life onboard would merit a book in itself. Perhaps the most important fact is that the entire expedition operated with forty-six people onboard, a village to ourselves, managing daily operations and even changing our destinations without needing to consult with NOAA headquarters—a surprise given my experience during NASA missions.

During the expedition a crew of twenty-four operated the ship, including eight NOAA officers who serve in NOAA's Commissioned Officer Corps (a service of the US military) and sixteen "wage mariners" who belonged to a union, consisting of engineers, technicians, and stewards.

There were also twenty-two people called "augmentators," which included the NOAA coordinator who managed the entire expedition, two science leads, and two mapping leads (employed by NOAA's Office of Ocean Exploration and Research, OER) and a science data manager (a scientist contracted for the expedition), plus nine ROV engineers and six video specialists employed by the Global Foundation for Ocean Exploration (GFOE). Officially, my role was designated as VIP, a title used for unpaid guests.

The ship left from American Samoa in the South Pacific, and during two weeks at sea, February 16 to March 2, 2107, carried out dives at thirteen seamounts. The route of the expedition was developed with input from American Samoa management agencies, a call for proposals from any interested scientist, and regional workshops. The Rose Atoll Marine National Monument and National Marine Sanctuaries suggested natural biological areas to explore.

Unexpected squalls from a tropical cyclone on the fourth day required an emergency retrieval of Seirios and D2 and then high-tailing it to the north. The coordinator and two scientists developed a new traverse plan, which was reviewed by the remote scientists. We returned to the south on the eleventh day to pick up the lost site, then completed the expedition at the port of Apia in Samoa, on the other side of the date line.

At the end of the voyage, we experienced two Friday sunsets and two Saturday sunrises. We had encountered a kind of transactional time warp in crossing the international dateline—an Excel chart was required to keep track of it; electronic photo and video time stamps were all confused.

A Transactional Perspective of the *Okeanos* Exploration Subsystems

Teamwork onboard during the expedition transcends organizational boundaries: The NOAA officers, wage mariners, and ROV contract engineers work as a single team to carry out the dives safely, guided by the interests of the scientists. For example, one may find ROV engineers working directly with wage mariners in physically deploying and retrieving Seirios and D2. Similarly, the NOAA Commanding Officer (CO), OER coordinator, and mapping lead, and scientists collaborated to schedule daily dives and re-planned the route as necessary. During the 9:00 a.m. daily briefing on the bridge, the CO and NOAA OER members reviewed weather charts and considered how condition of the seas might affect carrying out the planned traverse. Briefings generally required only five or ten minutes, everyone standing except the CO. After polling for issues, he would call, "Break!" and pairs or small groups would converse to work out the identified issues (e.g., how proximity to a sanctuary affected ship operations). The efficient meetings reflect how completely ship, ROV, and science activities were distributed, coordinated, and generally routine.

To represent functional relations among the diverse activity systems during an expedition, I adapt Wilden's (1987) notation and analysis using a *dependent hierarchy* (Figure 4.3). This diagram shows the overall exploration system as consisting of multiple subsystems with their own integrity—different institutionalized practices constituted by roles, activities, technologies, procedures, etc. training, funding, and career paths—working together as a single team during the expedition, most visibly and intensely during a dive.

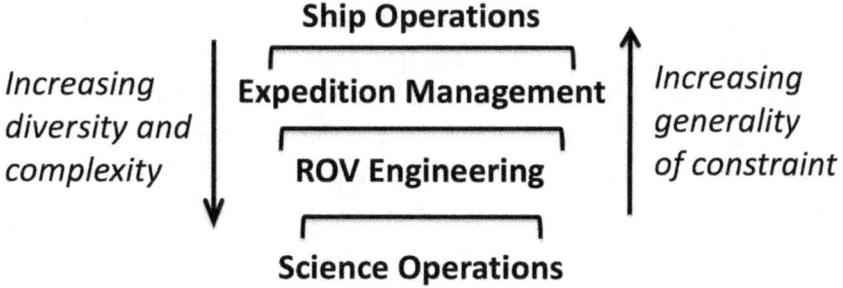

Figure 4.3 *Okeanos* exploration system dependent hierarchy.

To verify the validity of an analysis, Wilden uses the *Extinction Rule*: "To test for the orientation of a dependent hierarchy, mentally abolish each level (or order) in turn, and note which other level(s), or orders(s), will necessarily become extinct if it becomes extinct" (74). Each "subsystem level" provides an environment for those below to exist, that is, to carry out their activities during the expedition:

- Without the ship and its infrastructure, these telepresence scientific expeditions would not exist (e.g., the satellite dish enables real-time interactions with the remote scientists).
- Without the expedition management provided by NOAA's OER, the ROV engineering team and the two scientists would not be collaborating onboard, and the remote science team's organization, logging tools, and practices would not exist.

The term "existence" refers specifically to the organization and character of each subsystem in activities during expeditions, not its origin, history, or future. In particular, *OE* was constructed to collect underwater acoustical data in support of anti-submarine warfare operations; its ownership and use could change again. NOAA's OER operates ten research vessels, with many other forms of data collection and services, including National Weather Service satellites. Even the relatively specialized GFOE non-profit organization serves other activities, such as undersea filmmaking and shipwreck archaeology. Scientists typically work on several projects with different sources of funding; they are usually volunteers, not employed by NOAA. Thus the individuals and groups participating in the activities shown in Figure 4.3 have obligations and concerns apart from *Okeanos* expeditions, which underscores the question, how do they constitute a coherent exploration system, with practices that developed, but mostly persist, over a decade of expeditions, with different people playing the roles?

Such a complicated activity may suggest a hierarchical command structure, but who or what group is at the top in control? The scientists do not have authority over ship operations; and although the ship's crew and the NOAA OER expedition leader can veto operations when the constraints they manage require (e.g., safety, politics), neither the crew nor the expedition leader may decide D2's path or sampling. Although one could imagine a dependency tree, with science operations at the top (inverting the diagram), it would suggest that the other activities are subservient or only exist for the sake of the more complex system, a form of reductionism. For example, other functions of ship operations and expedition management (e.g., to serve mining interests by scanning the seafloor overnight) would be obscured by only viewing them through the interests of oceanography in a dependency tree. This point is illustrated further in the section "Imaginary Oppositions."

Rather than breaking the expedition into parts and wondering how it "comes together" (an inter-actional view) or identifying some authority that controls the others (a form of "self-action"), we use Figure 4.3 as a way of "seeing functions together," with the levels corresponding to groups having different formal organization, roles, and activities, acting within the environment provided by those represented higher in the dependent hierarchy. Crucially, *each subgroup's expedition activities exist physically and temporally, and have meaning, only within the larger whole*—the exploration system in action. Although most salient during dives, the work system depicted by Figure 4.3 has extended and developed over a decade of expeditions, incorporating new sensors, online tools, and purposes (see section "A Broader View of the Dependent Hierarchy of the Okeanos Exploration System").

We say that the relationships of the activities among the subsystems are *transactional* because the constraints flow in both directions and pervade the entire exploration system. Nevertheless, the "higher" levels are more general and flexible. The ship's function is primarily to go from point A to point B, whatever the expedition requires, while keeping everyone alive with food, water, and basic utilities. Aside from challenges of the weather and aging ship, for the crew every day is much like the rest. ROV launches and recoveries are also routine and by the clock, though on the seafloor they are cooperating with the scientists. Expedition management relates logistic and technical activities, primarily in organizing expeditions and advising during abnormal situations, but never strictly supervising or directing the subgroups. The scientific work is a more diverse, opportunistic activity, as it involves different disciplines investigating the varied seafloor and biosphere, relating interests, theories, and projects. During an expedition a plethora of specific requests and constraints affecting dive sites, traverse paths, and how to use D2 to collect data ripple through the entire system.

In a work system, one group's activities constitute an "environment" for others by providing the services they require. Thus responsibilities and expectations develop and reinforce local actions into the coherent practice of a single team. For example, ROV engineers expect ship operations to be predictable after the bridge's acceptance of their movement requests (unless notified of difficulties). The scientists expect that GFOE will maneuver the ROVs to satisfy the agreed-upon daily plan and keep them operable for the full expedition. Figure 4.3 thus provides a way of seeing the different group–activity systems as an "extensional-durational" whole: "Our own procedure is the transactional, in which is asserted the right to see together, extensionally and durationally, much that is talked about conventionally as if it were composed of irreconcilable separates" (Dewey & Bentley 1949: 120; see also Andersson, Garrison, & Östman 2018, chapter 2).

Although the operations of the *Okeanos* exploration consist of cooperating and often collaborating institutionalized organizations (e.g., NOAA/OER, GFOE, universities), typically levels in a work system are not formally distinct corporations, agencies, etc. More generally, Wilden says the different activity levels are "goal-seeking systems" (e.g., ship operations seek to preserve the infrastructure while satisfying the interests of NOAA and the scientists).

In a broad exposition of his analytical framework, *System and Structure*, Wilden ([1972] 1980) characterizes *structure* as consisting of frameworks, channels, coding—more generally "types of relationships between subsystems." *System* consists of processes, transmissions, messages—more abstractly, "how regularities are used" and "relations between relations." The essential point, which I elaborate subsequently, is that although for design and accounting purposes we commonly view subsystems as distinct, independently existing entities, this labeled separation—making a whole process into named things—exists only in our conceptual activity of describing and notating, characterized by Wilden as "in the imagination." To understand how the exploration system succeeds, it must be "seen together," as activities extended in space and time (Ryan 2011; Garrison 2001: 285 ff.).

The Functional Trans-Actions of a Dive

A ship is a perfect work site for an ethnographic study—places, roles, and activities are all well-defined and repeat daily. I spent most of my time sitting next to the scientists in the control room (Figure 4.4). You see here the operations at the start of the day as Seirios is to be deployed off the stern using the A-Frame crane; D2 is deployed portside with another crane.

Seated up front in the control room, the engineer on the left is the ROV navigator (ROV NAV), who communicates with the bridge to keep the ship aligned with Seirios and D2. The ROV Pilot flies D2 using hydraulic thrusters, and the ROV Co-pilot aims Seirios cameras and assists in operating D2 when retrieving samples. To the right, off this image, the cinematographer controls the zoom camera on D2. The two scientists (called "Watch Leads") and I sat in the

Figure 4.4 *Okeanos Explorer* Control Room, showing morning deployment of Seirios (top middle), ROV (top right), inset of bridge deck officer (top left), ROV engineers, and scientists sitting in the back.

back. Everyone has a choice of over forty video and graphic displays that enable tracking the status of the rovers and provide views through cameras on Seirios, D2, and onboard.

The NOAA bridge deck officer works within the broader maritime environment to make ROV operations possible. Using software to control the robotic ship, he is constrained by the topside physical environment (weather, sea conditions), resources and capacities (fuel, propulsion, life support), and crew assignments. The videos broadcast to the ECCs and through a browser provide stereo sound, with the engineers and scientists on different channels. Thus, we can hear (and see indirectly) how the engineers coordinate with each other, the bridge, the cinematographer, and the scientists sitting behind them. Like television celebrities hosting a holiday parade, the narration from the scientists is continuous during the dive, explaining what we are seeing and doing to the unseen audience of remote scientists and the public. At times, a remote scientist will call on the shared phone line, which is broadcast in the narration channel, usually providing information relevant to what we are seeing—identifying it, characterizing its habitat or significance, and relating it to other species. Usually the remote scientists use the chat room for most of these remarks, which at least one of the Watch Leads is monitoring.

Figure 4.5 shows the recurrent lines of communication during a dive. By protocol, each person only speaks with certain other people. For example, the Watch Leads only address the ROV Pilot; they never make a request directly to the cinematographer. And in this group, only the ROV NAV communicates with the NOAA bridge deck officer. Different voice loops are dedicated to different subgroups.

At one point, we see the ROV NAV glance over several displays, including one overhead, and then turn to the ROV Pilot, saying, "You should have another five minutes ...." The ROV NAV's remark indicates that he is monitoring the relative locations of the ship and D2; he knows that a sampling activity is underway that prevents moving D2. As D2 moves forward, he will contact the bridge to move the ship forward in accord with the planned path and pace of the scientists' investigation. Each request specifies a certain heading, speed, and distance. If the ship is currently executing such a path, D2 will need at some point to move along so Seirios doesn't get ahead of it.

Responsibilities during a dive are fixed and relatively role-specific, associated with actions only particular individuals or groups may take, such as moving

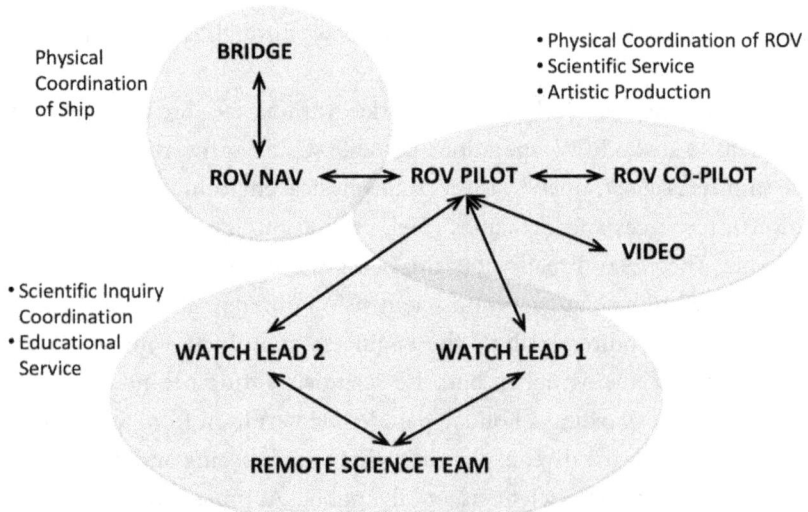

Figure 4.5 Lines of communication during a dive.

the ship, maneuvering D2, zooming the video, controlling the arm (ROV Co-Pilot's role), and logging the dive in a shared online tool (SeaScribe, accessible to any member of the science team). Responsibilities are with respect to some activity/subsystem, in service to other people. These relations correspond to the lines of communication; for example, the ROV Pilot is responsible to VIDEO for providing sufficient time to "image" a sample with the zoom lens, creating a close-up for the scientific database.

At one point, we hear the geologist say, "Chris Kelley is going to like this," revealing how he conceives his service to the remote science team, and his expectation that Kelley is watching or will be interested to examine the recorded data later. More broadly the entire team onboard is providing a service to students, future scientists using the dive's database, commercial fishing interests, and environmental protection agencies.

The design of the work system nicely illustrates the claim that "knowing is co-operative and is integral with communication" (Dewey & Bentley 1949: 97). Referring to Figure 4.5, people within each oval are *collaborating* in a specific activity, with broader durational–extensional *coordination* occurring among them. Thus, ROV NAV/Bridge activity is *coupled* to the engineers' activity, which is *coupled* with the scientists' activity. The whole system is like a collection of elastic bands tugging at each other, as they negotiate physical and intellectual constraints. A striking characteristic of this overall system is that we can't easily identify anyone as being completely in control of the dive operations: Control of D2's location and orientation is transactionally distributed with varying authority throughout the exploration system, including the remote scientists, who may call in with a request or whose narration requires holding D2 in place a while longer.

Furthermore, D2 is effectively a sensory-motor extension of our bodies—we see through the zoom lens, we manipulate and retrieve samples through the arm. Everyone moves with and through D2, up along the traverse path—a physical–intellectual choreography.

As mentioned, a wide variety of tools are used for communicating during a dive—visual, verbal, and written; some are shared, some private. These include the videos, the status displays, scientists' narration and audible communications with the engineers; the open telephone line; the formal species identifications in SeaScribe; and the chat room. Negotiation of interests and actions occurs throughout in visible reporting and requesting.

An example sequence in the chat room illustrates a common type of conversational exchange:

MJ: As a geologist, I ask a dumb question: I understand that the nautilus is a cephalopod, like the squid and octopus?

BM @AS: The eggs are laid singly, attached to bottom ... Nautilus are long-lived, slow-maturing ... compared to other cephalopods.

AS @BM: Thank you! very interesting!

BM @MV: You are better qualified to answer MJ's question than am I.

MV: yes. Nautilus is a cephalopod, but ...

Here the geologist (MJ) explicitly refers to his discipline and expresses deference to those with other expertise. But his remark may also be interpreted as signifying his awareness of needing to demonstrate competence as a selected, distinguished representative of the scientists onboard. (The answer comes from BM, partly in response to a prior question from AS, followed by BM deferring to MV as more knowledgeable to speak about cephalopods.) "Being scientific" is an ongoing accomplishment of individuals, the science team, and through activities of the engineers and NOAA Officer Corps. New technologies for gathering and interpreting data, including especially robotic observation and communication methods, require new work practices, and thus reinventing what *being scientific* means (for elaboration, see Clancey [2012]). Accordingly, the "reality" of the ocean (as we know it) is inter-dependent with how we "come to know." The exploration methods and practices (activities of *knowing*) affect

TEAM	SCIENCE		ENGINEERING			SHIP
POSITION	Remote Scientists	WLs	ROVP & ROVC	VIDEO	ROVN	BRDG
CONCURRENT REAL-TIME ACTIVITIES	**Science** Telecon, Chat room, & SeaScribe logging—shared focus on identifying what we are seeing. [Collaboration]		**Cinematography** Tight choreography relating ROV position and camera—shared focus on clarity and quality of video [Collaboration]		**Operating Ship** ROVN calls for repositioning ship; Bridge reports on weather effects—shared focus on relation of ship to Seirios/ROV [Cooperation]	
	Data Interpretation Chat & Phone Interaction [Collaboration]	**Gathering Scientific Data** Request view, close-up, sample—shared focus on satisfying scientific interest [Cooperation]				
		Operating ROV ROVN advising pilots about operations—shared focus on safety of ROV & tethers [Collaboration]				
PUBLIC VIEW	Shared ROV main camera and Seirios main camera looking at ROV					

Figure 4.6 Robotically mediated work system design.

what is examined, described, and measured (aspects of the ocean claimed to be *known*); and vice versa, as known interests, needs, and opportunities shape tools, organizations, and operations.

Figure 4.6 is another way of representing graphically how one activity area provides an environment for another.

Each subgroup—designated in Figure 4.3 as science, engineering, ship—is responsible for the quality of a different aspect of the dive: scientific guidance and interpretation; D2/Seirios operation and video recording (cinematography); and movement and stability of the *OE*. But some activities overlap, such as gathering biological and geological samples, as well as operating the ship during a dive (in which ROV NAV gives specific movement directions to the Bridge Deck Officer).

The activities functionally compose to create a scientifically coherent investigation of the region, while preserving safety of the ROVs and ship. The overlap among groups reveals how relationships are forged through and within activities. In this graphic, *collaboration* is defined as working together as peers on a common project (e.g., scientific research; operating ROVs); *co-operation* involves people engaged in an activity but with different intentions, perhaps functionally related, often across organizations. In particular, gathering scientific data involves cooperation between the university scientists and GFOE engineers—the former to specify interests and the latter to determine what is possible and execute operations. The *OE* bridge is not involved in science or operating D2 directly, but cooperates with those activities, tacitly aware of D2 and knowing something about the planned traverse route and duration. ROV NAV collaborates with the bridge deck officer in moving the ship, but of course the officer has responsibility and authority for all ship movements and how they are carried out. It is common to talk about "shared goals" in activities, but the notion can be subtle, with different aspects of "sharing." The ROV Pilot and Co-Pilot share the goal with the Watch Leads of gathering scientific data, but they have distinctly different roles and subgoals. The scientists select sample candidates according to their interests, while the ROV engineers decide whether a candidate sample is retrievable and have their own subgoals and methods for grabbing and storing it.

Finally, the diagram helps us realize that "robotically mediated" refers to much more than the robotic system, D2. The mediation—the functional instrumentality of the exploration system—is distributed throughout the system of roles, technology, and protocol-regulated activities.

Student Activities in an Exploration Control Center

My ethnographic study of the *Okeanos* exploration system actually began by observing university classes at the Harbor Branch Oceanographic Institute's ECC during 2015. My interest was to help Pomponi and other teachers understand how the ECC functions as a learning environment and how teachers might facilitate the students' experiences while observing dives together.

During one expedition the students and teachers were watching and talking about a series of dives during a week, while the students were charged with creating a taxonomic catalog of the life encountered. A lecturer provided a broad overview of oceanographic field science, illustrated by physical samples HBOI had collected during past decades. Afterwards, the teachers sat among the students and participated in searching on the internet for information and photos, commenting on what they were seeing, and (infrequently) posting remarks and questions in the chat room. Three high-resolution screens on the front wall displayed the chat room, the main video from D2, and either a context video from Seirios or the quad-display with status of the ROVs.

The group often listened intently to the onboard scientists' narrations, which was broadcast loudly in the room. Inevitably their conversations would overstep the narration, as they became engaged among themselves and ignored the broadcast audio. The students and teachers were observing the same vistas as the science team at nearly the same time and effectively constructed their own scientific narration, as in this exchange:

> ECC teacher: Look how long that's been there, how clean it is.
> (Watch Lead): (Yeah) that's what I was thinking.
> ECC graduate student: That's exactly what he was thinking.
> ECC class student: How was something like that formed?
> ECC graduate student: That's a really good question … [explains]

The graduate student was observing the class and expedition, often standing in the back of the room. When the onboard scientist made a remark that circumstantially fit what a teacher in the classroom had said, the graduate student snapped back in a joke, "That's exactly what he was thinking." Everyone laughed, implicitly acknowledging the discordance—even though everyone in the ECC heard what the scientists and engineers broadcast, nobody outside the room could hear what the students and teachers were saying.

In an ECC we are observing the observers, but we are also a constituent part of the exploration system. The ECCs are being "played to" as part of the audience of the narrated streaming video and products later posted on the web. The scientists onboard, ROV team, and bridge deck officer, as well as the scientists who call in or post, are at least tacitly aware that their actions and remarks are public and being recorded. But students and facilitators in the ECC are also able to post remarks or questions in the chat room; when this occurred, scientists onboard responded to HBOI postings during their narration.

The chat room enables students to observe what the participating scientists are seeing and thinking and learning from each other. Everyone is seeing this world together for the first time, and the scientists' guidance, interests, surprises, and questions are visible for all to reflect on. Indeed, we might say that for all participants: "Observer and observed are held in close organization" (Dewey & Bentley 1949: 131).

The *Okeanos* Exploration System Is Designed for Learning

In summary, NOAA has created a sociotechnical exploration system for collaborative learning among the scientists, students, and the public. We can view D2 itself as being a tool for collaborative inquiry, just as Mars rovers are multidisciplinary collaboration tools for field science. Together with the software tools for planning, programming/control, and visualization of operations, these robotic systems provide a sense of presence, in which we project ourselves into the viewpoint of the rover as it moves, sees, and manipulates life and objects on the sea floor. In learning the practice of observing, imagining action, and its execution, we become present through the robot, not as spectators, but transacting directly with the sea environment (cf. Clancey 2012, chapter 6, "Being the Rover"). This common embodiment in the physical place of the seafloor (and Mars surface) brings engineers, scientists, students, and the public together in a special, powerful way. The *Okeanos* exploration system is particularly effective because tele-operated control enables real-time contributions by everyone. All experience some form of personal agency in the exploration. (Mars operations are carried out in "batch mode," using fully programmable instruments; data is returned about a day after a restricted science team formulates requests.)

More generally, we can view the exploration system as being designed for learning, pervading every aspect of the work system: planning, cinematography, sampling, and narrative. In the ethnographic report to NOAA following my participation during the American Samoa Expedition, I suggested how learning opportunities might be facilitated or elaborated:

- **Exploration Command Centers**: The ECC at the NOAA Daniel K. Inouye Regional Center in Pearl Harbor, HI benefits from being placed immediately outside the cafeteria where people encounter it daily. A NOAA employee is present during dives to explain what is occurring, as well as to welcome school and other visiting groups. Such facilitators serve as mediators between the narrated, visible dive operations and the people present, enabling feedback to the onboard scientists. To be available to the public, the ECCs require more volunteer facilitators.
- **Online Educational Materials**: Previously, NOAA's website has naturally focused on the facts of each expedition and the oceanography. The *Okeanos* system also provides an excellent opportunity to explain how engineers use technology during scientific investigation (e.g., radar). Recently posted logs are revealing technical aspects of the exploration system and the diverse activities of scientists, engineers, and NOAA officers.
- **Open Remote Science Teams**: The telecons and shared media make data gathering and interpretation open to everyone during the mission. Making the sample curating after the dive and subsequent analysis public would reveal to students that "scientific discovery" involves much more than looking and sampling during a dive's traverse.

Imaginary Oppositions: System Levels in a Dependent Hierarchy

To better understand the intent of the dependent hierarchy presentation, it is useful to know that Wilden's analysis was partly motivated to dispel what he called *imaginary oppositions*, such as the familiar mind–body dichotomy (Figure 4.7). For example, technology is created and used within less constrained orders such as social systems, on which its existence and proper functioning depends. What we call the biological "self" has different boundaries from the "psychic self or social role." Epistemological boundaries exist in the imagination of an observer, not nature itself (Wilden ([1972] 1980): 220–1).

Wilden's summary is helpful: "Only in the imaginary—of common folk and scientific parlance—can these categories be seen as symmetrical, binary opposites rather than as relations between levels of a larger system. The higher term (e.g., body) is the environment that the other term (e.g., mind) depends on for subsistence and survival" (Wilden 1987: 82). One might refer again to

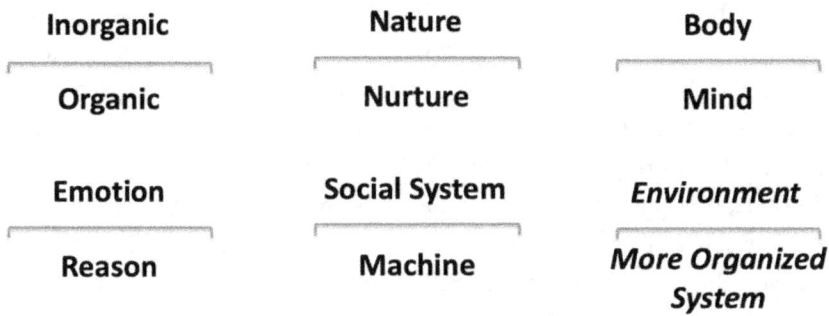

Figure 4.7 Imaginary oppositions shown as dependent hierarchies, most generally showing a designed or natural system/organism in an environment. (Concept adapted from Wilden, 1987: 82).

Dewey and Bentley's (1949: 120) remark about "seeing together" what is typically decomposed into "irreconcilable separates."

Perhaps the most useful, general principle is shifting from *either–or* analyses to understanding systems contextually with *both–and* development and reciprocity (including simultaneity). Different organizations or systems within a functional whole (e.g., the layers in Figure 4.3, as well as biological subsystems in an organism) are in "a reciprocal and co-constitutive exchange" (Wikipedia 2019), such as how emotional experience orients and shapes a conceptualization of "being in a situation." Garrison (2011) stated this similarly: "Transactional thinking requires us to comprehend the organism-in-environment-as-a-whole; the same holds for mind-(or self)-in-social-environment-as-a-whole" (311). Every more organized system (the lower systems in the Figure 4.7 dyads) may be viewed as being in a dynamic "organism–environment" relation with a less-constrained context that makes its existence possible, providing a source of problematic situations, challenges, and opportunities, and also providing resources for their resolution as the more organized system develops.

But we must be careful in how we adopt the transactional perspective in characterizing a system. It is tempting to suggest that the transactional perspective is "best," namely, "all human exchange is best understood as a set of transactions within a reciprocal and co-constitutive whole" (Wikipedia 2019). Our understanding of an "either–or" mentality should lead us to take pause. Transactional and interactional descriptions of a system adopt different modeling perspectives/viewpoints. Their value depends on the context and our purpose. Analytic methodology can fruitfully incorporate *both* TP (transactional perspective) *and* IA (interactional analysis). In particular, in designing a work system, we can model automated system flows by an IA (as in a dataflow diagram), while understanding and considering that the relation of people to each other and automation will emerge in the practice, a TP (the automation may also adapt in response to people's behavior and the environment).

In short, the opposition of IA and TP exists only in the imagination; implying that TP is superior or "truer to reality" adopts a false dualism. TP is not more objectively the "correct" way of describing a work system in particular or always the "best" perspective, but it may be more useful for certain purposes, bringing out different aspects of the system, such as its resilient, adaptive, and dynamic qualities. Indeed, another well-known remark by Dewey and Bentley (1949) suggests that we may start with an interactional perspective and refine it after we have identified subsystems, roles, protocols, and practices: "Transaction ... represents that late level in inquiry in which observation and presentation could be carried on without attribution of the aspects and phases of action to independent self-actors, or to independently inter-acting elements or relations" (136).

Inquiry is usually iterative; our appreciation of relations develops over time and as new aspects are revealed by events and their patterns. Our descriptive language changes and interesting nuances are realized that may be useful for our purposes, which may involve teaching, redesigning a work system, inventing new kinds of automation, providing guidance to long-term planners, and so on. I conclude with such a broader TP of the exploration system.

A Broader View of the Dependent Hierarchy of the *Okeanos* Exploration System

Figure 4.8 broadens out from the ship-oriented perspective shown in Figure 4.3 to include the physical–biological and political–economic environments. These are less-organized systems than the ship's operation and the expedition policies and management of NOAA's OER (for simplicity, the ship subsystem is not shown; it is implicitly included here in the OER management of exploration and research). Again, these are not like layers in a cake, but coupled systems: Influences flow in both directions throughout the system and aren't isolated to levels; for example, political–economic interests and policies of commerce and the government influence expedition routes and what the scientists study.

NOAA, including the OER, is part of the United States Department of Commerce and thus must serve business interests, for example, studying the

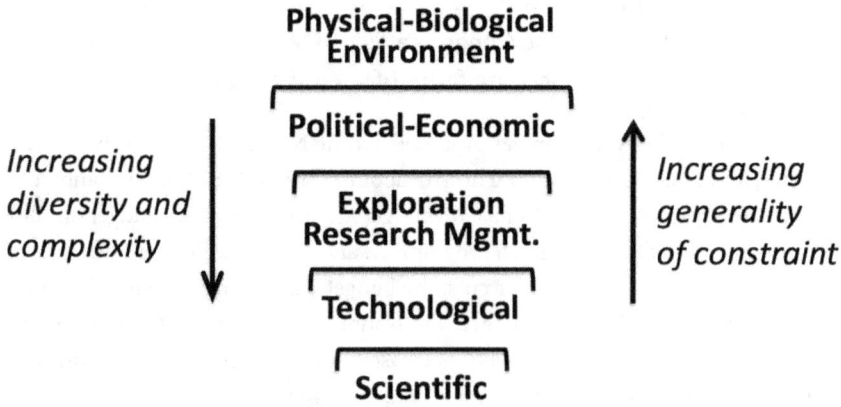

Figure 4.8 Broader view of the dependent hierarchy of the *Okeanos* exploration system.

ecology of fisheries in the North Atlantic. Scientific motives transcend what we might call "pure science"—scientists may select sites that they believe should be set aside as preserves in which fishing might be prohibited. Some oceanographers may want to reveal and document how trawling for shrimp by dragging nets destroys everything in their path, as has occurred along the continental shelf of Florida. Consequently, *Okeanos* expeditions may be *both* scientific *and* political, as well as economically and pedagogically oriented.

Each level of the exploration system coexists and is in a reciprocal relation to others, establishing a broader system of mutual conditions. Because these are open systems, effects may be expressed throughout the overall system. Perhaps most obviously, technological capability and scientific inquiry are co-developing; for example, expeditions reveal to scientists what instruments might be useful, just as the pace and location of traverses reveal to engineers what map and radar instruments and displays, planning programs, and mobility are useful during expeditions. For example, success in using the thermal probe in one location may prompt studying another area, but also modifying its capabilities and/or how it is deployed.

Political and economic interests and policies may be influenced by climate changes to ocean properties (especially temperature) and hence affect biological habitats. Consumer preferences shape economic interests, which may lead to over-fishing and new government regulations.

The term "constraint" in the dependent hierarchy diagram refers to resources, guiding values, beliefs, perceptions, and methods that organize a system in accord with certain functions or qualities of the whole. For example, political beliefs of the US President and Congress affect NOAA's funding and may seek to discourage or even prevent certain forms of scientific inquiry:

> The [Trump] administration has proposed cutting NOAA's budget to about $4.5 billion for fiscal year (FY) 2020, a drop of about 18%, nearly $1 billion, compared with the agency's FY 2019 enacted budget ... The proposed budget would terminate most climate research programs ... and eliminate climate competitive research funding. Among other cuts, the budget would terminate the National Centers for Coastal Ocean Science, the National Sea Grant College Program, and some Arctic research products; decrease funding for ocean exploration and research efforts; and eliminate coastal zone management grants.
>
> (Showstack 2019)

In conclusion, the study of the *Okeanos* exploration system demonstrates how exploration can be understood as an ecology of systems influencing each other. The physical–biological and political–economic constraints are most general, providing an environment in which exploration enterprises (e.g., NOAA expeditions), advanced technology development, and scientific research may exist. These more diverse and complex subsystems of interests, data, models, and guidance then affect policies and (commercial) operations in the government agencies that support exploration. The exchanges throughout may at first be described as interactions in a flow of funding, data, control, and information within the exploration system (e.g., Figures 4.5 and 4.6). But when we inquire about the history of scientific work, such as how the origin and locations of expeditions change over nearly a decade, we find a transactional perspective fruitful, as it leads us to discover reciprocal relations and mutual influences. We realize in particular that terms such as "collaboration," "sharing," and "mediated," which are often used informally in robotic research, can be more precisely understood by examining the roles and activities of people and automation within a work system. And regarding the scientists who worried about the inter-actional limitations of the new robotic system, although they might not state it this way, their satisfaction with the *Okeanos* exploration system is an expression of its transactional nature.

Acknowledgments

I am grateful to the onboard scientists, engineers, and ship's crew who welcomed me to the *Okeanos Explorer* during the American Samoa Expedition (*Okeanos*

EX1702) and explained their practices and experience. I particularly thank the Commanding Officer, CAPT Mark Wetzler, and Operations Officer, LT Aaron Colohan, for describing the history and operations of the ROV deployment/recovery and ship navigation/control. NOAA's Senior Expeditions Manager, Kelley Elliott, along with Brian Kennedy in the Office of Exploration and Research, provided essential support in enabling my participation and onboard arrangements. Kelley also provided extensive background information to help me understand the intricacies of the exploration system. Matt Jackson and Santiago Herrera, the two onboard scientists, gave important perspectives on the unique opportunity that these expeditions provide in enabling scientific studies of great interest to their communities. Air travel support to and from American Samoa was provided by Florida Atlantic University/HBOI through the Cooperative Institute for Ocean Exploration, Research and Technology program funded by NOAA and managed by Shirley Pomponi, whose original interest and support made this research possible. Supplementary data/imagery are provided courtesy of NOAA's Office of Ocean Exploration and Research expedition repository:

https://oceanexplorer.noaa.gov/okeanos/explorations/ex1702/welcome.html

This report was prepared in my personal capacity and represents my own observations and conclusions, which are accurate to the best of my knowledge, and do not necessarily represent the views of NOAA or any other institution.

Democracy, Education, and Transaction: The Importance of Play in Dewey's Thought

Andrea Fiore

Introduction

In chapter 15 of *Democracy and Education*, Dewey introduces a theory of play with implications worth developing in order to highlight the significance of play in his thought (1916/1980). This chapter shows that for Dewey play is a transactional activity/category bound to social–political life helpful for developing social intelligence in a democratic community. The discourse starts from the main elements of Dewey's pedagogy and moves toward play as a transactional activity/category, and finally, play in connection with the social and political sphere.

Dewey's Pedagogy: Play and Transaction

Play and the Main Elements of Dewey's Pedagogy

Some of the main elements of Dewey's pedagogy can be summarized as follows. First, the individual is embedded in her/his environment since birth. Second, the mind does not exist either before or independently from experience of the world but emerges and develops within experience. Third, by active doing the child appropriates her/his social nature, and, thereby, the connection between the self and the world comes to light and continues strengthening. Finally, since human life is a continuous reorganization of experiences, Dewey defines education as "the direct transformation of the quality of experience" (1916/1980: 82). Therefore, child education mainly consists in developing and consolidating the connections of the self with the environment, particularly the social dimension.

In this regard it is worthwhile to recall that emotions play a crucial role that is important for both the child and the adult as we will see below.

According to Dewey, the educational process is based upon doing, not at all separated from thinking, and considered as experience par excellence. Doing has high pedagogical value insofar as it: (1) puts the human being into direct contact with the concrete culture of a given society, (2) leads to solutions of new problems, and (3) fosters the individual's development while building her/his unique intelligence. Doing includes play and work, the main human activities/categories in education, which Dewey defines as "active occupations" that bind pupils to the concreteness of life (1916/1980: 208).

For Dewey there is no antithesis between work and play (1916/1980: 210). This is a key point in *Democracy and Education*, in which he argues: (1) play and work have the function of educating the child to integrate herself/himself into society as well as into the natural environment, which is crucial to adult life, and (2) there is no antithesis between ludic and serious dimensions of life. The difference between play and work is "largely one of time-span, influencing the directness of the connection of means and ends" (1916/1980: 210). Play cannot be considered merely as a training for adulthood. On the contrary, it continues across a human being's entire lifespan.

Even though it is difficult to find an exact definition of what constitutes play, scholars in different disciplines have identified its main features (Eberle 2014; Henricks 2015). Transaction is not mentioned. Henricks, for example, considers theories that look at play as action (or possibly self-action) and interaction judging the former not fully satisfying (Henricks 2015: 25). However, such an approach emerges from the pages of *Democracy and Education*, especially when compared to Dewey's other major works.

In *Knowing and the Known*, Dewey and Bentley suggest treating all human behavior "as processes of the full situation organism-environment" that is to say transactional processes (1949/1989a: 97). This statement implicitly suggests that play is one of those behaviors. For example, a billiard game by itself may be understood interactionally. However, considered within its social and cultural account the game displays a transactional character (1949/1989a: 126).

Play as Transactional Activity/Category

The transactional character of play as activity and category emerges from the following three aspects: play involves elements mutually integrated, possesses a strong experimental nature, and has aesthetic and artistic value.

Concerning the first aspect, transaction has no detachable and independent elements, which is true for play that cannot be considered as an abstract activity or category, because its mutually integrated elements arise from playing itself (Graham & Kirby 2016: 14; Stoller 2018: 49). This aspect is important for defining play as a transactional activity/category rather than self-actional or inter-actional.

Another remarkable aspect is the strong experimental nature of play when it enters the Deweyan "Circuit of Inquiry" forming, thereby, new habits. This can be described by a story. Let us imagine a child taking a walk next to a lake. She spontaneously picks up a stone and throws it toward the water in a *specific* way. Because of its flat shape, the stone bounces on the surface once, then it splashes and sinks into the water. The stone, water surface, arm, movements, and hand are elements of the same situation whose meaning and function before the gesture of throwing is differentiated by inquiry. From this activity new meanings may readily arise.

For example, let us now imagine the child throwing the stone in the water for the first time, so her behavior can be considered nonreflectively produced by previous habits. These habits encompass grasping and throwing as possible operations of the hand and arm, the fact that a stone splashes in the water, and so on. Yet, the bouncing of the stone upon the surface is an unexpected event that, once focused, the child will experience as a completely new. She may then repeat the action possibly trying to make the stone bouncing more than once. To succeed, she will look for suitable stones (i.e., flat and light), coordinate her movements, and learn to know how much effort to make. In other words, a nonreflective behavior generates a problem that needs an experimental outlook to solve and perhaps leading to a new habit. In this case, the new habit consists in the skill of throwing bouncing stones on the water or, more widely and importantly, of seeing and experiencing in some objects of the world something she has never experienced before. Throwing stones on the water transforms the child's quality of experience making her aware of "some of the connections which had been imperceptible" (Dewey 1916/1980: 83). In addition, her behavior has become an organized activity with "a directing idea which gives point to the successive acts" (Dewey 1916/1980: 211; Vanderstraeten 2002: 235).

So far, I have described an activity that Dewey would have defined as sound (or healthy) fully fledged play. By contrast, he describes forms of confused, unproductive, and even pathological play. Insofar as play is a mere mechanical movement or discharge of physical energy it is unfruitful from the educational point of view (Dewey 1916/1980: 210–11; 1933/1986: 287). Furthermore, play without a sound emotional quality might become pathological, such as gambling (1916/1980: 213). This is not authentic, nor sound play. On the contrary, sound play leads human beings to develop a deeper sensitivity toward the world, and it helps to creatively build new habits.[1] This leads us to the third aspect for which play is transactional, that is its aesthetic and artistic value.

In Dewey, the word "aesthetic" means what the ancient Greek term αἰσθητικός indicated; that is, "sentient, perceptive, feeling, sense, and sensitivity" (Andersson, Garrison, & Östman 2018: 29). Art is, according to Dewey, the way to fully "feeling" and "perceive" the world, therefore, to fully integrate it with our human being. Thus, "aesthetic" and "artistic"[2] are two aspects of the same meaning, namely, the experience in its full accomplishment. However, to be aesthetic and artistic, experience requires emotion.[3] Not all experiences have these qualities but play and art do (Dewey 1916/1980: 212; 1933/1986: 348). Especially in child education play familiarizes the individual with meaningful activities, namely, activities in which means and ends are tightly interwoven, mutually interdependent, and coordinated, and in which the emotional quality constitutes the connecting factor of experience. Moreover, as we have seen, play transforms the quality of experience, and this is what play and art share (Patton 2014: 244).

Both art and play are always a matter of constructing and re-constructing the world, producing something new in an emotional framework. Every artist, as well as every player, re-elaborates objects and situations, giving them new meanings and eliciting an emotional response (Dewey 1934/1987: 73). The artist plays because she/he gives new meanings to things and situations in a free,[4] creative, full and balanced (sound), emotional, and imaginative way, as child's imagination "makes what it will of chairs, blocks, leaves, chips" (Dewey 1916/1980: 211).

The actor who pretends to be Hamlet, becomes Hamlet, by performing in a play his character, actions, and emotions (Huizinga 1938/2014: 145). A violinist draws vibrations from her wooden instrument forming a Bach *Partita* or a jazz improvisation. A painter or a sculptor use different tools and materials to produce something absolutely new, such as Van Gogh's *Sunflowers* or Paige Bradley's *Expansion*. These examples show there are many ways to develop a deeper sensitivity toward the world, enhancing our capacity to genuinely know and understand it. (It is worth noticing that the same term, *play*, in English indicates different meanings with, however, something in common. This is also the case of the French verb *jouer* or German *spielen*.)

In *How We Think*, Dewey claims that the development of intelligence and knowledge depends upon carrying out observations in a specific way. According to Dewey, intelligent observation is a process that shifts the attention from something already known and familiar toward something else completely new and unfamiliar usually consisting of a problem to be solved. This movement is understood as a drama or a story, in which a balanced mixture of familiar and unexpected can be found. In addition, it must include an emotional "thrill" that creates a strong interest for the plot. The scientific method involves such intelligence. Dewey says that "scientific observation does not, however, merely replace observation that is enjoyed for its own sake. The latter, sharpened by the purpose of contributing to an art like writing, painting, singing, becomes truly esthetic, and the persons who enjoy seeing and hearing will be the best observers" (1933/1986: 322). Play, in its aesthetic and artistic sense, involves the foregoing process of intelligence (Henricks 2015: 51). Further, it is important to notice that in play, understood, for example, as a drama or a football match, spectators participate and are not merely detached and neutral observers (Eberle 2014: 214). The result of a match as well as the performance in a drama is also strongly dependent on the spectators.

Dewey claims education is a necessity of life and a social function in chapters 1 and 2 of *Democracy and Education*. Since play is an educational activity/category, its value and importance is conducive to human growth within social and political life. However, this process is not merely the reproduction of some already-existing cultural, social, or political form. It consists, instead, in the intelligent reorganization of experience that promotes the development of the individuals deeply integrated, in a transactional way, in their social and political environment (Rømer 2012: 136; Graham & Kirby 2016: 11). Play is an activity and a category of this sort. Now, let us see how tightly it is connected to (or merged in) social–political sphere.

Play, Transaction, and Social–Political Life

Play and Politics in Aristotle: A Non-transactional View

In Aristotle, both play and politics rest upon an inter-actional, not transactional, view. Aristotle argued that whoever is outside the community is like "an isolated piece at draughts" (Aristotle *Politics*: 1253a). In other words, the Greek philosopher underlined the relational character of the human being and thought of the political community as a sort of game in which every piece moves according to previously established rules.

In Dewey's view, however, the relational and political dimension and play have a very different meaning. The individual is not considered a piece or part *of a whole* but is integrated *within a transactional whole*. Nor is community reduced to a system of given rules, to which the individual has to submit. Social and political relationships rather are works in progress and an unfinished business. Rules are certainly important in play (paradoxically, this is one of the reasons why play can be so serious). In Dewey's view, however, rules emerge during the active relationship with reality (1888/1969: 231–4). Thus, it becomes apparent that, by playing, the rules aside, both children and adults experience a continuous reorganization of the relation between the self and the environment and this is fundamental for social and political life. This reorganization happens in a transactional way. In play, as well as in political life, the roles of the components and their meanings are bound to the whole situation. There is no play without players, no political life without citizens. Play arises from a transactional web of relations in which human beings and things participate.

Huizinga, Henricks, and Dewey: Towards a Transactional View in Play and Politics

Huizinga claims that play is one of the most primordial aspects of human beings' communal existence (1938/2014: 4). Henricks agrees with the Dutch author,[5] depicting Huizinga's *Homo ludens* as "an attempt to identify the defining qualities of play and to demonstrate its broadest range of significance" (2015: 4). Moreover, Henricks highlights the fact that, according to Huizinga, modern societies have lost the "vital, creative spark" of play-element. Dewey seems to share Huizinga's view when he claims that our ancestor's lives were permeated by play, which created both symbols in the form of collective objects and behaviors with strong emotional qualities (1925/1981: 73). But Dewey is also aware of the difficulties in employing play in education in modernity the same way as in primitive societies, that is "through the dramatic plays in which children reproduce the actions of grown-ups and thus learn to know what they are like" (1916/1980: 10). In advanced societies, Dewey holds, play often needs to be organized through the formal education. It does not mean, however, that play loses its value of free and creative activity, but only that the informal and spontaneous association cannot by itself "transmit all the resources and achievements of a complex society" (1916/1980: 11). Transaction brings to light the ancestral social and political significance of play, and this is true especially with regard to contemporary democracy. To show this, let us make a brief comparison between Henricks and Dewey.

The relation between play and political life looks like what Henricks calls "play-communitas combinations." These are specific forms of shared social behavior connected to certain group activities or events in which play is included divided into the two notions of "communal play" and "playful communitas." The former refers to "what people can do together" (2015: 66), as, for instance, the actor in a troupe, while the latter focuses on what the community or a social group ask to players, for instance when they participate in a party, banquet or reunion. "If communal play features spirited collective assertion," writes Henricks, "then playful communitas features acts of bonding that are animated by play's feisty spirit" (2015: 66). Even though play-communitas displays a character strongly related to the political sphere in Henricks's view communal play seems to indicate shared action and interaction, but not transaction. I believe, instead, that play as activity/category resulting from an examination of Deweyan thought is wider and deeper in its social–political implications than Henricks's notion while play's transactional character better fits in with a democracy.

Dewey's Transactional Play and Social–Political Life

Play and social–political life share the same transactional matrix. As observed above, Dewey's integrated approach provides us with a more consistent and reliable account of both play and the political sphere. This is true because interaction does not constitute a thorough explanation of what and how things really happen in either political life or play. To say that players do not exist without play, and likewise citizens do not exist without political community, does not mean only that people are transactionally involved in what they are experiencing at the present. Connecting more with Dewey's view than Huizinga's, we can see that the transaction refers also to the relation between past and present. In other words, to say that play and social–political life share the same matrix is to say that people of a given society cannot exist without the heritage of their ancestors. This means that the stratified forms of culture are embedded in present life, and play is not only a means to know them but also a fundamental way to discover the deep social nature of play itself. In Dewey and Bentley's (1949/1989a) terms, this means we must "see together, extensionally and durationally, much that is talked about conventionally as if it were composed of irreconcilable separates" (67).

Human beings are *ludens* because they are social (Vanderstraeten 2002: 241). Besides a continuous reorganization of the relation between the self and the environment, by playing both children and adults experience the transactional nature of the exchange with other, past and present, human beings. This reorganization is directed toward better ways of dealing with the world.

At this point, it is worth observing that the resemblance of play and the social–political sphere is not merely a matter of similarity in structure. Political and social life are actually permeated with play as a ludic category. Dewey makes a point of not separating play and work. Nor can play be separated from political and social life. When play is considered only as a break from working, as an amusing and relaxing activity in contrast with the other (and more serious) function of maintaining personal and collective life, then it is tantamount to taking one step back with regard to both Dewey's ideas and a well-functioning society.

To sum up, firstly, the citizen cannot be considered as a "piece" existing previously and separately from her/his community. The former does not exist without the latter, just as the player does not exist without play. Secondly, play has been integrated into human communities since ancient times, so that the transactional tie of members in a society, even over its history, comes to light through the play-element and contributes to the ongoing reorganization and adaptation of political life. In addition, "Play is where old ideas are discarded and new ideas are 'tried on'" (Graham & Kirby 2016: 13). Because of this, play fully fits in with the dynamics of a democracy and is important in democratic education.

Play, Democracy, and Education: A Transactional Approach

Play and Democracy

Democracy, for Dewey, is an open process in which all citizens need to continuously adjust themselves to new problems and issues while developing answers that are necessarily provisional. In democracy there are some basic patterns (such as a wide participation, fundamental liberties, free debate, and so on), but people and events constantly change due to the constitutive openness of this political form. According to Dewey, in democracy the individual and society are intertwined. In play the individual is fully involved, ends and means are inseparable, and emotions have a pivotal role to such an extent that should they be removed, play itself would no longer exist (Eberle 2014; Henricks 2015). A player cannot be extraneous to what she/he is playing as in a democratic society citizens cannot be extraneous to their community. The same cannot be said with respect to other political forms in which the individual is alienated from public life (Dewey 1888/1969: 240, 242–3). In both play and democratic public life emotion functions as the glue binding together individuals and community giving the individual's behavior (when the emotion is sound) a specific (i.e., bound to the situation) and possibly fuller meaning. Dewey argues that the educational significance of play consists in its being a means of developing social intelligence (1916/1980: 216).

The main reason for which play is helpful to developing social intelligence is its transactional and experimental character. As we have repeatedly observed, all the elements of play acquire their meaning and function only within the play-event; their meaning and function must arise in it. Moreover, when enters the "Circuit of Inquiry," play creates new habits (and re-creates old habits giving them new forms). So, in play there is nothing that exists as a thing-in-itself. Even a football pitch, a chessboard, a ball, or a pawn are only "dead" things until they enter the real game (Vanderstraeten 2002: 237–8; Stoller 2018: 50). Play becomes what it is, and how it is, just when the elements involved start to function transactionally in a certain way (e.g., as we have seen with throwing stones on the water). Play, especially in its creative artistic form, habituates human beings to an organized and transactional behavior, and helps us to abandon confused and unproductive behaviors (Dewey 1925/1981: 68). Considered as a transactional activity/category play includes two fundamental elements helpful to develop social intelligence in democratic education: imagination and emotion.

The Role of the Imagination and Emotion

Rømer considers imagination the driving force of any transaction. Imagination is the "ability to make the absent become present" (Rømer 2012: 141). This ability is crucial for democratic education and involves transactional play. Following Dewey's discourse in chapter 18 of *Democracy and Education*, Rømer argues that the constructions of imagination play out in the gap between actor and spectator. As an actor, one is directly involved in a given situation or role in the world, while the spectator is whoever is placed in a different role and situation and observes from a distance the events involving the actor. Both the actor and the spectator, if taken as separated, hold positions "that are incapable of exchanging imagined interests in a crisscross of communication." To fill the gap and put actor and spectator in actual communication requires the "play of imagination." This is, for Dewey, the aesthetic concept of dramatization. This means that teaching and learning are "about making the distant present, to suck into the classroom the 'environing conditions'" (Rømer 2012: 135). Take as an example the subject matter of "unemployment." It is difficult to grasp the meaning of this concept for concrete human life if the positions of people linked to it (e.g., unemployed, social workers, employer, etc.) remain separated. "The educated point of view […] is the intelligent and pluralist working of the faculty of imagination, permitting all kinds of positions and habituations to be exchanged, e.g., how different groups cope with unemployment, distinctions within the notion of unemployment, consequences for the economy and for politics, etc." (Rømer 2012: 142).

In a pluralistic and manifold society imagination is a transactional educational tool to help empathically understand the differences existing among groups to overcome the obstacles that prevent citizens and people of different cultures, traditions, religions, and even languages from really participating and integrating within a democratic community. Imagination makes use of transactional play in the artistic form of drama or dramatization.

Although Nussbaum (2013) does not explicitly use transaction she seems to share Rømer's account, particularly when she claims that play and playfulness can promote and strengthen democratic values, such as reciprocity, respect, and trust, toward the other's world. Nussbaum holds that this is possible through music, poetry, drama, and literature in education.

For Dewey (1916/1980), "The engagement of the imagination is the only thing that makes any activity more than mechanical" (244). However, imagination naturally involves emotion. Therefore, as in a game or a drama, a person who participates in political life does not behave in a mechanical and abstract way. For example, when a person votes she/he does not get rid of her/his own life experience, character, emotions, in a word, the self. On the contrary, the entire self is involved in and contributes to this event, which therefore assumes a specific meaning. Through this example Dewey intends to point out that in democracy rules and political procedures do not make sense if they are not associated with meaning. As we have seen, emotion (especially in art) deeply integrates human beings with the environment, making the experience highly meaningful. The importance of the emotion for play and political life rests upon two main notions, bounded each other and both involved in transaction: the "dramatic rehearsal" and participation.

Dewey descries imagination as "dramatic rehearsal" in chapter 16 of *Human Nature and Conduct* and consists in carrying out mental experiments in order to select the better course of action. This process of reasoning is motivated by emotions and leads to a response in which the competing elements are selected and balanced (1922/1988: 132–8; Morse 2010). Dramatic rehearsal involves imagination as well as emotion and helps to transform action into "intelligent action" (Vanderstraeten 2002: 239). On the other hand, participation "requires that an actor reacts to the meaning of the acts of the other" (Dewey 1925/1981: 141; Vanderstraeten 2002: 240; Andersson, Garrison, & Östman 2018: 5). Play and political life share these two elements. Therefore, not only children's play and playfulness at school are educational means which habituate young human beings to meaningful activity and can develop a deep sensitivity toward the world, but both can help to do this in adults too.

Play as Transactional Activity/Category in Democratic Education

Some practical circumstances in which transactional play is supportive of democratic education can be readily pointed out. For Dewey teaching is an art, and the teacher and artist share the attitude of combining playfulness and seriousness (1933/1986: 348–9). So conceived, the teacher's task consists in attuning different elements arising within the teaching–learning process (teacher's role itself, the students, subjects, materials, environment, and so on) employing a balanced combination of seriousness and playfulness (Skilbeck 2017). This can be considered a transactional attitude helping students develop the capacity to manage a variety of unstable elements in democratic life. Another case, bound to participation as reaction to the meanings of the world, is public art and architecture permeated with the play-element with transactional and educational value. The *Millennium Park* in Chicago, as described by Nussbaum (Nussbaum 2013: 300), is a good example. The park, its sculptures, fountains, and buildings push the visitor to see and experience the self, others, and the environment through new perspectives.

Empirically considered, play as an educational tool offers a number of examples in which the role of transaction is often neglected or not explicitly acknowledged (even though included). This is the case, for instance, of both Nussbaum's accounts cited above. This is also the case in *Michael Rosen's Book of Play* (Rosen 2019).[6] Rosen nicely summarizes (without knowing it) the notion of transactional play in education, especially when he writes that, instead of treating his book as an object containing instructions or knowledge, the reader "can treat it as something you're *having a conversation* with" (Rosen 2019: 12). The sheets of paper with printed symbols and letters become (are) something (perhaps someone) I am speaking to and something to be experienced instead of simply read. People in a democratic society need to see and experience their world in this way, and they need to be educated to cope with unexpected change and learn flexibility. This is exactly what transactional play can help to do. Here the poet Rosen echoes the philosopher Dewey about the role of imagination, the shift from familiar to unknown, and the experimental nature of play. All that has to be included in democratic education in order to find out creative solution for communal problems is imagination.

Conclusion

Human life is permeated with play. We cannot consider it only a way to make life light or a rest from labor. Play is much more, especially when considered transactionally. It is an activity, or category, through which (or in which) human beings can find self-realization and fulfillment in their lives. Since sound play affords a deeper and wider look at the world people who experience play (especially in its artistic sense) become increasingly aware of the possibilities the world offers and they can develop more suitable habits for coping. There is no inner force pushing a human being to play (self-action), nor can play be reduced to rules and playthings that move the "mechanism" of human relationships (inter-action). Instead, as I have shown, play is based upon the organism–environment transaction. This attitude is the same in a democratic society where understanding one another means that objects obtain "the same value for both with respect to carrying on a common pursuit" (Dewey 1916/1980: 19; Vanderstraeten 2002: 240).

6

Applications of Transactional Methodologies for Analysis of Teaching and Learning Processes

Pernilla Andersson and Johan Öhman

Introduction

Investigating teaching and learning processes is methodologically challenging when considering the complexity and variety of different sociocultural contexts and the different experiences teachers and students bring to the classroom. This chapter presents how such methodological challenges can be met by a combination of John Dewey's pragmatic philosophy and theory of transaction, Ludwig Wittgenstein's work on language games, and a German and Scandinavian *didaktik*-tradition (Klafki 1995). A German and Scandinavian *didaktik*-tradition (*didactics* in English) implies a research-focus on the relation between teaching and learning with a particular interest in the educational content, encompassing learning of knowledge, socialization in relation to particular values as well as person-formation. The teacher is here regarded as an autonomous practitioner who makes decisive didactical choices within the scope of the curriculum. This means that didactics is not only about teaching a given content but also involves a critical stance toward the content that is taught as well as the purpose of teaching. The role of didactic research is to support teachers as professionals by making inquiries into the reasons for making certain selections of content and methods in relation to a particular context and thereby providing a basis for critical reflection (Wickman 2012). In this chapter we refer to this role of didactic research as providing knowledge that is helpful for teachers to sharpen their "didactic gaze" and developing their teaching practice. When the goal is to provide this kind of support, both Dewey's pragmatic philosophy and theory of transaction and Wittgenstein's work on language games are quite useful.

This chapter builds on work done by the research group SMED (Studies of Meaning-making in Educational Discourses) based at Uppsala University and Örebro University in Sweden (Andersson 2019). The combination of German and Scandinavian didactic theory, pragmatism, and a transactional perspective implies a particular interest for the consequences of education in practice; therefor, the group has extensively explored ongoing teaching and learning processes. Different teaching and learning practices that have been studied include: mathematics, science education, physical education, sloyd, environmental and sustainability education, religious studies, social studies, business management and economics, early childhood education as well as other forms of practices where learning happens, such as study visits, social media, nonformal education, and extracurricular activities. The empirical materials in the different studies include transcribed video-recorded observations, field notes, audio-recordings of smaller group discussions and students' written assignments. For the purpose of analyzing learning of knowledge, socialization content as well as the conditions or scope for person formation in these teaching and learning practices the group has developed special analytical methods. In this chapter we present different transactional methodologies, and exemplify how they have been applied.

A Transactional Methodological Framework

In contrast to understanding the world as comprised of interacting *substances*, educational researchers using a transactional methodology approach the world as *events* where different participants transact (Dewey 1929/1958, 1932/1985). Furthermore, as opposed to understanding learning in terms of *causal connections* between different elements (presupposing a division in independent elements and a kind of "freezing" the state of things), learning is seen as a *process of continuity and change* and the relation between actions and consequences as *mutually constitutive*. From this transactional perspective, meaning is something that emerge in transactions rather than existing in our minds—people "know with their habits not with their 'consciousness.' The latter is eventual, not a source" (Dewey 1922: 182–3). As a methodological consequence, transactional researchers focus on what is happening in encounters involving different participants (people, artifacts, environment) rather than on investigating inner feelings, thoughts, and knowledge before and after teaching.

Based on Dewey's theory of action (1929/1958, 1949/1989a) and Wittgenstein work on language games (1953/1997), Leif Östman and Johan Öhman claim that meaning-making and learning can and ought to be investigated through analysis of how language is used in social practices (Öhman & Östman 2007; Östman & Öhman *forthcoming*). In contrast to a mainstream cognitivist understanding where language is separated from people and their actions and looked upon as a tool used to connect meanings with reality (a third-person perspective), language is here understood as integrated in people's actions and the mind is something that is reflected in the use of language (a first-person perspective).

In their research Östman and Öhman (*forthcoming*) create an alternative to the conventional cognitivist understanding of individuals' previous knowledge and experiences as fixed entities located in the memory. Relating to Dewey's principle of continuity (1938) they claim that the past, present and future can be observed in communicative actions (i.e., in events). They show how previous experiences are reflected when re-actualized and related to circumstances in a contemporary event, and how the future always is present here and now in people's actions through the existence of a direction, goal, purpose, or an idea about future consequences.

Finally, drawing on Rogoff (1995), Östman and Öhman suggest that the significance of the individual, social and institutional dimensions must be treated as an empirical rather than a theoretical question, i.e., how the different dimensions are shown in the individuals' actions in a specific event. The reason for this, they claim, is that neither individual experiences nor sociocultural dimensions can be isolated as "a priori" or given status as independent primary factors (as in many mainstream approaches). Individual, social, and institutional aspects of meaning-making need to be treated transactionally as dimensions of the same process, simultaneous, and mutually constitutive.

Practical Epistemology Analysis

Based on the transactional perspective presented above, the research group SMED has developed a number of analytical methods among which *practical epistemological analysis* (PEA), developed by P-O Wickman and Leif Östman (2002) can be described as a key method. The method draws on Wittgenstein's idea of language games and is used to analyze learning.

In short, *practical* epistemology refers to the epistemology of different *practices* while PEA means to investigate learning as changes in individuals' way of interacting with their environment. Four concepts are central to analyze and describe the learning process: "stand fast," "encounter," "gap," and "relation." The concept *stand fast* captures what different individuals already know (e.g., previously acquired habits) in the particular moment and situation. This becomes visible in the way students use words without hesitation, ask questions, etc. The concept *encounter* is used to capture how the individual and her/his (natural, social, and/or cultural) environment mutually affect each other. The encounter can occur in relation to teachers, other students and/or artifacts, or something else material. In these encounters, students can stumble across difficulties that they need to handle to "move on," i.e., continue the activity. The concept *gap* is used to identify and describe these situations. The gap becomes visible when students hesitate, ask questions, guesses, etc. To handle the difficulty the student needs to create a *relation* between what stands fast (what the student already knows) and what is new (what students' do not know) in the encounter. The relation closes the gap and helps the student to "solve" the difficulty (i.e., the student *makes meaning*). It can, however, also be the case that the gap is closed immediately and does not become visible for the researcher. In other cases the student does not get through the difficulty and the gap lingers.

In educational activities there is always a purpose—a specific idea about what the students should or want to learn. The purpose can be initiated by the teacher but also by the students and it can also change when, for instance, a classroom discussion takes a new direction. The purpose of the activity, therefore, needs to be determined and analysis related to this purpose. The purpose can be obvious, for example, from the students' and teacher's conversation but it can also be necessary to clarify the purpose by asking the teacher and students. Important to note is that the purpose can change during the activity and that students also can be involved in directing this change, for instance in classroom discussions.

Different Didactical Research Problems and Applications of Transactional Methodologies

This section exemplifies various uses of transactional methodologies, i.e., specific combinations of analytical methods and theoretical models. The different examples come from previous studies conducted within the research group SMED (2006–18) and are chosen in order to represent a variety of didactic research-problems to which different transactional methodologies have been found to be suited. These themes of research-problems are:

1. To capture the *complexity* of learning processes involving different educational purposes and *forms of knowledge* that occur simultaneously.
2. To investigate, identify and *illuminate critical situations* and moments in learning processes and when the meaning-making can take different directions.
3. To investigate and *illuminate teachers'* and others' *actions* and their influence in individual learning processes.
4. To identify and illuminate different *selective teaching traditions* as they appear in educational practice.

The Complexity of Learning Processes

Teaching and learning processes are complex. Different purposes of education and different forms of knowledge occur simultaneously and are difficult to separate in educational practice. The complexity could, for instance, involve the role of knowledge in ethico-political classroom discussions or the role of the body and aesthetics in learning sports. In this section we have chosen a study of classroom discussions about climate change to exemplify how the complexity of facts and values in learning processes can be investigated from a transactional perspective.

In pluralistic and participatory (as opposed to behavior modification) approaches to environment and sustainability education, one way of finding answers to value-related issues or recognizing different standpoints is through peer discussions in classroom practice. Even though such approaches seem to be increasingly used, there are many questions regarding how and what they contribute to students' learning. One concern is that they take too much time from the learning of scientific knowledge. Another concern comes from studies indicating that students seldom include scientific knowledge in discussions and when they do it is not used in a critical and reflective way. There is, however, a lack of empirically based knowledge regarding the role knowledge plays in students' ability to formulate arguments and take a stand in value-related environmental and sustainability issues.

With the aim of contributing to this research gap Rudsberg and Öhman (2015) used a transactional methodology consisting of a transactional understanding of Toulmin's model of argumentation and PEA, to analyze classroom discussions about climate change. More specifically the study focused on if, how, and what kinds of knowledge students used as well as how this knowledge was related to the claims they made in the discussions. This approach involved an analytical focus on what happened in the encounters between the assignment designed by the teacher, the sustainability issue at hand (in this case climate change) and the participants in the classroom discussions. In short, this involved: (a) identification of gaps that occurred (including the kind of gaps and how they emerged) when participants interacted in argumentation; (b) analysis of the actions in form of responses, agreements, answers, or rejections that followed the gaps; (c) analysis of the relations between recalled knowledge and the problem at hand that the students created when participating in the discussion. The students' previous experiences (facts and values) about climate change were identified as they were expressed and re-actualized when related to questions, claims, etc. by peers and the teacher in the situation. Furthermore, the analysis focused on the function of different kinds of knowledge that the students used in argumentation in the classroom activity. This included re-actualized knowledge as well as knowledge gained in the ongoing discussion and how the previous knowledge gained new meaning in a new situation (continuity and change). As a result, the study showed that students used knowledge from many different subject areas such as environmental studies, history, politics, biology, and human geography to construct their arguments, *at the same time* as they developed their argumentative abilities.

Transactional methodologies have also been used to capture other kinds of complex aspects of learning processes, such as how learning of argumentative abilities and progression of learning facts presuppose each other in classroom practice (Rudsberg, Öhman, & Östman 2013); how children's learning of gravity and the shape of the earth are affected by individual previous experiences and the sociocultural setting simultaneously (Lidar, Almqvist, & Östman 2010); the role of the body in teaching and learning "how to sail" (Andersson, Östman, & Öhman 2015); and the importance of esthetical judgments when learning sports (Maivorsdotter & Wickman 2011).

The support these studies provide teachers as professionals consists of detailed analysis of classroom dialogues, including extracts from verbatim transcripts. Extracts from classroom dialogues or other places where teaching and learning takes place were selected on the basis that teachers are likely to be familiar to similar situations. The researcher's first-person perspective (see previous section "A Transactional Methodological Framework") means taking the same perspective as the teacher has in the classroom and is therefore helpful for teachers to sharpen/develop their "didactic gaze." In the illustrative example above this means: developing the ability to identify strengths and weaknesses of discussions as teaching method, pay attention to if and how students use different kinds of knowledge when building arguments, supporting students to use knowledge in a critical and reflective way and justify when it is a wise decision to spend valuable time for discussions.

Critical Moments in Learning Processes

The studies presented in the last section illuminate the complexity of learning and that the students' meaning-making could take different directions depending on different conditions in the situation. Thus it can be argued that it is important to investigate, identify, and illuminate critical situations and moments in learning processes where the meaning-making can take different directions. In this section we have chosen a study of entrepreneurship and sustainability education to exemplify how critical moments in learning processes can be investigated with a transactional methodology.

In the field of environment and sustainability education research there has been a debate that has been described as "a tension between instrumental and emancipatory educational objectives" (Wals 2010). To ensure that environment and sustainability education avoids "business as usual" it has been argued that more instrumentalist approaches are needed, and on the other hand it has been argued that such approaches are incompatible with emancipation and critical thinking as educational objectives. With this background, it could be argued that it is important to identify and analyze moments in educational practice that can facilitate change and contribute to "business as un-usual" without compromising emancipatory educational ideals.

Drawing on a transactional methodology consisting of PEA combined with Glynos and Howarth's logics of critical explanation and Laclau's concept of "dislocation" Andersson (2018) demonstrated how such (dislocatory) moments can be a critical turning point in students' understanding at the same time as they provide scope for emancipatory aspects of education. The approach involved an analytical focus on the encounter between individual business students' previous experiences (of what acting "sustainably" entails), their personal feelings about sustainability issues, the assignment about preparing for an entrepreneurship exhibition, and the teachers' comments in the ongoing classroom practice. The analysis of the transcribed classroom discussions focused on what "running a business sustainably" became in the classroom activity and how a "dislocatory moment" was critical in the change toward what could be described as *business as un-usual*. More specifically, the moment involved a situation when the teacher gave an example that made the complexity of sustainability issues clear to the students and that the principle of "buying products locally" in the particular case was irrelevant from a sustainability point of view. The loss of a guiding principle called for the involvement of students' personal feelings (emancipation) for socioecological sustainability dimensions when finding other principles that were more relevant from a sustainability point of view, which also became visible in the way the students worked with the assignment. The students' previous experiences about "doing business sustainably" were re-actualized and became visible when related to the new assignment in a context that was novel to the students. In this way the transactional approach made it possible to identify students' previous experiences of "acting sustainably," as well as how and when it changed during the course of the lessons.

Transactional methodologies have also been useful to illuminate in detail: political moments in educational practice (Håkansson, Van Poeck, & Östman 2019); critical moments when students learn a specific epistemology (Lundqvist, Almqvist, & Östman 2009); and critical moments in toddlers' learning in encounters with their physical environment (Klaar & Öhman 2012; see also Klaar & Öhman, this volume).

These kinds of transactional studies provide knowledge that can help teachers create conditions for moments that are critical for students' meaning-making. The support consists of detailed descriptions and micro-analysis of situations that are of particular importance from an educational point of view, but are hard to see without the help of video-recordings and the time to do a careful and detailed analysis. In the illustrative example above the micro-analysis can be of particular help for teachers to identify opportunities for emancipatory aspects of education and "business as un-usual" and how to create conditions for and take care of "dislocatory moments" when they occur.

Teachers' and Students' Actions and Their Influence on Individual Learning Processes

Investigating teachers' and other students' influence on individual students' learning processes is methodologically challenging. In this section we have chosen a study of science education to exemplify how a transactional approach can meet this challenge.

A common way of investigating the teacher's influence on students' learning in educational research has been to study students' conceptual development—from an everyday to a scientifically correct understanding. However, the interview method has limits when it comes to acquiring knowledge about the learning *process* in relation to teaching. To contribute knowledge about the relation between the teaching practice and students' learning, Lidar, Lundqvist and Östman (2006) used a transactional methodology consisting of PEA in combination with a teacher moves model to analyze students' learning processes, in situ. Teacher moves are actions that get a specific function for an individual student's learning in relation to the purpose of the activity. The labeling of the "moves" is connected to the specific function they have in students' learning processes.

A teacher move can, for instance, be a confirming action in the form of a subtle nod confirming that a student sees and does the right things. The first step in such an analysis involves distinguishing events with (at least) three transactions of interplay. What is focused on is sequences in the empirical material showing an event involving: (1) an individual's action before the teacher's action, (2) a teacher's action, (3) an individual's action after the teacher's action. An action that affects the student's action/learning in relation to the purpose of the activity is labeled "a move." In the final stage the function of the teacher's action is analyzed.

Lidar, Lundqvist, and Östman (2006) used this methodology to study how students learn how to do laboratory work and to working in a scientific way. More specifically, the transactional analysis involved focus on the encounter between the students' previous experiences (of what could be expected from a scientific experiment), the experimental material (water, saltpeter, etc.), the task of the experiment ("Cold and hot water as solvents") and the teacher's actions. In one of the lessons a group of students ran into a difficulty when the assignment involved a question about "*what* happens?" and they thought that "*nothing* happened." In other words, a gap emerged when students' previous experience of what could count as something that "happens" was not fruitful to describe something that dissolves (saltpeter in water). Furthermore, the analysis focused on what kind of teacher actions that were more or less successful for the students to create a new relation to the term "happens" and thereby learn what was worth paying attention to when working as a scientist.

The analysis of the student and teacher dialogues from the laboratory work showed that the students never used scientific concepts in a scientifically acceptable way. This means that if the aim was that students should learn to use scientific concepts correctly one could draw the conclusion that no learning had taken place and that the teacher's actions were unsuccessful. However, the transactional methodology facilitated seeing other kinds of learning that took place, which in this case involved learning what could be worth paying attention to when doing laboratory work, that is, learning how to observe like a scientist. The transactional analysis illuminated how learning takes place in small steps and might not be so much about new concepts as of learning a new kind of attentiveness. The transactional approach made it possible to show in detail which kind of actions lead individual students further and which actions were unsuccessful, in the specific situation.

Transactional methodologies have also facilitated detailed analysis of: how teachers influence socialization processes in science education (Lundqvist, Almqvist, & Östman 2009); how teachers integrate education and care in preschool practice (Klaar & Öhman 2014); and how teachers/educators and students influence discussions about different perspectives on a sustainable future (Öhman & Öhman 2013, Van Poeck & Östman 2019).

These studies support teachers in that they show which kind of teacher actions seem more or less successful for leading individual students further in particular situations. In the illustrative example the "generative moves" (teacher summarizes what in the experiment that is important facts to pay attention to) were more fruitful than the "re-orienting moves" (teacher pointing out that there can be other properties worth investigating) when it came to learning how to do laboratory work. The labeling of different teacher moves also contribute to a professional language that help teachers talk about teaching in a more nuanced way.

Different Selective Teaching Traditions in Practice

Within institutionalized educational practices patterns of specific ways of selecting educational content and choosing teaching methods are created over time. These patterns can be described and investigated by using the concept of *selective teaching traditions*. Different selective traditions have previously been identified through analysis of texts, such as textbooks and policy documents. By means of a transactional perspective it is possible to also investigate selective traditions in ongoing practice, and in this way it is also possible to explore the function of the traditions in students' learning processes. In this section we have chosen a study of laboratory work in science education to exemplify how this can be done.

In science education, two different selective traditions have previously been identified, the academic and the romantic (Östman 1996). The main aim of the academic tradition is that students should learn scientific concepts and methods.

With regard to the romantic tradition, the main aim is to make students learn from science, which means a focus on the human relation to nature and possibility of including moral and political dimensions in science teaching. By means of a transactional methodology consisting of PEA and the teacher moves model, here combined with the concept of selective traditions, Lundqvist, Almqvist and Östman (2012) made a close case study of one teacher's teaching in relation to these established traditions within science education. This implied a focus on the encounter between the teacher, the students, the assignment, and the artifacts used (different materials) in the lesson. Students' previous experiences of being a good student in science were re-actualized and became visible when related to the new assignment "Properties of materials" where they through their talk and actions showed a focus on writing down correct answers. Since the purpose of the activity was "to learn how to do laboratory work" (rather than knowing and writing down the correct answers) the teacher made different actions to change the students' habits of just writing down correct answers to the habit of the scientific method (to first do an investigation); for instance by offering the students a thermometer when students talked about measuring the boiling and melting points. The students' new habit of making investigations was captured in a statement by two students who already knew the answer to the question of what material it was: "Are we supposed to pretend that we don't know what kind of metal it is?" In other words, the students had learned that becoming a scientist means investigating before knowing.

Transactional methodologies have also been used to investigate: selective teaching traditions with regard to and similarities and differences in science vs physical education with a focus on teachers' motivating work and the potential consequences with regard to what kind of students are "created" in educational practices (Östman et al. 2015); how a pluralist selective tradition appears in environmental and sustainability teaching practice (Rudsberg & Öhman 2010); if, to what extent and how students adopt a way of thinking about environmental issues which corresponds to their teacher's selective tradition (Sund & Wickman 2011 a, b).

These studies support teachers by making them aware of how particular selective traditions appear in educational practice, which is hard because they are taken for granted. To make an informed didactic *choice* requires awareness of alternatives. By providing knowledge about how particular selective traditions appear in practice and comparing them with alternatives, teachers get a tool for critical reflection upon their own teaching practice and a basis for a professional development of their teaching. In the illustrative study presented above this implied illuminating in detail how students were socialized in an academic selective tradition in comparison to what a romantic selective tradition would entail.

Concluding Comments

In the introduction to this chapter we described that the development of the transactional methodological framework was driven by the ambition to provide the teaching profession with a basis for making didactical choices. The methodologies strive to use a similar gaze as the teacher in a classroom setting (a first-person perspective). In this way the transactional research can offer results teachers can recognize and use to sharpen their "didactic gaze" and develop their teaching practice. In this chapter we have presented examples of what this could entail by describing how a transactional analysis offers the possibility of capturing critical moments in classroom practice where meaning-making can take different directions and provide detailed analysis of teaching and learning processes. In most of the studies presented in this chapter a teacher has planned the activity with a specific purpose in mind. In some of the studies the purpose changed during the course of the lesson and students were active in redirecting toward new learning goals. Sometimes no teacher was involved at all. The studies include a variety of different school subjects, age groups, teaching methods, formal and informal education as well as extracurricular or voluntary activities where teaching and learning also take place. The studies demonstrate how transactional methodologies facilitate studies of how *individual* previous experiences and new challenges transact in ongoing *social* and *cultural* practices. It can therefore be argued that transactional methodologies have much to offer when it comes to addressing blind spots in mainstream cognitivist and behavioral educational research.

7

Analyzing Teachers' Functional Coordination of Teaching Habits in the Encounter with Policy Reforms

Malena Lidar and Eva Lundqvist

Introduction

In this chapter, we will explore how a transactional approach can shed light on continuity and change in teaching practices. Our starting point is that teachers develop personal habits of acting based on their having been educated in, being in, and working in contextual situations created by earlier generations of teachers and traditions within the school subjects and scientific disciplines. Teachers, like any other human being, act in relation to what they are used to and what they have previously known and valued. On an individual level, one could say that habits are what constitute continuity in teaching practices. However, when teachers are faced with new requirements in their practice, for example a policy change, their habits may be challenged and possibly adjusted—or new habits may be formed. New policies may require a re-modeling of the teaching habits so that these habits become functional in relation to the new requirements. In this way, continuity and change may be perceived as a coordination process integrating existing habits and new elements of teaching practice. In this chapter, we will illustrate this process in transactional analyses of one teacher's reasoning, as she talks about how she organizes her experiences in everyday practice when working with the enactment of a state-mandated policy reform.

One common approach to studying teachers' meaning-making and professional knowledge is to examine their beliefs or views concerning a phenomenon (e.g., Coenders, Terlouw & Dijkstra 2008; Cotton 2006). Beliefs are said to form the core of what a teacher thinks and to direct how classroom action is performed (Lumpe, Haney, & Czerniak 2000). Wallace and Priestley

(2011) point out that teachers tend to enact reforms in relation to their own beliefs. Although the definitions of teachers' beliefs are not entirely uniform, one common characterization is that beliefs are "the cognitive structures that teachers bring to bear on classroom decision-making" (Wallace & Priestley 2011, p. 360). Such analyses could include teachers' individual views as well as sociocultural dimensions, but these aspects are often understood as parallel structures and thereby the focus is typically on one or the other, not both.

In the challenge to embrace both continuity and change when studying the meaning-making teachers do while coordinating their teaching habits with new requirements, we take our point of departure in the interplay between the individual and his/her environment. Because individuals' actions change the (physical, social, and/or institutional) environment, and because a shift in activity is a response to changing conditions, functional dynamic coordination is a continuous back-and-forth process in which individuals continuously readjust their actions to a changing environment (Dewey 1938/1997). Instead of seeking to explain teachers' individual beliefs or knowledge as something underlying their responses to reforms, we look at teachers' meaning-making and actions using a transactional epistemology (Dewey & Bentley, 1949/1989a). Our approach views teachers' responses as being related to the habits that they use in their everyday practices and that become visible in how they talk about those practices. Using this approach, meaning-making or knowing is not seen as something entirely reducible to a process within the minds of human beings; instead it is something practical, something we say or do (Biesta & Burbules 2003; Quennerstedt et al. 2011; Wickman & Östman 2002).

Here, we consider teachers' statements about what they do in their everyday teaching to be expressions of their teaching habits, because their talk is an expression of how they make situations intelligible. Habits are what make up teachers' dispositions to act and make meaning in their encounter with the environment (Nelsen 2014). Here, the focal aspect of the environment is constituted by the content of a reform.

Habits are the default mode of human experience and are nonreflective rather than reflective (Ryan 2011). The nature of habits is, in other words, not solely that of practices connected to something a person does repeatedly, but a foundational aspect of human activity that is always present, but not obviously controlling the person's actions. We begin thinking about our different options when we find ourselves in a troubling situation, i.e., when our habits no longer provide an automatic response to a change or a need in the environment (Östman, Van Poeck, & Öhman 2019b).

When our experiences from encounters with the environment come into conflict with our habits, coordination is required that may result in a need for modification of these habits. In the context of educational changes, such as policy reforms, teachers' habits may be challenged. If a teacher's teaching habits do not correspond with how he/she perceives the new requirements, tensions may arise requiring coordination, where the existing habits are evaluated in relation to what is new in the requirements and vice versa. Dewey presents the "intelligent or artistic habit" as the ideal, where habits are plastic and adaptable to new situations while still retaining their usefulness (Dewey 1922, p. 88). Habit formation is illustrated by Östman, Van Poeck and Öhman (2019b, p. 52) in a model describing the process of consolidating, transforming, and creating a new habit. Creating a new habit begins with a disturbance in the environment, that is, when our experiences do not harmonize with our habits. This gives rise to a problematic situation, which in turn triggers an inquiry process. A crucial part of the inquiry is to define the problem and try to solve it. If the process is successful, this may result in new ways of acting, which include new knowledge, skills, and values. The outcome is the start or re-creation of a new habit. Using Dewey's words, we chose to talk about the process of organizing experiences as "functional coordination" (Garrison 2001). This points to the fact that making progress and organizing experiences involve a back-and-forth transactional process of actions and undergoing of actions. When teaching an entire class of pupils, the teacher's actions depend on a complex network of factors. The teacher must consider the purposes and conditions in the situation in relation to all of the participating individuals as well as make judgments concerning the new purposes, content, and methods suggested by reforms. Thus, for teaching to function in practice requires coordinating many considerations.

A Background to the Empirical Case

We will illustrate this transactional approach with a special focus on the idea of functional coordination using analyses of interviews with one teacher over four years, exploring responses to a number of policy changes in Grade 6[1] compulsory school science teaching. The policy changes included a new curriculum with associated subject plans and connected to this, the introduction of national testing and grading in science education. In Swedish schools, national tests had previously been carried out in math and Swedish in Grade 6, and in more subjects in Grade 9, but for Grade 6 science education this was a brand-new activity. Grades were formerly assigned first in Grade 8. The main reasons for introducing national tests were to support teachers in making fair, equitable assessments and to provide a basis for analyzing the extent to which knowledge requirements were being met at different levels. Additional aims for the national tests were to support teachers' work by concretizing curricula and to improve student achievement (Skolverket 2011). Even though the test was centrally administered, the responsibility for marking the tests was placed on teachers at the school level. After two years of the new national testing regime, a new government was elected, and it decided to make administering the national tests voluntary for schools. After another year, national testing in science education in Grade 6 ended altogether, among other things, due to pressure from the teachers' union, which claimed that the test was too time consuming for teachers to administer and assess. However, the requirement to assign the students grades still remained.

The data used to illustrate the situation originate from a comprehensive interview study with sixteen science teachers from a diverse set of schools; the interviews were conducted on four occasions during a period of four consecutive years: 2013–16. In all of the interviews, there was an overarching focus on the teachers' views on science and science education and their enactment of the reforms. Additionally, the different interviews had slightly varied approaches, investigating whatever was the current state of affairs. In between the second and third interviews, the national tests in science became voluntary. By interviewing teachers over time, we could track changes in how they reasoned about their teaching in relation to the reforms.

Adding new elements to the curriculum is something that brings expectations of a change in teachers' practices. This becomes particularly accentuated when there is an external test meant to evaluate whether the students have acquired the intended knowledge. In the analyses, we explore the consequences of educational policy reform by examining how one teacher reasons as she organizes her experiences in everyday practice. The coordination work is analyzed in terms of this teacher's descriptions of her work with the educational reforms, especially the national tests. We treat the reforms as disturbances that cause problematic situations that teachers approach as affordances and challenges in their habitual practices. Östman et al. (2019a) stipulate that disturbances are what create learning situations, in that disturbances lead to problematic situations, which call for a coordination process in the form of inquiry. Disturbances may be of different kinds, e.g., an intellectual disruption or a change in physical surroundings. Regarding national tests, when the content of the national tests causes a disturbance in understanding, it means that teachers cannot proceed as they normally do without reflecting and, thereby, beginning an inquiry. The reflections could touch upon, for instance, whether the content and the methods they normally use in teaching are consistent with what the pupils will be tested on. The national tests could also mean that the physical surroundings need to be altered, for example because time management or assessment is affected.

In the following, we focus on what aspects of this teacher's existing teaching habits were coordinated with the new requirements in the presented reforms. We call the teacher Astrid, and we selected her statements for the sake of illustration, as throughout all four interviews she clearly expressed how her encounters with the reforms had challenged her teaching habits. The statements she gave are not unique, but it should be noted that they do not represent the dataset as a whole.

Astrid was working as a schoolteacher in Grade 4 to 6, having done so for twelve years when we met her for the first time. Because grading had not been done at this level before, assigning grades had not been included in her teacher education, nor had she had the opportunity to practice it before.

Coordinating Habits in the Encounter with Reform

We met Astrid for her first interview just after the first round of national tests, which was a couple of weeks before grades were to be handed in. She then expressed that she had difficulty figuring out how to work in accordance with the new subject plans, and she struggled to find acceptable methods. During the first interview, she explained that she was primarily using textbooks to plan her teaching, but predicted she would increasingly use the national tests. The new subject plans were not entirely in line with Astrid's teaching habits concerning what science education should include in Year 6. She had noticed, for example, that systematic investigations were now a central content area:

> I will be working a lot more with systematic investigations and practicing that, instead of just doing … Before, I did more of what I wanted to do, some fun experiments, and tried to point out things you could see around the school, in a fun way, and then discuss what caused them.
>
> *(Interview 1)*

This is an illustration of how Astrid's habit of working with "what she wanted to" was disturbed, and she described the need for a change. She mentioned that the students were too young to work with science in this way. Instead, she said she would prefer working with students and discovering that science is exciting, working with investigation, teaching them a few concepts, and giving them experiences that introduce them to the joy of learning science. The new requirements were a disturbance; they caused a problematic situation that triggered a coordination process. For Astrid, conflict was involved in trying to balance her habit of working to make science teaching fun and exciting with what she perceived to be stipulated in the new subject plans.

She expressed this ambivalence regarding the reforms as follows:

> I don't think my teaching will be better because of the national tests or grades. However, I think it will be better because of the planning and that I control the content. That is naturally a result of having to assign a grade.
>
> *(Interview 1)*

Astrid was doubtful the tests would improve her teaching practice and was also worried about whether the tests would govern and change her teaching in a way not in line with how she wanted to teach. She showed awareness of the national expectation that these reforms would improve students' learning outcomes. Her way of making meaning of this situation can be understood as her doubting that measuring results was the best way to improve teaching, and she described her former teaching as more joyful. Still, she saw the affordances of the national tests and grading, in that her mastery of the content would improve. Thus, this problematic situation included several considerations to be investigated and coordinated. Astrid discussed her old way of teaching in relation to the new requirements, trying to find functional ways to confidently continue with her teaching. Being forced to assign a grade entailed being able to motivate one's decision. Planning differently and mastering the new content occurred through a transaction integrating the individual teacher and changes in the environment.

To Adjust with the Students' Best Interests in Mind

Because administering national tests was an entirely new activity in the Swedish schools in science Grade 6, there were no routines or specific guidelines for how to work to prepare students for the tests. Some teachers considered it to be a test for all three Grades 4–6 and, as such, a way of calibrating to ensure that their teaching covered the right content. Even though Astrid was not fully convinced of the benefits of national testing, she chose to prepare her students thoroughly for the tests. She and a colleague at the school designed preparation materials for the students:

> Yes, it's because I want them to be successful on the national tests. But there I end up with a conflict of interest, because I don't think it's very interesting. […] I have to adapt a little bit to what the tests look like, so I try to cover everything so my students have a chance to succeed. So that it's not because of me that they don't pass the test, because I haven't taught them, or not taught them in the right way.
>
> (*Interview 1*)

The problematic situation still concerns the fact that testing students and measuring their knowledge are not in line with Astrid's teaching habits, which included trying to make science class enjoyable. For instance, she described how she and her students used to build a model of the solar system, to scale, and that doing this took a lot of time. She explained that she could no longer spend that amount of time on "having fun." In her reflections on her previous habits in relation to the new requirements, she described how she wanted to live up to the students' and parents' expectations, and part of that commitment was doing what is best for the students. In the coordination process between her previous ways of assessing students and what she, after considering different options, regarded as functional in relation to the new requirements, she chose to prepare her students as a way of showing care, even though the preparation took a lot of time away from regular teaching.

The Coordination of Content and Methods

In the second interview, Astrid reported that she had learned a great deal and changed her teaching considerably. However, she stated that much of the content included in the Year 6 national tests was being introduced too early. According to her:

> I will be teaching completely differently. First, I will adapt, for example, the A part in the test, so that they will have a proper chance to perform a little better. Then I also think that some tasks [on the test] have helped me better understand the idea of how to work with some things in the core content. It has been easier to interpret the knowledge requirements, I think, when you have some examples. It is obvious that I have to adjust to what is new […] I'm still totally convinced that

it would be better in primary school just to feel that science class is great fun and then, when they enter the next stage in school, they can start with this.

(*Interview 2*)

After the first round of national tests, Astrid gradually began to use the tests as a tool in interpreting and working with the new subject plans. Even though the testing disrupted her habit of working to make science fun, she worked transactionally to coordinate and organize different experiences. It is obvious from her reasoning that this was a back-and-forth process, and that she had noticed both affordances and challenges associated with the new requirements. Working with the national tests was a catalyst in her transactional meaning-making around the core content in the syllabus.

In interview three, the issue of systematic investigations was addressed again, and now Astrid's habits had been challenged and she had revised her teaching to some extent. She talked about the tests as having helped her to concretize how to work with that kind of content:

> I found it difficult before to get students to decide themselves on an investigation, because I couldn't think of what kind of things, I was thinking backwards, I constantly had a goal that I wanted them to reach [...] I thought it was very difficult to specify a task that allowed the students to get there. But there in the tests, there were a lot of such assignments, where they posed questions in different ways that actually made me think, I understood how to do it. So I've changed a lot and work a lot more like that now.
>
> (*Interview 3*)

This excerpt shows a greater level of detail in what Astrid addressed as a problematic situation: how to understand what could be included, on a relevant level, as the content area for systematic investigations. Naturally, the subject content in the printed test text remained, but in the coordination process, Astrid's way of understanding the subject content and her way of acting upon it had changed, thus, transactionally, the environment, regarding the meaning of the subject content, had also changed. In this way, the tests provided her an exemplary model that contributed to the inquiry and coordination process toward determining how to render the demands in the subject plans intelligible. When this work was consolidated, a new habit was formed.

When Astrid learned that the tests had become optional, she was ambivalent about this decision. Her school chose not to give the tests, which she felt unsure about because the tests had given rise to both good and bad outcomes. In the third interview, she first stated that making the text optional was very bad, because they had been important to her professional development:

> I think it was a really good implementation in the curriculum. I suddenly got it "Yes, this is what they mean" [...] some tasks are really good, tasks I've reused in my own reworked form, not taken them because they're confidential, but I've taken the idea behind the tasks to include in what [the students] are supposed to practice.
>
> (*Interview 3*)

After three rounds of tests, she concluded that she had "in principle changed everything" and that tests had the benefit of confirming whether you had taught the right content and made a reasonable interpretation of students' achievements.

Consequences of Experiencing New Things

One incident that we as researchers have often returned to in our discussions of the interview material occurred during the third interview with Astrid, when another teacher at the school, Elisabeth, passed by and also participated in part of the interview. Elisabeth had not worked with the tests the previous years. Looking at the two teachers' different outlooks from a transactional perspective, there was a striking contrast between having and not having administered the national tests. Earlier during the interview, Astrid had talked about having changed her way of teaching to a great extent. To ensure she was working in line with the new requirements, she now began already in Grade 4 and felt strengthened by the experience. She gave several concrete examples of changes, for example that she now knew what to address when working with the carbon cycle and how to get the students to plan for their own investigations. She appeared to be very confident in her professional role. Elisabeth had taught Grades 4 and 5 earlier when the tests had been given and described how she had been very stressed about administering the national tests. While teaching Grades 4 and 5, she had not managed to embark on the science content in Grade 6, even though she had participated in reflection meetings about the science tests the two preceding years, when her class was in Grades 4 and 5.

The disparity between the approaches of these two teachers, who were working at the same school in similar positions, highlights the importance of the teacher's experiences and the coordination that occurs when teachers put educational policy reforms into practice. During the four years of the present study, Astrid, whose students took national tests, struggled with coordinating what she experienced as new in the reforms with her existing teaching habits; she also found new functional ways of teaching. This work had entailed a coordination process, where careful selection of what content and methods to include and exclude in relation to her existing habits. Although Elisabeth had encountered the content of the national tests through the curriculum, this had not caused a disturbance in her habits and thus had neither triggered a coordination process nor caused modification of her habits.

In the last interview, when looking back, Astrid expressed the following:

> From the beginning I thought it was really a shame and very sad, but now I think maybe that it's raised the level. I think it has become more scientific [...] to have a scientific approach, I think that's is very positive idea that's come into my teaching.
>
> (*Interview 4*)

Astrid's habits were transformed and revised while she struggled to coordinate the content of the reforms with her teaching practice. She showed a great deal of ambivalence toward the reforms. The reforms generally aligned with what she valued as good and reasonable ways of teaching, but she said that her teaching was still not synchronized with this view. Her habits of teaching had thus been modified to come closer to what she thought constituted desirable teaching. She found, for example, that the questions on the national test could inspire her to find new ways to teach and assess students. However, the amount and level of the assessment practice was not consolidated:

> Yes, exactly and so it's this with the parents who can come and question and wonder and "What do you mean?" and that you always have to have to be able to fill things out to show them. This means that many assignments are written. Because I don't dare just trust what I previously could only get a sense of, if you know what I mean.
>
> (*Interview 4*)

Astrid experienced tension between what she expressed as an increased need to assess the students, at the expense of letting students just be amazed, have fun, and not feel the pressure of being assessed. She felt that what was required of her in assigning the grades necessitated justifying how she had assessed the students' efforts. Thus, the process of coordinating the new requirements with previous habits included modification of the assessment practice toward including activities establishing greater accountability.

Final Comment

In writing this text, we wanted to illustrate an approach to visualizing continuity and change in teaching practices through investigations of teachers' functional coordination between existing habits and new requirements. Using a transactional approach, as an alternative to cognitive approaches, in analyses of teachers' talk about their actions offers a way to understand complex meaning-making processes, as this action-oriented approach simultaneously takes the social and cultural dimensions of meaning-making processes into account (Quennerstedt et al. 2011). Here the different dimensions are transactionally integrated in action rather than being interactionally parallel and analyzed one at a time.

The coordination process is a transactional interplay between the individual and the environment (constituted by physical as well as sociocultural aspects/elements). In this text, we have scrutinized the interplay occurring in the encounter between one teacher's habits and the new requirements presented in the national curriculum and national tests. These encounters produced different problematic situations as well as different "meanings" of the reforms and the habits—depending on which habits were part of the encounter as well as which environment was taking part in the transaction.

In this illustration, we choose to focus on one teacher who had radically changed her teaching practice due to the reform requirements. Other teachers from the larger dataset, who had faced the same requirements, had shown other priorities and judgments regarding what their teaching needed to include (see also Lidar et al. 2020; Lundqvist & Lidar 2020). Some teachers felt that these requirements were completely in line with what they were already teaching, and others made the judgment not to change what they thought was functional just because of new tests and grading. For Astrid, whom we chose to focus on here, the reforms clearly created a disturbance that we were able to follow while she was undergoing a back-and-forth process, coordinating her experiences of good teaching with new requirements.

The section of the environment that we focus on here (the national curriculum and the national tests) was the same for all teachers over the years. The fact that Astrid changed her habits can be understood as part of the inquiry process that occurs when one plans teaching over time. In these processes, Astrid created new meanings concerning the curriculum, the test, and her previous habits.

A few problematic situations, in relation to which Astrid labored with coordination, are foregrounded in the illustrations above. The way systematic investigations were presented in the national tests came into conflict with the way she had been teaching by using experiments and practical work. At first, she discussed this in terms of making science class "no fun anymore," but gradually she began to appreciate the benefits of making students plan their investigations—benefits she had not been aware of previously. Another aspect she struggled with was her feeling that the students were too young to work with systematic investigations in this way and too young to be graded. Her previous habit had been to work without so much formal assessment, and the requirement to administer national tests and assign grades had caused a disturbance. Her efforts to merge the new requirements and an approach that would allow her to feel satisfied with her own work and accountable for the results resulted in a practice in which she felt the need to assess her students more often and give more written assignments.

Astrid's coordination process was particularly elucidated when it could be compared to a colleague's encounter with the reform. The disparity between the approaches of these two teachers led us to think about the importance of the experiences a teacher has when he/she engages the practical consequences of educational policy reform. What at first seemed to mostly be a new workload in Astrid's case turned out to be a learning opportunity that she felt had strengthened her in her professional role. We do not wish to claim that following state-mandated prescriptions to the letter makes someone a better teacher. Rather, our claim is that making reforms functional, or successfully implementing reforms, presupposes that teachers will have sufficient time to make the reform continuous with their teaching habits.

One general observation from our interviews with teachers about these reforms is their experience of lacking time. Time was also the main argument for ending the national tests in science in Year 6. During the period under study, the national tests were compulsory for just two years. This is a short amount of time in which to revise professional habits. It takes a considerably more time to learn how to work with and assess new requirements since teachers have a great deal of new information and administrative work to handle. However, it is striking that when teachers get used to working with particular materials or content, they gradually adapt and find functional ways to go forward. Time constraints may not be a problem when reforms are transformed into teaching habits. Instead, the reforms might even serve as a tool that promotes teaching and professional development.

8

Learning through Encounters with the Physical Environment

Susanne Klaar and Johan Öhman

Introduction

This chapter uses transactionalism to clarify how learning can be understood as actions and re-actions in encounters with the environment. We will explain how learning can be understood as an action-centered inquiry process that intertwines earlier experiences and previous knowledge with present and future unknown, but not unexpected, experiences. In these learning processes the learner, with personal feelings, and desirers, encounters problems and handles these problems, learns more about them, and learns new ways of managing old problems and future challenges.

However, the learner does not act as an isolated atom. From a transactional perspective learning processes take place in and through encounters integrating the individual learner in the social and physical environment. The social environment involves the cooperation with peers, teachers, and new ways of acting together with other people while the physical environment involves artifacts and natural phenomena and processes. We will have a specific focus on the physical environment where the learners act and re-act in relation to the surrounding material world. We will show how the transactional understanding of learning is particularly useful when it comes to clarifying very young children's learning processes and contents when they explore their physical environment. Young children often, very explicitly and observably, use their bodies as they act and re-act with the physical environment, and their actions are often more bodily than verbal. These nonverbal encounters make it necessary to turn the gaze toward how learning processes and content can be understood with limited access to verbal expressions. Thus, in this chapter we will have a particular focus on young children's (toddlers') early learning when they encounter their physical environment and learn in and through bodily experiences.

We will use data from a previous research project among 1–3 years old children in an ordinary Swedish preschool practice to illustrate our transactional approach. The research project involved young children's learning about nature in preschool environments. The children were video-recorded when they were taking part in outdoor activities in the preschool yard. We have chosen three events. The first event takes place one day in autumn, when Andrea slides down a wet slide with waterproof trousers on and gets very surprised over the speed. The second event takes place on an icy hill on a winter day. Robert has a sledge, he is walking toward the top of the hill, but rain, and cold temperatures have made the hill very slippery this day. In the third event, Robert, Joanna, and Elaine explore pallet collars that are going to be used for growing plants. It is early spring and Robert is struggling with climbing over the edges to get in and out of the still-empty pallet collars.

A Transactional Perspective on Learning in and through Physical Encounters

When we are young there are a lot of things in the world that we have not yet encountered and learned about. When a toddler encounters the physical environment in the preschool playground the physical environment offers possibilities for new experiences, discoveries, and investigations and consequently opportunities for learning new things. In order to understand such learning processes, we turn to Dewey's transactional perspective and especially the concepts of *experience, habit, resistance, functional coordination*, and *inquiry* (Dewey 1922). We will start our elaboration of these concepts by meeting the three-year-old toddler Andrea and her teacher on the preschool yard a rather wet autumn day:

> Andrea starts walking up the stairs towards the top of a slide to be able to slide down. It is a rainy day and she has waterproof vinyl trousers on. Andrea reaches the top of the slide; she sits down and starts to slide downward. The ride down the slide turns out in a very high speed and Andrea finishes the ride out in the sand that lays around the slide. Andrea gets up, looks very surprised, turns to the teacher beside her and expresses: "Wow, it was really fast!" She looks at the slide once more and states: "It is wet!"

The event shows Andrea going down a slide and expressing her experiences about the ride. She looks very surprised over the speed and expresses a reasonable conclusion about why the slide is so slippery. Thus, with facial expression and with words, Andrea expresses feelings and emergent knowledge about the relationship between speed, "tickling in the stomach," slippery surfaces, wet surfaces, and inclined planes.

In this way, Andrea's *experiences* are made visible *intellectually, practically,* and *emotionally*. Dewey explains how these "modes" of experience are mutual and interwoven:

> It is not possible to divide in a vital experience the practical, emotional and intellectual from one another and to set the properties of one over against the characteristics of the others. The emotional phase binds parts together into a single whole; "intellectual" simply names the fact that the experience has meaning; "practical" indicates that the organism is interacting with events and objects which surround it.
>
> (Dewey 1934/1980: 56)

If we explain Andrea's experience on the slide using Dewey's modes of experience, we can understand how her emotional expression of amazement combines intellectual meaning-making about wet and slippery surfaces and practical fast sliding-action into a single whole. The situation shows something central in all learning processes when using a transactional perspective, namely, how emotions, cognitive reflections, and practical doings are all parts of the same process, inseparable but still with the possibility of highlighting one at a time if necessary. With this understanding of experiences as part of a learning process in mind, we continue with the question about how to understand the continuity of experiences in learning.

Learning New Habits

In the event above Andrea seems familiar with the sliding situation; she has done it before. We will here clarify how the things she learns in and through her experiences can be understood as new *habits*. Habits can be seen as embodied knowledge about how to act in different practices with specific purposes and react to different circumstance in the world: "We walk and read aloud, we get off and on street cars, we dress and undress, and do a thousand useful acts without thinking of them. We know something, namely, how to do them" (Dewey 1922: 177–8). We do not have to reflect constantly; in most situations we can rely on our habits. How to act to be able to slide is part of Andrea's habits; it stands fast for her in the event described above.

In the same way as Dewey's concept of experience involves practical, emotional, and intellectual aspects, his idea of habits covers much more than practical actions: "*the principle of habits … covers the formation of attitudes, attitudes that are emotional and intellectual; it covers our basic sensitivities and ways of meeting and responding to all the conditions which we meet in living*" (Dewey 1938/1997: 35). Thus, our habits can be understood as an already-formed repertoire of responses to all kinds of changes in the environment. However, for toddlers every day is full of new, unknown, and not yet recognizable situations. Compared to an adult, the toddler has many habits still to be acquired. Dewey (1922) clarifies:

> The reason a baby can know little and an experienced adult know much when confronting the same things is not because the latter has a "mind" which the former has not, but because one has already formed habits which the other has still to acquire. The scientific man and the philosopher like the carpenter, the physician and politician know with their habits not with their "consciousness." The latter is eventual, not a source.
>
> (182–3)

The toddler who slides down on the wet surface with waterproof trousers on for the first time might have previous experiences of a ride down a slide on a dry summer day, and therefore become puzzled when the unexpected happens. The child has not yet formed a repertoire of responses to changes of surface. The adult might recognize the feeling of speed from earlier experiences with times spent at a water park, but the young child becomes very surprised. But, as Dewey emphasizes, the difference between the child and the adult does not lie in their mental capacity but rather in their repertoire of habits. Throughout life people experience encounters with the environment every day. The more experienced adult has already formed a large amount of habits and is in most situations able to act with no need for hesitating or questioning: "The more numerous our habits the wider the field of possible observation and foretelling" (Dewey 1922: 175). In this way, the adult encounters the physical environment with an extended repertoire of responses to "chose from" and use, while young toddlers more often encounter new situations where old habits do not work.

Habits, Continuity, and Resistance

Dewey holds that the fundamental aspect of life is action: "the organism, is always active; that it acts by its very constitution, and hence needs no external promise of reward or threat of evil to induce it to act" (Dewey 1932/1985: 289). Young children are a striking illustration of this fact and they constantly create encounters with their physical environment and learn new habits. These habits extend the possibilities to act in new encounters and make new experiences. In this way the process of learning new habits can be understood as simultaneously continuous and constantly changing process. Dewey explains this as the *principle of continuity*:

> As an individual passes from one situation to another, his [sic] world, his environment, expands or contracts ... What he has learned in the way of knowledge and skill in one situation becomes an instrument of understanding and dealing effectively with the situations which follow. The process goes on as life and learning continue.
>
> (Dewey 1938/1997: 44)

With Dewey's help, we can understand Andrea's learning process by observing how she habitually starts to climb toward the top of the slide. We can tell that she recognizes the activity, she knows how to do it, and she has done it before. These already-formed habits are useful for her as they in the present situation act as a bridge between what she expects is to happen and what actually happens.

When Andrea has finished her fast sliding tour she turns to the teacher and expresses her experiences verbally. In the following we attend to show how the principle of continuity in learning described by Dewey above also can be understood in situations which do not include verbal communication. Imagine a toddler who has just learned to walk. The toddler experiences its ability to stand on its two feet and move around—the habit of walking is acquired. When the toddler has learned how to walk (s)he continuously practices this new habit. To be able to walk makes it possible to encounter and explore the environment in extended ways. But to understand and investigate nonverbal learning offers the teacher or researcher a particular challenge. We will therefore now demonstrate how the transactional perspective is applicable also when no words are spoken, and we will extend our understanding by adding the influence of *resistance* from the environment on the learning process.

In this example we will follow a video-recorded event with Robert, twenty-two months old, when he encounters a changed physical environment during a winter day in the preschool yard.[1]

> It is a winter day with a temperature just below 0 C. The day before there was a great snowfall, but during the night the temperature has risen which has made some playing surfaces outside icy. The toddlers (1–3 years of age) are playing outside. Some of the children have got sledges and they are sliding down an icy hill. Robert approaches the hill with his sledge and he starts walking towards the top.

When observing Robert, we can see how he walks in his usual manner. He uses his already-formed repertoire of responses to the environment; it stands fast for him how to do when walking up a hill. The actions and the consequences are purposive, there is no questioning or doubt, and the situation continues without disturbances. In the beginning of the situation, where Robert is approaching the hill, it works for him to walk in the same way he has done before: acting by the use of previously formed habits.

However, on some occasions, the previously formed habits are less purposeful, and they do not make it possible to act in desired ways. This is what happens to Robert when he approaches the top of the hill with his sledge:

> Robert starts walking towards the top, but when Robert is nearly at the top of the hill, he slowly starts to slide backwards.

In this case the physical environment presents an unexpected obstacle. Robert confronts *resistance* from the physical environment and we can observe how he experiences it as a practical problem. Even if Robert has previous experiences of walking up the hill, and he might even have the same clothes and shoes as earlier, the ground has changed during the night and it is not possible to reach the top by using old habits when walking on ice. For a toddler like Robert, these kinds of situations offer important opportunities for extending his repertoire of habits. Robert has to create new and more purposeful relations to be able to act in this new situation.

Functional Coordination: To Act and Re-act in, with and because of the Environment

In situations where old habits do not work there is a need for explorations and investigations to establish continuity—we need to try out different actions to overcome the resistance from the environment. Robert's purpose is clearly visible in his actions; he wants to reach the top of the slippery hill. But since Robert has already formed a repertoire of responses to the environment that do not work to fulfill his purpose, he has to change his actions, and the process of finding new ways of responding to the tricky environment begins.

> When Robert starts to slide down, he quickly bends his knees, putting one hand on the ground. Very slowly, he takes one small step at a time, still with bended knees, and he finally reaches the top.

When Robert acts according to his habits, he undergoes the consequences of the actions and slides down. To walk as he has done in previous situations turns out to be less useful for him when he is heading for the top of the hill today. He *re-acts* and the re-action involves a change. Instead of walking straight up he corrects his body, he lowers his center of mass by his bending his knees, putting one hand on the ground, and walking very slowly. In this process, Robert acts outside his habits and explores, investigates, and changes his actions in order to make the consequences more purposive.

We can understand this process in terms of a *functional coordination* between the individual and the environment (Garrison 2001). The process consists of an active phase—where we *do* things, we act, and a more passive phase—where we *undergo* the consequences of our actions. The process of doing and undergoing the consequences is a nonlinear and reciprocal process where the environment takes part as inconstant and mutable rather than static or neutral (Dewey & Bentley 1949; see also Van Poeck, Östman, & Öhman 2019). The environment makes Robert change his actions; he bends his knees and walks; his actions on the slope create more friction making the environment less slippery.

If we look back at the event where three-year-old Andrea encounters the slippery wet slide, looks very surprised, and comments on the speed and wet surface, the sliding down consists the active phase, while the passive phase, where the child undergoes the consequences of this action, emerges as high speed and maybe a tickling in the stomach. Andrea is able to talk about her experiences and expresses her new understanding. When it comes to Robert trying to reach the top of the slippery hill, we can, even though his actions are nonverbal, observe how he actively walks toward the top of the hill on the very slippery surfaces, wearing his winter boots. The more passive phase where he undergoes the consequences of his actions is materialized in the process of sliding down, backward. This is followed by a new bodily action, where he readjusts his actions to the unfamiliar conditions of the environment.

These examples illustrate the functional aspects of habits underlined by Dewey: "habits are like functions in many respects, and especially in requiring the cooperation of organism and environment. // ... natural operations like breathing and digesting, acquired ones like speech and honesty, are functions of the surroundings as truly as of a person. They are things done by the environment by means of organic structures or acquired dispositions" (Dewey 1922: 14). Robert functionally coordinates his actions with the environment when he, with his clothes and shoes, explores, investigates, and changes his actions as the slope mutually changes making it possible for Robert to continue his walk toward the top of the hill. In a similar way Andrea's encounter with the physical environment can be seen as a coordinated function of the wet surface, the waterproof vinyl trousers, and Andrea's "doings," wherein Andrea learns new habits.

The Inquiry Process: To Handle and Maybe Solve a Problem

Above we have used a transactional terminology to describe Andrea's astonishment when experiencing a new relation to the environment and also how Robert practically responds to changing conditions in his natural surroundings. In the following we will show how a more detailed understanding of young persons' struggles with challenges from the physical environment can be reached by viewing these efforts as a process of *inquiry* (Dewey 1938). Once again we turn to Robert and his explorations of the preschool yard:

> It is spring and the preschool teachers have brought out pallet collars where they, together with the young children, plan to grow vegetables and wild strawberries. This is the first day with the pallet collars in the yard and there is still no soil in them. The toddlers start to play with the collars, and they climb in and out of them. Robert approaches one of the pallet collars, but the edge is too high for him and he is not able to climb over it. He tries to get inside by lifting up his right knee and then his left knee, and then his right knee once more. He then lifts his legs sideways, but none of these attempts are successful. He watches his friends Joanna and Elaine playing inside another pallet collar, and he approaches them. He tries once more, and eventually a teacher lifts him over the edge into one of the pallet collars. The toddlers play inside the pallet collars for a while and then they start to climb outside again. Robert is now stuck inside and is not able to get out. He looks at Elaine when she climbs out, and then he walks to the same corner of the pallet collar where Elaine climbed out. At that corner, he lifts his left leg, puts it on the edge of the collar and leans forward in a way that makes

him change his center of gravity. He tips over the edge and is able to put one foot on the ground outside the collar. He leans over a little bit more and is soon able to lift the right leg over the edge, and he gets out. Immediately he walks toward another pallet collar and does all the movements all over again; and he is now able to climb into the pallet collar, and out again.

In this event, Robert starts a process where he repeatedly acts and re-acts to solve a problem. The edge is too high for him and acting by the use of previously formed habits does not work. This can be described as a situation where our "expectations are disrupted by an unexpected problem" (Ryan 2011: 21). Andrea, sliding on a slippery wet surface, expresses her sliding-experience in words, while Robert expresses his expectations bodily, but there is no doubt that his expectations of climbing over the edge of the pallet collar turns out to be a problem that has to be solved. Robert starts an inquiry process by investigating and exploring how to get inside. He uses his own body in different ways and he also watches the other toddlers climbing in and out.

Dewey explains these kinds of explorations of the environment as inquiry processes involving questioning and answering the question (Dewey 1938). The inquiry starts with a problematic question or activity, continues with problem-solving activities, trying to answer the question or turn the activity toward fulfillment. Dewey (1938) describes this problem-solving as a process which requires a new balance: "The state of disturbed equilibration constitutes *need*. The movement towards its restoration is search and exploration. The recovery is fulfilment or satisfaction" (Dewey 1938:27). Robert's inquiry is triggered when his old habits are not good enough for handling the new situation—there is a problem to overcome, and he has to find a new way of responding to the environment. During the whole situation, Robert tries (eight!) different ways of climbing over the edge of the high pallet collar. Finally, by lifting his legs very high and leaning forward, almost losing his balance, he solves the problem and can move on with his activities.

Thus, in the event where Robert climbs over the edge of the pallet collar, he learns a new habit when he re-adjusts his body and is able to manage the height of the edge. As this new action turned out to be useful, he can extend his repertoire of habits and act more purposeful when responding to similar problems in future situations. This way of providing new answers when the environment resists answering our questions immediately are what we call "learning by experience" and we can understand whole events like these as "educative experiences" (Dewey 1938/1997).

Conclusion

In this chapter we have described different events where toddlers encounter and learn in, from, and about the physical environment. We have used the examples to show how learning can be understood in terms of a problem being solved by investigating and exploring new ways of acting when handling resistance in an unexpected environment. We argue that this transactional perspective on learning is particularly useful in Early Childhood Education and other similar pedagogical contexts involving young children. First this is due to the way the transactional perspective focuses on actions and explains toddlers' learning as inquiring processes, starting in what is already known and exploring new ways of encountering the physical environment and second that this perspective allows for an understanding also of embodied learning.

In the beginning of this chapter we clarified the need for action-centered ways to understand toddlers' learning. We conclude by highlighting the individual aspect of action-centered learning and emphasize relations among individual learning, teachers teaching and the educational practice, and setting. From the perspective of sociocultural learning theory toddlers' learning is explained in terms of their encounters with the physical environment with focus on how artifacts, the teachers, and the peers take part and contribute to their learning. The sociocultural perspective has in this way contributed to important knowledge on the ways the environment influences learning. But as claimed by Hodkinson, Biesta, and James (2007), there is a "tendency for individual differences and individual learning to disappear, with the focus on social interactions, activities and participation" (p. 417). We argue that our transactional gaze makes it possible to take both individual actions and the sociocultural context into consideration when illuminating the process of learning new habits. The transactional perspective positions individual learning within the sociocultural setting, taking the individual, the material, the social, and the cultural dimension under equal and mutual consideration. Seen from an individual point of view Robert's interpretation of the pallet collars as high obstacles to overcome is crucial for how he approaches them, and in this situation he becomes a problem-solving person who needs to handle resistance from the physical environment. Of course, the teachers and peers, as well as the clothes, ice and pallet collars also take part in Robert's learning by challenging him, inspiring him, and allowing for inquiries. Thus, the transactional perspective puts focus on how actions are interweaved with encounters with the environment as a whole and how this leads to a continuous growth of children's repertoire of habits.

When the environment responds in unexpected ways Andrea expresses her experience verbally while Robert articulates his experiences only with his body. By using the transactional perspective, it is also possible to observe embodied learning. Thus, we do not have to take verbal, cognitive, intellectual processes that cannot be made visible in practice as a starting point when explaining toddlers learning. Nor do we require any predetermined assumptions about how the environment effects the learner. Instead, we can understand this learning from what is observable in bodily and nonverbal encounters. In this way, a transactional perspective clarifies learning as an inwrought, mutual, and double process that includes both the learner and the environment. The learner's experiences are practical, intellectual, and emotional, all visual in the "doings" when the learner encounters the physical environment and solves problem by creating new habits and in this way extends the ability to act in the future.

The transactional perspective emphasizes the importance of offering young children a challenging physical environment which stimulates them to experience, inquire, and learn new habits. The authentic events chosen in this chapter all derive from an earlier research project in an ordinary Swedish preschool. The events involve both teacher-planned and spontaneous activities which in various ways trigger young children's learning. In the first situation, Andrea gets an opportunity to express a poignant feeling during free outdoor play—wow, it was really fast! It was an unanticipated and unexpected experience for her and she looks very surprised over the fast ride. In the second situation where Robert encounters the icy hill, there is a change in the environment that affects his body, which trigger him to act in new ways and learn new habits. Like the first situation, this change in the environment was unexpected. In the third situation, where Robert tries different ways of climbing in and out of a pallet collar, he experiences a disruption, a problematic situation, in which he cannot proceed without an inquiring process. The situation is not unexpected for Robert, but he needs to explore and try new modes of bodily movement. This situation was more planned by the teachers, since they noticed the children's interest and waited to fill the pallet collars with soil and start the planting activities.

Thus, one important pedagogical implication of transactional perspective is that it is imperative to provide situations where the children can try, and try again, test new ideas, experience, explore, and investigate making it possible for them to learn new habits. Sometimes these situations happen spontaneously when children are allowed to encounter a rich and varying environment. But it is also important that teachers plan activities that challenge children in different ways. When organizing such learning activities, it is essential to take children's previous experiences and interest into account in order both to create a continuity of experiences and to make the children motivated to face the challenge. As we have indicated above, there is always an emotional aspect of experience and what we should strive for are activities and situations where the children are challenged but at the same time feel joy and are excited to learn new things. As Dewey holds, we cannot simply transfer our good habits to the next generation, we must also provide a fruitful environment for such habits to grow:

> We must work on the environment not merely on the hearts of men. To think otherwise is to suppose that flowers can be raised in a desert or motor cars run in a jungle. Both things can happen and without a miracle. But only by first changing the jungle and desert. Yet the distinctively personal or subjective factors in habit count.
>
> (Dewey 1922: 22)

The Dramaturgy of Facilitating Learning Processes: A Transactional Theory and Analytical Approach

Katrien Van Poeck and Leif Östman

Introduction

People often encounter challenges for which no ready-made solutions exist. How to tackle major problems such as climate change or Covid-19? How to organize traffic in a city, acknowledging diverse interests? How to design user-friendly, affordable prostheses? How to turn an idea into a business plan?. In the face of such challenges appeals are made to creativity and innovation while learning is often seen as vital for making this possible. A key question, then, is how to make it happen. How can fruitful learning processes be *facilitated*?

With the facilitation of learning[1] we mean the whole process from planning/designing the learning practices to the actual performance of it in the service of creating something (a solution, an innovation, etc.). How exactly that "something" takes shape (e.g., the choices made in a new traffic plan) cannot be determined in advance, but nevertheless the facilitation of learning processes in the pursuit of developing it requires careful and well-considered steering (e.g., to keep the focus on aspects relevant for traffic, to make sure that choices are made). This chapter investigates how learning facilitators[2] work to accomplish their goals.

We aim to contribute to knowledge creation on this topic by presenting and illustrating a transactional theory and analytical approach for in situ empirical investigations. We combine and integrate a dramaturgical, transactional, and didactical approach. Dramaturgical analysis (DA) is used to study social interactions with a focus on how these are affected by the setting in which they occur. We incorporate such attention to what a setting does to a practice in our approach by taking inspiration from existing dramaturgical frameworks. But settings are not static; they dynamically take shape and transform as people act within and upon them. We draw from transactional pragmatism in order to capture what settings do with people as well as what people do with settings *simultaneously* and *reciprocally*. Finally, we have a didactic[3] interest to gain insight in the *facilitation* of learning. This requires attention for what facilitators do—both in planning and in performing the activities—and how this affects the participants' learning. Therefore, we employ transactional didactical theory on teaching and learning.

We will elaborate this approach by explaining our dramaturgical take on facilitating learning, presenting our transactional theoretical perspective, and then illustrating how this can be analytically applied with empirical examples from a study of workshops where people gather to create sustainable agro-food practices. We conclude with discussing the specific kind of knowledge we can develop using this transactional approach.

A Dramaturgical Take on the Work of Facilitating Learning

DA takes various forms that share a common focus on how social interactions are affected by the context in which they take place. DA frameworks are developed for conducting empirical analyses drawing on metaphors borrowed from drama: script, roles, setting, staging, performance, acts, scenes, etc.[4] Early, influential DA contributions are, for instance, Kenneth Burke's (1945/1969) book "A Grammar of Motives" and Erving Goffman's (1956) research on role playing in social settings. More recent work includes DA of organizational routines (Feldman 1995), policy deliberation (Hajer 2005; Nahuis 2009), and nonformal learning (Van Poeck et al. 2017; Plummer & Van Poeck 2020). These examples illustrate the variety of fields and phenomena that can be explored with a dramaturgical lens.

A shared characteristic of diverse dramaturgical frameworks and studies is their *performative* focus on revealing the influence of the contexts in which actions take place. Maarten Hajer emphasizes how every act takes place in a particular "contexture" that influences the quality of that act and his analytical focus on how the design of a setting affects the meaning-making within it, that is, how it affects "what is said, what can be said, and what can be said with influence" (Hajer 2005: 626) is aimed at revealing precisely that. We use the dramaturgical vocabulary because this performative approach aligns well with the below elaborated transactional perspective. There is some variety and ambiguity regarding how to understand the performativity of settings in DA, more precisely about the extent to which the setting is assumed to determine actions. We draw on work that is non-deterministic. Hajer (2005), for example, argues for investigating how settings and actions "*interrelate* to produce a particular staging of public involvement" (p. 630—emphasis added) and reveals through his analysis how "scripts [...] *codetermined* the [...] performance" (p. 632—emphasis added). As we explain in the next section, an explicit *transactional* perspective allows investigation into how settings and actions take shape and transform simultaneously and reciprocally.

Feldman (1995), Hajer (2005), and Nahuis (2009) offer inspiration to analyze the facilitation of learning as encompassing scripting, staging, and performance. *Scripting* refers to the framing of an event in terms of the purposes it seeks to achieve (Feldman 1995), the roles of characters in the play, cues for appropriate behavior (Hajer 2005), and access conditions (Nahuis 2009). The *staging* of a setting refers to the deliberate organization of interactions (Hajer 2005) through tools, methodologies, activities, rules of the game, artifacts (Nahuis 2009), etc. *Performance* refers to what actors do within and upon the staged settings to pursue the scripted purposes (Feldman 1995).

Applied to facilitating learning, this threefold analytical focus allows us to grasp both the *preparatory* work of planning/designing a learning setting in advance and the facilitation of learning as it is performed, *in action*. Scripting involves formulating purposes regarding what the learning process is expected to pursue, clarifying the roles of facilitators and participants and establishing cues for appropriate behavior. Staging a setting consists of, on the one hand, staging fruitful *tasks* for the participants and, on the other, staging the *scene* on which the activities take place. Performance can be understood in terms of a variety of facilitator *moves*, i.e., actions performed by a facilitator that bring about, for example, a change or enforcement in the direction of participants' learning. As we will show, it is not so that the scripting and staging of a setting are confined to the preparatory stage. Scripting and staging also occur in performance.

A Transactional Theory on Facilitation and Learning

DA offers us a framework and vocabulary to study the work of facilitating learning from planning to performance while aiding in understanding the *influence* that occurs among setting, the actions of the persons performing in it, and the meaning-making that thus becomes (im)possible. In this section, we employ a transactional perspective to further elaborate on this influence and subsequently apply it to how to understand learning and facilitation.

A Transactional Perspective

John Dewey and Arthur F. Bentley (1949/1989a) introduced the concept "transaction" to label their way of understanding the mutual influence of individuals and environments. In contrast to a mechanistic, *inter*actional perspective where things are described in terms of linear and causal interconnections between the subject and the environment as independent, already-known entities that inter-act (Ryan 2011), a *trans*actional perspective sees humans as always already in relation to the environment. Dewey and Bentley speak about "organism-in-environment-as-a-whole." Both become present and acquire meaning simultaneously and reciprocally.

Before we continue to unpack the transactional perspective on the mutual influence within organism–environment transactions, we need to clarify Dewey's concept of environment. Dewey distinguishes the "environment" from the totality of what he calls the surroundings. Only some aspects of the surrounding conditions, he argues, become actualized in action and thereby become an environment. Thus, people and their actions are not seen as being determined by their surroundings but assumed to also actively (re)construct them through this process of "environing." Environments are constructed in action. But at the same time as the environment is (re)constructed in actions, the environment (re)constructs the acting person. Through transactions "between a live creature and some aspect of the world in which he lives," Dewey (1934/2005: 45) argues, a mutual adaptation of persons and environments emerges.

This mutual influence and adaptation occur *in an event*. What we call an "event" consists of an active phase—doing—and a passive phase—undergoing the consequences of doing (Dewey 1934/2005). The reciprocal and simultaneous influence between organisms and environments thus occurs in and through alternating doings and undergoings. This should, however, not be understood as just "doing and undergoing in alternation, but [...] in relationship" (p. 46), as an "intimate union" (p. 54). This intimate union makes up the event. It is important to recognize that the doing and undergoing phases can either occur within a particular moment or durationally spread. Sometimes one undergoes the consequences of doings instantaneously following the initial actions. Sometimes doing and undergoing are dispersed in time.

Besides the mutual adaptation of persons and environments within events, the transactional perspective also illuminates another mechanism of influence, one that occurs *between events*. What is undergone affects further doings since the receptivity in the undergoing phase should not be understood as passivity: "The consequences undergone because of doing are incorporated as the meaning of subsequent doings" (Dewey 1934/2005: 65). This process of influence *between* events makes up the principle of continuity (Dewey 1938/1997). Meaning-making can be seen as cumulative: Meaning made in previous events functions as a means for the meaning made in the present. "The junction of the new and the old," Dewey (1934/2005: 63) argues, "is not a mere composition of forces, but is a re-creation in which the present impulsion gets form and solidity while the old, the 'stored' material is literally revived, given new life and soul through having to meet a new situation." What is previously done and undergone is re-actualized (Östman 2010) and thus affects further doing. As Dewey ([1934]2005: 52) concludes, "What is done and what is undergone are thus reciprocally, cumulatively, and continuously instrumental to each other."

Facilitation of Learning in a Transactional Perspective

Any learning process involves a *"privileging"* (Wertsch 1998) which steers learning in a certain direction, toward certain outcomes. One aspect of privileging concerns which phenomena to focus on and which ones to neglect. Here the privileging is about attentiveness and environing: The participants, in transaction with the world, make certain phenomena in the world present, i.e., they create an environment out of the surroundings. Privileging also concerns what to *do* with the created environment. Here, too, the privileging involves inclusion and exclusion, i.e., a choice between alternative possible doings. The "careful and well-considered steering" that we argued to be vital for facilitating learning processes can thus be understood as a matter of *governing privileging in connection to a purpose*. It is about steering the participants' attentiveness (and, thus, the environing) as well as what to do with the environment in the service of what one aims to create.

To facilitate learning is thus to govern the privileging process. More specifically—and connecting the abovementioned aspects of privileging to our dramaturgical take on facilitating learning—the work of a facilitator is to offer participants a setting consisting of a *scene* and a *task*. In transaction with the offered scene, the participants develop a specific attentiveness and, thus, an environment. In transaction with the offered task, the participants give shape to an inquiry—an investigation of/experimentation with the environment—that, if successful, leads to a productive learning outcome. Partly, this scene and task are offered through the facilitator's preparatory work, e.g., by selecting content to disseminate, deciding on how to divide participants into subgroups, or preparing questions. But facilitators also continue to stage the setting *in the performance*. Drawing on our earlier-developed transactional teaching theory and didactical research on teacher moves (Östman, Van Poeck, & Öhman 2019b), we call the facilitators' actions that change the participants' privileging in performance *"facilitator moves."* A move can be directed either toward students' attentiveness to certain phenomena in the world (environment) or toward their manner of acting upon the environment (inquiry).

Thus, when the participants act upon the setting offered through the facilitator's moves, a transformative transactional process occurs. Realizing this, it is vital for facilitators to be prepared to adjust the scene/tasks offered, or add things to it if they judge it to be necessary or fruitful for the participants' ongoing privileging. The information required for such judgments can only be obtained if the relation between the facilitator's doing and the undergoing of its consequences (i.e., participants' response) can be experienced. Hence, as illustrated below, an important part of facilitators' work is to organize events—the entanglement of doing and undergoing—in a fruitful way to make it possible to experience the consequences of her/his doing. An event thus has an important *explorative* function: It allows to explore the meaning of an intervention, which is constituted and becomes visible in the response to it. To explore is to experience the consequences of one's action as a facilitator and, as such, getting to know whether it had the intended effect. At the same time as one gets to know the meaning of one's action through the participants' response, also this response acquires its meaning in relation to the initial action. Thus, both actions acquire meaning simultaneously and reciprocally in the transactional event. The influence that occurs *between* events is also an important didactical resource. It has a *coordinative function* in the sense that it is the facilitator's next intervention (doing) in relation to the previous event (doing–undergoing) that co-constitutes the participants' ongoing privileging. After exploring the consequences of earlier doings, the facilitator can add something to the scene, reorient the task, etc. Optimally using the explorative and coordinative function of transactional events requires well-considered *didactical timing*, i.e., when and how to include "check-points" that allow to explore the participants' response to one's actions and coordinate the subsequent action in relation to that.

An Empirical Example

To illustrate the knowledge about facilitation that the above-elaborated theory and analytical approach can produce, we present some examples from an analysis of learning in workshops aimed at creating scenarios for Short Food Supply Chain (SFSC) initiatives. The workshops, facilitated by researchers in a project funded by an urban government, involved varied stakeholders: Farmers, retailers, cooks, civil servants, experts, etc. We focus on the (preparatory and in situ) work of facilitators.

We used practical epistemology analysis (PEA) to analyze learning in the SFSC workshops (see also Van Poeck & Östman 2020). The method, developed by Per-Olof Wickman and Leif Östman (2002), is well suited for delivering findings that can be used within a transactional theory (Shilling 2018; Östman & Öhman 2020) to explain the work of a teacher or facilitator. Underpinned by the later work of Wittgenstein and subsequently supplemented by Dewey, PEA investigates meaning as something we literally *make*. It investigates how meaning is created in action by identifying first the gaps that occur when people encounter a new situation and subsequently the created relations between what stands fast for a person—previous experience, earlier acquired knowledge, skills, values, etc.—and the new situation that is encountered. Gaps occur in every encounter yet are often bridged immediately. At times, however, the gap is too big to bridge automatically and people hesitate, start to guess, ask for help, etc. The gap then triggers an inquiry, urging the learner to stage new encounters to fill the gap, e.g., with a book, an expert, peers. Earlier experiences are re-actualized to make the new situation intelligible and the participants develop an expanded and more specific repertoire for action.

The scope of this chapter does not allow us to present the analyses or complete results. Rather, our aim is to exemplify the *specific* knowledge that can be developed through a *transactional* analysis of the dramaturgy of facilitating learning. PEA delivers findings that can be used to grasp facilitators' moves and the work of exploration and coordination. It does so by enabling us to identify events where a facilitator intervenes in an ongoing inquiry and to reveal whether or not these interventions had the consequences intended by the facilitator which, as explained, becomes visible in the facilitator's subsequent action.

The Preparatory Work of Scripting and Staging a Setting

As reflected in documents, interviews, and facilitators' explanations of the goals and expectations while introducing activities for the participants, the scripted purpose of the project was to develop, together with stakeholders, three well-developed scenarios for promising SFSC pilots and to create support for upscaling these. The project needed to be "hands-on" and "interactive" and it was meant to "create support among potential stakeholders in an upscaling process" and to "initiate a movement that goes beyond the actual project." In line with this purpose, the participants' role is scripted as "active actors" with "ownership" of the developed scenarios. The participants were told that they were selected "because they have good ideas" and can draw on their own experiences. They were invited to "think along about what's possible," to "formulate problems and solutions" and "help create various scenarios" and "a partnership."

The facilitators prepared a stage in view of the scripted purpose. While staging the scene, they gathered actors with diverse backgrounds and experiences to draw from. They also explored and documented examples of SFSC initiatives elsewhere for the participants to draw inspiration from. They staged the task of developing SFSC-scenarios through the organization of workshops with multiple subtasks, e.g., addressing specific questions (how to organize the logistics and communication?; what are the characteristics of the supply and demand-side of the SFSC initiatives?; etc.) and preparing a business model through the methodology "Business Model Canvas." While designing the workshops the staging of the scene continued through decisions about which actors to gather for the different scenarios-in-the-making, how to divide them into subgroups, etc. In this preparatory work, the facilitators anticipated the performance, including the transformation occurring when participants act upon an offered stage. For instance, they decided to organize consults with different groups of stakeholders (e.g., farmers, catering industry) separately before bringing them together because their earlier experiences made them realize that farmers tend to be reluctant to share ideas in a mixed stakeholder group.

Facilitation in the Performance

We will now present two excerpts from a workshop where the participants developed a scenario for a distribution platform to promote SFSC trade between local producers and catering industries, large kitchens, and retailers. The examples illustrate how scripting and staging continue to take shape *in the performance*, i.e., when the participants transact with the setting offered to them and illuminate the facilitators' work involved.

In a subgroup the participants discussed how to encourage more producers and consumers to work with SFSC. The *gap* that thus emerges for the participants is the result of the facilitator's preparatory work of formulating the questions to address. M1, chef in a top-end restaurant, repeatedly puts forward that it is a matter of emphasizing the high quality of products and of being proud to work with them. Thus, he creates *relations* between "quality," "pride," and "achieving the goal of more producers and consumers choosing to work with SFSC." W2, a dairy farmer, raises a new *gap* within this discussion. Drawing on her experiences, she argues that M1's argument does not hold in the case of milk since the convenience of prepackaged, sterilized milk is more attractive than higher quality fresh milk with limited shelf life. She says she has experienced that this fact makes it difficult to get a constant purchase of her products through SFSC. M1 continues to repeatedly raise the argument of "quality" and "pride" and he takes a lot of space in the discussion. The facilitator intervenes as follows:

1. Facilitator: And so, apart from that—because you [M1 and W3] have now indicated that in the catering industry it can grow and that it is more evident there to cook with products coming from the short chain—but are there other obstacles for your [W2] company to fully switch to the short chain? Apart from the fact that the purchases are constant? Do you still see-
2. M1: [interrupts] If it would become attractive, in fact the purchase would become very constant.
3. Facilitator: Yes, so that's a point you've made, but I wondered if there were any other, well doubts that [W2] experiences about switching to the short chain. Or reasons to say we are going to fully commit to it?
4. W2: I don't know ... yes, yes it is not that easy to organize that you know. Because you already have to run a busy company so it all adds on. I think, when it is up and running that it is not so ... but it is indeed the start-up phase ...
5. Facilitator: A period where you have to do a lot of things in parallel?
6. W3: Is it also the logistics, the transportation actually, that is difficult? Or also looking for-
7. W2: [interrupts] Gosh, all kinds of things. We just started to work with personnel. It is not so easy to just start to do that. Those are all such things that you know nothing about.

The facilitator (line 1) performs a so-called *"reorienting move"* (Östman, Van Poeck, & Öhman 2019b): It reorients the meaning-making from a focus on pride, quality, and how this opens potential for SFSC to grow in the catering industry, toward exploring possible obstacles. Obviously the response to her first move (line 2) is not perceived as fruitful, which becomes visible in her complementary reorienting move (line 3). Thus, by undergoing the consequences of her intervention she can assess it as inadequate and coordinate with a subsequent, adjusting intervention. What she does through these moves is to stage a setting in terms of a scene ("obstacles") and a task (to identify possible obstacles). This setting creates a *gap* for the participants, requiring an inquiry in order to fill it. The facilitator's moves have the consequence that the participants reorient their attention and activity but also that other participants become active actors in contributing to trying to fill the gap, e.g., by relating "obstacles" to "the difficulty to do a lot of things in parallel in the start-up phase" (line 4), especially "things that you know nothing about" (line 7). Taking departure from the facilitators' preparatory work, one can conclude that not only were the reorienting moves logically necessary in view of realizing the scripted purpose (creating well-developed and supported scenarios) and enabling actors to take on the scripted role (drawing on their own experiences to jointly formulate problems and solutions); the moves also established, amongst the participants, associated cues for appropriate behavior (distribute the speaking time more evenly).

The second excerpt illustrates how the facilitator stages a task in a way that allows the participants to deepen their inquiry. The participants are still addressing the *gap* how to make more producers and consumers to work with SFSC.

1. M1: [We can do this] by doing our best. That we cook the best we can.
2. Facilitator: Yes, yes but who is "we"? And who takes responsibility?
3. W3: Well I think the communication is important, isn't it? From farmers, but also from restaurants. If there would be a bit more information about the products and why you choose them.
4. [People talk interchangeably]
5. Facilitator: Should the distribution platform to do that?
6. W3: Yeah, I think often farmers, producers … Our PR isn't that good, we're not good at that. Now we're working on a website too. That was a real disaster, it still is a disaster. […] We cannot do that so well. That is not our core business, we are farmers so we cannot do that very well ourselves.

M1 relates "promoting SFSC" with "doing our best" (line 1). By performing a so-called *"specifying move"* (Östman, Van Poeck, & Öhman 2019b) the facilitator makes the participants to make that more concrete (line 2): W3 includes the responsibility of "farmers" and "restaurants" in the privileging and at the same time she creates a *relation* with the importance of "communication" (line 3). The facilitator's move in transaction with the participants' response thus set a scene (with attentiveness to the phenomena "responsibility" and "communication") and a task (to further specify and concretize). Undergoing the consequences of her doing, the facilitator takes in the new object that W3 added to the scene ("communication") and coordinates (line 5) with a *"generalizing move"* (Östman, Van Poeck, & Öhman 2019b). Thus creating a *relation* between the emerging attentiveness for "communication" and the workshop's overall aim to create a scenario by defining "what the SFSC platform should do" she continues to stage a task for the participants (clarify and concretize the scenario-in-the-making) in line with the scripted purpose and roles (designing promising pilots by drawing on available experience).

Conclusion

The presented theory and analytical approach are created in order to develop useful knowledge on fruitful facilitation strategies. By integrating a dramaturgical, transactional, and didactical approach, it offers researchers a framework to examine the work that facilitators do both in planning/designing learning practices and in performing them and, moreover, to investigate links between what is done in preparation and in situ. Furthermore, it enables investigation of the effects of facilitators' work on the outcome of the learning process.

The examples briefly presented here illustrate the kind of knowledge that can be created to offer useful insight into fruitful facilitation strategies. First, we can create *knowledge on how to fruitfully anticipate the performance in the planning*. While preparing a learning process, facilitators need to anticipate how the offered setting will be received by the participants and tailor their offerings accordingly. Making this "didactical imagination" functional demands familiarity with the content and the participants, their knowledge, values, conditions, etc. Although the scope of this chapter does not allow us to provide empirical evidence, we observed repeatedly that the anticipatory work of consulting different stakeholder groups separately in advance informed the staging of the workshops' setting. While planning the staging of a scene, for instance, it helped the facilitators decide how to distribute available expertise across groups. In situ we observed that facilitators repeatedly drew on what they heard in these consults to add topics to the offered scene.

Second, the theory and analytical approach allow to provide *knowledge regarding how to intervene in the performance so as to govern the staged setting and realize the scripted purposes*. When participants transact within a setting, a simultaneous and reciprocal transformation occurs. Facilitation in the performance, therefore, requires moves in order to continuously govern the staging of scenes and tasks in relation to the purpose. As in the first excerpt, this can be a form of governing in response to unintended or undesired developments. The reorienting moves were necessary to aid all participants in performing their scripted roles and, thereby, to realize the purpose of developing scenarios based on the expertise of varied stakeholders. Other possible forms of governing are illustrated in the second excerpt. The specifying move here functioned accumulatively rather than correctively as it made it possible to further elaborate the ongoing meaning-making by extending the staged scene. The generalizing move, then, made use of the extended scene in order to govern the progress toward the staged task. Through these moves the facilitator directed and deepened the participants' inquiry in a productive way. As reflected in the report delivered to the urban government, the obstacles raised were used to delineate the distribution platform's scope and "joint communication" was added as one of its activities. In transaction with the offered scenes and tasks, the participants constructed a well-developed and increasingly concrete scenario, which was afterwards selected for funding as a pilot project. Based on multiple analyses, we can identify and classify moves in relation to how they can be used to direct and deepen inquiries and thus create an important source of inspiration for facilitators of learning processes.

Third, the presented approach enables us to create *knowledge on how to plan a fruitful alternation of explorative and coordinative actions*. The examples reveal both the explorative and coordinative function of the facilitator's actions and show how she was able to immediately explore whether her doings had the intended effect and coordinate subsequent doings in response to that exploration. In this workshop, four parallel subgroup discussions took place. The choice to provide a facilitator for each group (instead of letting participants work independently with one facilitator moving between them) made it possible to carefully explore and coordinate (e.g., correct, extend) instantaneously in the pursuit of intended outcomes. We also observed examples of how the explorative and coordinative functions occur spread over time, when facilitators redirected some participants to workshops that developed a different scenario in a second meeting in response to observing that the initial choice in the first meeting was not fruitful. By identifying and classifying different ways of organizing the alternation between exploring and coordinating, as well as their effects, we can create insights that help facilitators to decide what way of doing this is preferable under which circumstances.

Our analysis shows that facilitating learning is not just a matter of *having* a script and a stage—and subsequently performing on it. It also highlights the importance of script*ing* and stag*ing* in the performance, i.e., in trans-action, and illuminates how this involves specific interventions of facilitators in order to steer the learning process toward the pursued purposes. As argued, this is not to be seen as a matter of steering the participants' knowledge, values, behavior, etc. toward a well-defined, *a priori*-determined result. Designing scenarios for something that does not yet exist and about which different participants have diverse ideas obviously requires a more open-ended, creative approach. Nevertheless, as our examples show, that also demands careful and well-considered steering of the process.

Acknowledgments

The analytical approach is the result of a project funded by the European Union's Horizon 2020 research and innovation program under the Marie Sklodowska-Curie grant agreement No 843437. The empirical case study was funded by Formas under grant 2016-00992_3.

10

Transactants in Action—Examples from a Craft Remake School Project

Hanna Hofverberg

Introduction

Paul's eyes sparkle with excitement as he explains what he wants to remake. We meet Paul in a craft classroom for the Swedish school subject, sloyd, where the Grade 8 pupils have been asked to remake new items from old clothes or used fabrics. This and other remake activities in the classroom are common in Sweden, where students are required to learn about sustainability (Hofverberg & Westerlund 2021). However, remake activities are far from a straightforward learning process. Therefore, it is relevant to study what actually affects the learning process and how it proceeds.

I will address the learning process of the remake as a transactional activity to show some of the complexity of the teaching and learning processes. In earlier studies with the same empirical data used in this chapter, I showed what influences the learning process (Hofverberg & Maivorsdotter 2018) and the materiality that students recognize and acknowledge as they learn to remake (Hofverberg 2020). Here, I deepen the analyses of the transactional activity to describe the concept of *transactant*.[1] This concept helps us describe what aspects matter when humans and their environments are affected transactionally.

In the first section, I describe the theoretical stances for "transactant." In the next section, I use empirical examples to explain and illustrate the concept. I conclude by discussing what the concept can help us acknowledge in educational research, for example in this case when remake projects are made an educational activity for environmental and sustainability issues.

Theoretical Stances for Transactant

The concept of "transactant" is rooted in Dewey's concept of transaction. *Transaction* is, in short, the process in which humans and their environments are affected by each other. In his early writings, Dewey (1938/1997) describes this process as a process of interaction. Dewey used the word *transaction* to emphasize how entities become present together—not as separated entities in some kind of bridging operation—but rather jointly in the activity. He writes:

> An experience is always what it is because of a transaction taking place between an individual and what, at the time, constitutes his environment, whether the latter consists of persons with whom he is talking about some topic or event, the subject talked about being also part of the situation; or the toys with which he is playing; the book he is reading (in which his environing conditions at the time may be England or ancient Greece or an imaginary region); or the materials of an experiment he is performing.
>
> (p. 43)

A transaction takes place with whatever constitutes a human's environment. The environment is thus a reciprocally transforming relation integrating the person with their environment. However, two persons may have different environments even if they share the same surroundings. An analysis of a transactional activity focuses on the co-constituting relations that the student and their environment create in the learning situation. This means that neither a student nor a material *is* but rather *becomes* in the transaction. As entities become together jointly in the transaction, the meaning that emerges from the transactional activity is also jointly produced. Ryan (2011) writes, "Whereas traditional philosophies separate the examining mind from the thing examined, transaction 'sees together' as dynamically interdependent *what* we know and *how* we come to know it" (p. i). The point here is in the joint process—"transaction sees together"—what we know and how we come to know it. I will discuss this from a crafting point of view and describe the crafting activity as a transactional process.

A common way of thinking about making activities such as craft is what Ingold (2013: 20) defines as a *project*. The common idea of a *project* is that we first have an idea of something that we want to make, and then we impose the idea internal in our mind upon the material world "out there." Ingold, however, rejects this idea and argues for approaching making transactionally. Rather than imposing the idea on a material out there, the craftsperson responds with the material in a back-and-forth transactional activity. This means there is no separation between an object and how that object is experienced (Dewey 1938/1997: 43–4). From a transactional point of view, what something *is* is what it is experienced *as*. This means that we do not acquire knowledge by standing outside of it, but rather we know what we know because we are already part of the world. But language sometimes fools us here. Ingold (2011) explains:

> We say "the wind blows", because the subject-verb structure of the English language makes it difficult to express it otherwise. But in truth, we know that the wind *is* its blowing. Similarly, the stream *is* the running water. And so, too, I *am* what I am doing. I am not an agent, but a hive of activity.
>
> (p. 17)

What Ingold helps us acknowledge is that there is no separation between action and knowledge production. We talk as if things are separated from us—the wind, the material, and so on—but in reality, we know the wind is inseparable from its blowing nature and that the material is what it is experienced as. In crafting, the craftsperson "sees together" in a back-and-forth transactional activity with the world. It is not a matter of describing or representing the world but rather answering to it (Ingold 2013: 108). To answer to the world, as Ingold puts it, or to "see together" as Ryan (2011) describes it, is, I would argue, a bodily activity with all senses responding in the transaction.

However, when studying learning activities, the risk is that the material or other nonhuman participation will disappear empirically due to the idea that humans impose action on dull material "out there." In other words, learning activities may be treated as "projects." To take this risk seriously, we turn our attention to how "seeing together" can be acknowledged in transactional activities. As support, I turn to a socio-material research interest on "matter," and more specifically, on the use of actant (Latour 1996; Bennet 2010; 2013) and quasi-object (Serres 2007).

Actants in Action

The concept of actant was originally introduced by Bruno Latour and is an important concept in actor network theory (ANT) (Latour 1996). ANT is concerned with tracing how things become assembled and enacted in networked webs and the effects of this (Fenwick 2015). In these explorations, Latour (1996) does not limit the analysis "to human individual actors, but extends the word actor—or actant—to non-human, non-individual entities" (p. 369). He explains:

> An actor in ANT is a semiotic definition—an actant—, that is something that acts or to which activity is granted by others. It implies no special motivation of human individual actors, nor of humans in general. An actant can literally be anything provided it is granted to be the source of action.
>
> (p. 373)

What the concept of actant then gives us is a term that points to a source of action, and this term includes both human and nonhuman entities. Jane Bennet (2013) clarifies it further:

> By actant I mean an entity or a process that makes a difference to the direction of a larger assemblage without that difference being reducible to an efficient cause; actants collaborate, divert, vitalize, gum up, twist, or turn the groupings in which they participate.
>
> (p. 149)

Accordingly, an actant is an entity that operates with others and makes a difference to the larger assemblage. To give voice to what affects the activity and makes it turn in a specific direction, I borrow the term *actant* and combine it with *transaction* to form *transactant*. A transactant is what makes a difference and has a force in the transactional activity (i.e., to the larger assemblage). I should clarify that the transactant is still rooted in a transactional activity. This means that the concept shows what has a force in a transactional activity—the activity in which humans and their environments affect each other. The transactant creates the reciprocal relations with other actants. Without an activity among a hive of actors or actants, it is not possible to talk about a transactant.

It is also not possible to know beforehand what will become a transactant. One must conduct an empirical study to see what actually influences the activity to turn in a specific direction. To illustrate how something is "environing" (Andersson, Garrison, & Östman 2018), I find it helpful to think of the joint-transactional process as an activity where—in the activity—subject and object is only an analytic distinction. Serres (2007) illustrates this phenomenon by giving an example of a football player and a ball:

> In most games, the man with the ball is on offense; the whole defense is organized relative to him and his position. The ball is the center of the referential, for the moving game. With few exceptions—like American football, for example—the only one who can be tackled is the one who has the ball. This quasi-object, designates him. He is marked with the sign of the ball./.../There

are objects to do so, quasi-objects, quasi-subjects; we don't know whether they are beings or relations.

(pp. 226–7)

In this example, Serres shows how the ball *becomes* with the player and the player *becomes* with the ball. They are not two entities interacting separately, but rather they are, as Serres points out, marked from each other in the activity. Further, Latour (1996) uses Serres's example to show that not every encounter has a quasi-object:

A ball going from hand to hand is poor example of a quasi-object, since, although it does trace the collective and although the playing team would not exist without the moving token, the latter is not modified by the passings/.../ As a rule, a quasi-object should be thought of as a moving actant that transform those who do the moving, because they transform the moving object.

(Latour 1996: 379)

To identify the quasi-object/subject, one must understand that they are both designated and transformed by each other simultaneously and reciprocally. The transactant is what designates what becomes, or what evolves as the key feature in the learning activity.

Why is this important? What is the purpose? To answer these questions, I point to two things that the concept of transactant can potentially help us acknowledge. First, in pedagogical activities, materials and technology are often treated as a means to an end. For example, in a remake project, students are expected to learn about sustainability through the act of remaking. Students might also use technology such an iPad to sketch a design or use a sewing machine to accomplish their design. In these examples, the recycled materials and the technology are there to fulfil an already-envisioned end. However, what often happens is that the material and the technology get easily overlooked, as they are simply there to fulfil an already-imagined pedagogical aim. Second, the material or technology will most certainly produce other effects and do other things apart from what is envisioned. The problem—and thus why this is important to acknowledge—is that, if we only pay empirical attention to the envisioned presupposed aim, we limit our understanding of what it means to learn. Further, it might also limit our understanding of what students are paying attention to and cause us to overlook other things produced in the activity. By paying transactional attention to the learning activity and empirically paying attention to what has a force in and influence on the learning activity, we deepen our understanding of the learning activity.

Transactants in Learning Activities

Here I illustrate the concept of "transactant" with empirical examples involving a school project from a Grade 8 class in Sweden in which pupils are learning to remake old clothes and used fabrics (Hofverberg 2019).

The first example involves Paul, who we met at the beginning of the chapter. Paul's eyes sparkle with excitement and he is sitting at his desk waiting for the teacher. When the teacher arrives, Paul hands her a piece of paper and says that this is exactly what he wants to do. The teacher reads what is on the paper, and the following dialogue ensues:

(1) Teacher: Have you made a paper pattern? You have to make a pattern so that you can cut it out. Look, that's a pattern [points to another student's pattern]. You have to draw it according to the size you want.
(2) Paul: This, exactly this [points to the fabric].
(3) Teacher: But you have to do it in paper first.
(4) Paul: But, but …
(5) Teacher: These measures, you have to do them in paper first.
(6) Paul: But I am not gonna cut it. I have measured everything, and I am …
(7) Teacher: But you don't cut the fabric directly, you first have to make a … paper pattern.
(8) Paul: But I'm not gonna cut it. I'm gonna use the whole thing of this.
(9) Teacher: The whole thing? This is gigantic. You cannot use all this fabric.
(10) Paul: But that is 150.
(11) Teacher: This is much more than 150. You cannot use all this. You have to make it smaller so you can manage to show me how you use the sewing machine.
(12) Paul: [silence].
(13) Teacher: It is too big. You'll have to make it smaller.
(14) Paul: But how is it then supposed to hold clothes for lazy laundry days?

In this activity, when we follow the back-and-forth movement of the process, there are several things that matter. What I would like to focus on is what makes the activity turn in a specific direction and draws, so to speak, the future into the present. What Paul envisions is a product that he will use for lazy laundry days (what this is in particular is not exactly clear from the transcript). Paul points to the fabric, saying "exactly this" (line 2). He responds to the teacher and utters that he does not want to cut the fabric at all (line 8). When the teacher says that he cannot use all the fabric (line 9), he responds with silence, and then after a while, he utters, "But how is it then supposed to hold clothes for lazy laundry days?" (14). If he cannot use the whole fabric, then his vision seems to be lost. Arguably, it is the huge fabric that is a key actor here, the transactant that turns the process in a specific direction. The transactant creates the reciprocal relation between Paul and the vision of what will be made. One could also argue that the teacher's response about making a smaller product also turns the activity into a specific direction, and that is true. However, Paul does not continue the remake activity with the curtain when he cannot use the whole fabric. Instead, he stops and starts the process all over again by re-imagining a new product with another re-used fabric.

In another example, we meet Anna. She has decided to remake an old pair of jeans and is thinking about making some kind of bag with the jeans fabric. When the teacher approaches Anna and asks what she will craft, she replies, "A toiletry bag." Then they start to discuss the design and construction. The teacher suggests that Anna could use wadding, but Anna has changed her mind.

(15) Anna: I'm not really thinking of making a toiletry bag anymore.
(16) Teacher: No?
(17) Anna: I don't know what it's called, but I don't want it to have a bottom [she holds up a toiletry bag from the bottom]. It's more like …
(18) Teacher: Will it be used to store things? Does it need to be able to stand upright?
(19) Anna: Yes … kind of like a wallet or something.
(20) Teacher: Yes, okay. So, it's not a toiletry bag.
(21) Anna: No.
(22) Teacher: What will you put in it?
(23) Anna: I don't know. Like a wallet or—I don't know what to call it.
(24) Teacher: Some kind of storage anyway.
(25) Anna: Yes, storage.
(26) Teacher: Yes, I can see what you're thinking. You just need to write some measurements and so on.
(27) Anna: But I've done that already.
(28) Teacher: Did you write it down? I didn't see them. Then you may now start on the pattern. That's when you draw on a blank sheet of pattern paper. You can find pattern paper on the cutting table. You can take some there. There's even a set square tool.
(29) Anna: So, it is good now? [pointing to her description].
(30) Teacher: Yes. But you must also write what the recycled material is.

Anna continues to draw the design on the pattern paper. A while later, she calls for the teacher's attention.

(31) Anna: I think that since I already have these edges, maybe it's better that I make a bottom, so it's a little more complicated. It's pretty easy to do, and then I'll use batting.
(32) Teacher: That's a good insight.

In this example, Anna has no clear vision of what she wants to do, or else she cannot express it in words to the teacher. She first talks about a toiletry bag (line 15) and then a type of wallet (line 23). The teacher asks certain questions about the design and the imagined qualities of the bag, for example whether Anna wants to use wadding so the bag can stand on its own. First, Anna refuses the idea of wadding and making a bottom, but as she continues to work with the design, she realizes that the bag she is about to craft may be too simplistic (line 31). She says that "since I already have these edges" (line 31), meaning that, as she cut off a pair of jeans the seams on the sides of the jeans are already there. If she does not make a bottom on the bag, the only thing she has to do is to sew one seam at the bottom of the bag and add a zipper. What is going on here is that, when she sees the design emerging while working with it, she realizes that the product is very simple, and she wants to make a more complicated bag. Here, it is the vision of making the bag more complicated that turns the learning activity in a specific direction and can, accordingly, be identified in this activity as a transactant. The transactant creates the reciprocal relations between the jeans and the vision of making a more complicated product. Given the school context, I interpret Anna's vision about making the object more complicated as an act reflecting the desire for a higher grade. From this perspective, the grade is what prompts Anna to continue because she believes that the more complicated bag will help her get a higher grade. In other words, Anna "becomes with" a good grade, and that is what guides her actions further.

In a third example, Martin is about to remake a potholder. He has chosen orange fabric from a pile of leftover fabrics that was available in the classroom. When we meet him, he has made a pattern of the potholder and is about to cut out the fabric. The teacher approaches Martin and the following dialogue takes place:

(33) Teacher: You cannot use that material for a potholder because it will melt.
(34) Martin: Are you kidding?
(35) Teacher: If you would have shown me, I could have told you that. Because some fabrics are not suitable for potholders.

(36) Martin: Which fucking fabric should I use then? There's nothing here.
(37) Teacher: Watch your language.
(38) Martin: There's nothing here that won't melt [pointing to the pile of material].
(39) Teacher: There's lots of material here that won't melt. But you can't use that.
(40) Martin: I won't use it anyway [referring to the potholder].
(41) Teacher: But the important thing is that you learn things, that you know about materials, and that you learn which fabric can be used for different things. What kind of fabric can withstand heat, Martin?

Martin does not answer the teacher's question. He removes the pins and the pattern from the fabric and throws it back on the pile of re-used fabrics. He starts to look for another fabric. A while later, he gets the teacher's attention by shouting her name and asks if the new fabric that he has chosen is okay. The teacher approves, and Martin continues to make his potholder.

Here, when we follow the back-and-forth movement of the process, the transactant—in other words, what turns the activity in a specific direction—is hard to identify. In this case, I believe the activity lacks a transactant due to Martin's actions or lack of actions. I will explain further: The aim and overall purpose of this activity is to remake products, but Martin does not seem to care. He started remaking a potholder in fleece, but fleece is a fabric that cannot function as a potholder because the material will not hold heat. Instead, it will melt. When the teacher points this out (line 33), Martin gets frustrated and swears. This is not because he really likes the material (as he utters that he will not use it later), but rather, I assume, because he now has to re-do it. Unlike Paul, Martin has no interest in doing a special product or in getting a higher grade, like Anna. He simply wants to get this activity over with, and therefore, it does not matter if the potholder is made out of fleece. But when the teacher argues back, he—in silence—does what the teacher says and replaces the fleece fabric with another fabric. In other words, there is no actor (human or nonhuman) that creates the reciprocal relations between Martin, a future vision, and the fabric.

These examples show how three students given the same assignment encounter the task differently and make different meaning from the activity. What the students pay attention to and become more transactionally integrated with differs, and this in turn affects how the remake activity reveals not only the student's existing self but also the student's future self. For Paul, he becomes transactionally integrated with the huge fabric and envisions using it as something in the future (for lazy laundry days). Anna envisions her future self as a student with good grades, which prompts her to craft a more complicated product. Martin does not seem to care much. He just wants to pass the course. Therefore, the potholder is not part of his future self.

Acknowledging Transactants in Educational Research

I have described the theoretical stances for "transactant" and with empirical examples, illustrated how the concept can be applied. The students, Paul, Anna, and Martin each handled the task of remaking differently. The transactant analysis of their learning activities concretely shows how their transactional processes evolved and what emerged as important: for Paul, it was the huge fabric, for Anna, it was to make a more complicated product, and for Martin, it was rather the lack of transactants. As such, they "crafted" different meanings from the activity. The reason why I use "crafted" here is to point out how the meaning from the activity not only emerged as verbal or abstract visions but also as embodied and materialized relations. We can also see that from the web of relations present in the activities, what matters is not a separated actant but a *trans*actant that points to the reciprocal and simultaneous relations that emerge in the activity. When investigating an educational activity such as this remake activity, the transactional analyses can help us to illuminate these relations and show how different transactants make a difference in the larger assemblage and produce different learning outcomes.

One such learning outcome relevant for educational research to acknowledge is how students respond to the material. It is often stated that, when crafting, one needs to "work with the material" meaning that one must be "friends" with the material—to get to know it and work with it. The material has to cooperate. Ingold talks about this as "answering to the material" (2013: 108). But sometimes it is really difficult to answer to the material when the material is no "friend" at all but rather a real struggle. To borrow an expression from Serres (2007), the crafting material "designates" the students and the encounter changes what is possible to craft or remake. From the examples I have given, we can see that Anna's vision of what to remake changes as she encounters the material. Paul's vision emerges when encountering the material—the huge fabric—but he needs to change his vision when he cannot do what he has imagined.

However, it is not only the students who are changed and transformed in the encounter—so too are the remaking materials. This is visible in the example with Anna. At first, she was uncertain about what to do and how to realize her design. For her, making a more complicated bag evolved as a transactant, and that steered the learning activity in a specific direction. But the jeans are also changed. Previously, the jeans had qualities—woven twill with thick cotton threads—that were suitable for trousers. Anna had to answer to these qualities as she crafted, but only some pieces were used. The other pieces were cast aside (i.e., continued their journey as other shapes with other purposes). Both the teacher and Anna did not pay explicit attention to how the main part of the jeans was not used. This was perhaps because the aim of the project was to make a new product, which required Anna to work with the jeans. But no pedagogical attention was placed on "threading back," in other words, acknowledging where the jeans had been before the remake project or where the material was going after the classroom activity. Therefore, what is acknowledged in a transactional activity has a great impact on what is considered as valuable knowledge.

One could argue that a lot more was going on in these learning activities, and this is most certainly true. But the point of zooming in on the learning activity is not to capture everything but rather to acknowledge what has a major effect on the direction of learning and what draws the future into the present. This is valuable to articulate from at least two pedagogical viewpoints. First, it makes it possible to critically discuss the outcome with the envisioned pedagogical goal. Second, by focusing on what is included and given attention in the activity, it is possible to acknowledge what meaning is made but perhaps not explicitly acknowledged during the activity or else given little attention. For example, in Paul's case, the hugeness of the fabric turned out to be the transactant that made him want to make this special product. However, his concerns about remaking a special product produced other effects; for example, it took him about four lessons to decide what to do. It also produced many emotions. He was very happy and excited when he came up with his idea, but when that was not doable, he was disappointed. We do not know if Paul is displaying environmentally aware behavior, and if so, how? But what we can say is that Paul fully engages in the project as he becomes transactionally integrated with the remake material.

If we think about the remake process as a transactional activity, many new skills and techniques are required of the students. They will have to coordinate their actions to the surrounding world and for a specific purpose (even if the purpose is emerging or changes in the process). When studying these coordinating actions, it becomes clear that the students learn to follow and answer the material in transaction. As shown, the products may turn out to be too difficult to make within the framework of the task—factors such as grades may be involved or the characteristics of the fabric may hinder the activity.

This chapter highlights the complexity of the teaching and learning processes involved in remake projects by applying the concept of transactant. In examining this complexity, it is possible to illustrate what the students "become with" as they learn to remake.

11

Sensing Together: Transaction in Handicraft Education

Jonas Risberg and Joacim Andersson

Introduction

This chapter presents an analysis of the teaching of craft in a Swedish secondary school. Handicraft-oriented education (call "sloyd") is a compulsory subject in Sweden. The curriculum and syllabus include several learning aims, as well as descriptions of what different cultural techniques, values, and knowledge sloyd teaching should include. Our analysis focuses on how a teacher tries to help students to judge work processes using craft-specific terms and tactile-aesthetic awareness.

This chapter focuses on two ideas of pragmatism's account of experience. The first is that human beings are capable of experiencing the world directly, together with all the visceral, sensory, and emotional "stuff" that comes with it—Dewey's radical empiricism. The second is that human organisms coordinate different experienced "stuff" into functional wholes—the theory of inquiry. In this chapter, three transactional principles derived from these ideas are employed to analyze how teachers and students develop sloyd-specific values and knowledge as they engage in cultural techniques. To a certain degree, the process of learning basic techniques, such as sawing, hammering, and filing includes an extensive drilling of individual motor skills. This is dependent on shared cultural knowledge and values and is often referred to as "tacit knowledge." Our transactional view complements the individual and cultural perspectives of what we here call by-the-hand learning by starting in a first-person perspective of teachers' and students' work to find out what lies at-hand in their encounters with materials. The analysis is based on video observations of student–teacher–body–material–tool encounters. The main aim with empirically foregrounding the sensing together aspects of "seeing together" (Ryan 2011) is to reveal the sensory work that is involved in a teacher's and students' practical inquiries, such as what the materials feel like when they are touched.

Sensing Together

Classical pragmatism embraces the notion that human beings experience actual things in their immediacy and that certain qualities of such experienced situations can gain further meaning through the process of inquiry. James uses the term "pure experience" to underline that "the objects in immediate experiences are valid enough" (Shook 2011: 20–1). For example, breathing fresh air and drinking clean water are things immediately valued and enjoyed. Although such sensed qualities of the world have value, Hickman (2007) notes that "it is notoriously difficult to retain moments of aesthetic insight. Even the most intense delights have a way of turning to dust in our hands" (p. 137). Learning, then, requires that we seek out ways to secure "what would otherwise have been immediate and transitory" (p. 148). The theory of inquiry, which focuses on the process of securing pure experience for further use in continued transactional events, not only accounts for sensed qualities of the world (here and now), but also for sensed directions in the world (an expanded usage of sensed qualities). We argue that the qualities of current situations and the directions of future actions can be analyzed through observations of how teachers' and students' sense together in the sloyd process.

Moreover, the specific sensed relations between material, tool, and body movement in craft education constitute a shared context of use. When teachers and students coordinate that context on the basis of a shared sense, crafting can be described as a certain knowledge of sensing together. The examples in this chapter show how a teacher and his students share a common tactile exploration by literally sensing together. Our analysis emphasizes this process as a teacher's and students' practical knowledge from a transactional perspective, in that they sense together what novices might regard as distinct separates.

According to Ryan (2011: 4), Dewey and Bentley (1949) "wanted to develop a comprehensive theory of sign-behavior ranging from simple cues and gestures to the complex language of science and mathematics." Ryan (2011: 26–7) also summarizes Dewey and Bentley's transactional theory of knowledge as three crucial principles:

1. Since experience is our window to the world, attention to how things are actually experienced is vital to any account of knowledge and objectivity.
2. Neither rationalism's self-evident truths nor empiricism's sense-impressions faithfully capture the dynamic of actual experience. In different ways, they commit the philosopher's fallacy of supposing that the product of some reflective theory about experience initiates actual experience.
3. Attention to actual experience suggests that its default mode is nonreflective instead of reflective—dominated by habit rather than self-evident truths or brightly lit sense data. Perceptual content is not discretely parceled into things and thoughts. It is an integral unity, a gestalt or fit that is had rather than known.

These three principles together with the above elaboration of pure experience and inquiry are important for our operationalization of sensing together, i.e., how we explain craft-specific empirical situations as a certain embodied learning. The twofold purpose is to show how sensing techniques and experiences of sensing together are given a central role in sloyd education and how objectives are realized as outcomes of problem-solving activities. Learning sloyd is not just about learning to handle tools or use different materials. It is also about learning to make experiences as an active participant (producer and user) in a shared context of use. Our analysis shows how material objects emerge as certain objectives (e.g., sensed directions) in situated action and depict three aspects of sensing together actions in this process. The three aspects are equally informed by the three transactional principles and our video observations of how the teacher and students are sensorially engaged in their problem-solving activity.

1. Reaching out. Firstly, to know an object you need to have experiences of it. Therefore, we focus on actions where the participants use certain body techniques to become sensorially aware of the material and the situation. Dewey's immediate empiricism argues that it is what is experienced that is important (Ryan 2011: 24). James's radical empiricism claims that the objects of immediate experience are valid (Shook 2011). In this connection, we also show how students are guided by the teacher to make first-person experiences of a crafting. Reaching out thus refers to how the materials are encountered jointly and how tactile sensations are experienced.
2. Taking data. Secondly, we focus on actions that show how the teacher supports students in making meaning of certain tactile experiences. Here, as Hickman (2007: 137) notes, students must seek out ways to secure "what

would otherwise have been immediate and transitory." Likewise, Dewey reminds us that data is taken and not given. Taking data thus refers to what is supposed to be experienced in any particular moment.
3. Creating objectives. Thirdly, we focus on actions that show how tactile experiences are used to create new objectives, i.e., how the teacher and students use the sensed qualities of the situation to direct future actions (expanded usage of sensed qualities). Creating objectives therefore refers to how certain sensed experiences incorporate meaning into future doings.

Empirical descriptions of these three aspects of sensing together actions support an elaborated explanation of what it means, practically, to be sensorially engaged in a certain problem-solving activity. Furthermore, they help us to see that education often starts with nonreflective experience.

Method

For the analysis we reviewed sixteen 60-minute sloyd lessons. The lessons were video-recorded in the context of a five-year project called Teaching and Learning Practical Embodied Knowledge. The recordings were collected over a three-year period of following two classes of secondary school students. During the lessons an action camera was attached to the teacher's chest. This helped us observe the teacher as an active participant walking from bench to bench and creating a web of learning encounters (see Andersson & Risberg 2018). The arrangement also facilitated a close-up and detailed view of the student–teacher–body–material–tools transactions.

In sloyd education, students face the challenge of accomplishing very practical and individual tasks. They nevertheless depend on the teacher to progress as participants in a sloyd-specific culture. In order to design and craft even the simplest of products, students have to rely on very basic techniques. Carving, hammering, and sawing constitute an embodied knowing that is achieved and in-habited through hard and prolonged work consisting of encounters with material and tools, people, and purposes. Although the students in our analysis were knowledgeable about such basic techniques, they were not yet able to make sound judgments and decisions in the crafting process. Therefore, the teacher needed to engage in the students' assignments, as well as engage the students in the process. In this context, the students' most frequent concerns were questions like "what should I do next?" Andersson and Risberg (2018) show that an important part of a teacher's answer to such questions is a systematic use of students' hands and fingers (e.g., "lend me your hand") when giving instructions. For the analysis in this chapter, we reviewed the sixteen lessons and re-examined situations in which such sensing together became overtly observable and a joint concern for the teacher and students. In doing so, we built up a collection of forty sensing together situations that clearly included tactile exploration. On the basis of that collection, we analyzed how the teacher and students explored features of body–material–tool encounters.

An Analysis of Sensing Together

The analysis is presented in two sections. In the first section we analyze a teacher–student encounter that includes the three aspects that we point to in relation to "sensing together." In the second section we highlight specific features of some of these aspects by presenting complementary situations of body–material–tool encounters. Taken together, the two sections represent a visualization and description of some of the main characteristics of how students learn to develop practical reasoning through specific experiences of physical material, such as how they learn to think *in* the material in which they act, rather than *about* it. All the presented extracts include questions from students about what to do next. Such questions are understandable given that students are often faced with assignments that are presented to them as procedural. In the following we show how the teacher responds to these questions by enacting a first-person view of the material and then encountering the material together with the students as he engages them in different craft techniques. By means of full body responses to their "what to do next" questions, the students are taught that a particular sensing is central to the crafting process, how certain qualities can be experienced in the material and how actions can be realized as outcomes of (i) reaching out, (ii) taking data, and (iii) creating objectives.

Reaching Out, Taking Data, and Creating Objectives

The situation in extract 1 is initialized by a female student calling for the teacher and asking about the next step in her process of carving a texted sign out of a piece of wood. The teacher stops at her bench but does not give an immediate verbal answer to her question. Instead, he grabs the chisel that the student is using and starts to feel the surface of the wood with his fingers.

Extract 1, Smoothing out a rough surface[1]

[Teacher scrolls around with fingers on the surface of the wooden plate]

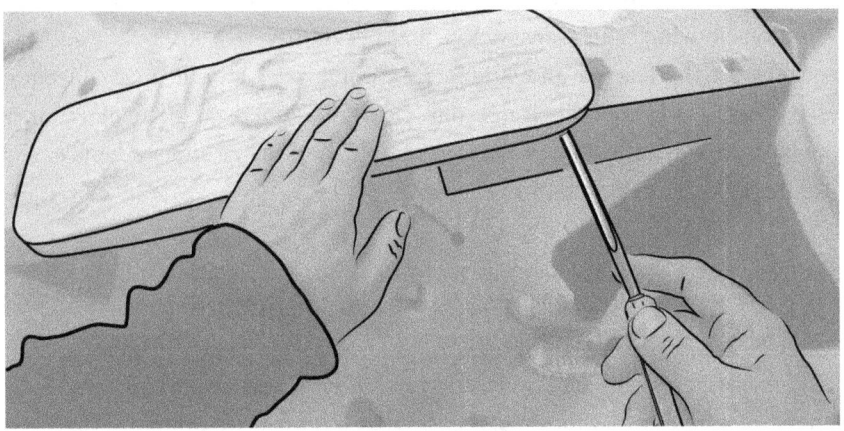

01 T—Yes, just take, if you ... if you could try yourself, be a bit critical ...
[Teacher scrolls around with fingers on the surface of the wooden plate]

02 T—And just feel a bit there where you have-
[Teacher feels a narrower area]
[Teacher drops the tool in his right hand and grabs the student's hand]
03 T—... if you feel a bit like that, right?
[Teacher starts to scroll with the student's fingers on the surface of the plate]

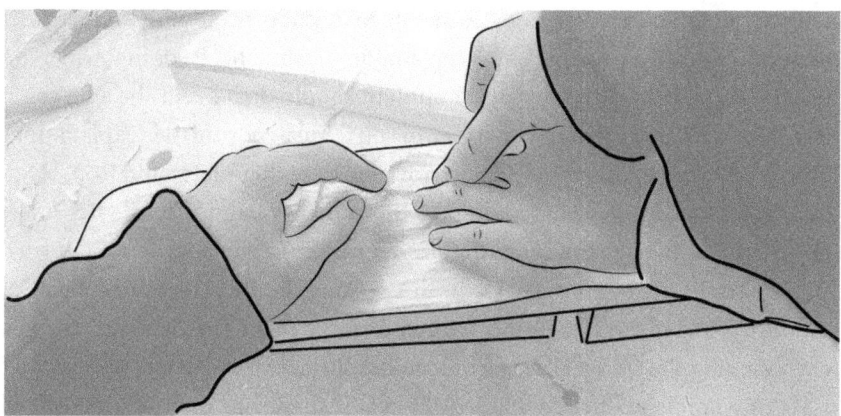

04 T—Feel neatly and carefully so you don't get any slivers in your fingers
   [Teacher moves the student's fingers very gently around the carved areas]
05 S—Yes
06 T—And feel a bit there, for example there is a peak there, right?
   [Teacher holds the student's hand and scrolls her fingers at a certain place]
07 S—Mm
08 T—So just smooth out those kinds
   [Teacher releases the student's hand and points to the place where they felt the peak]

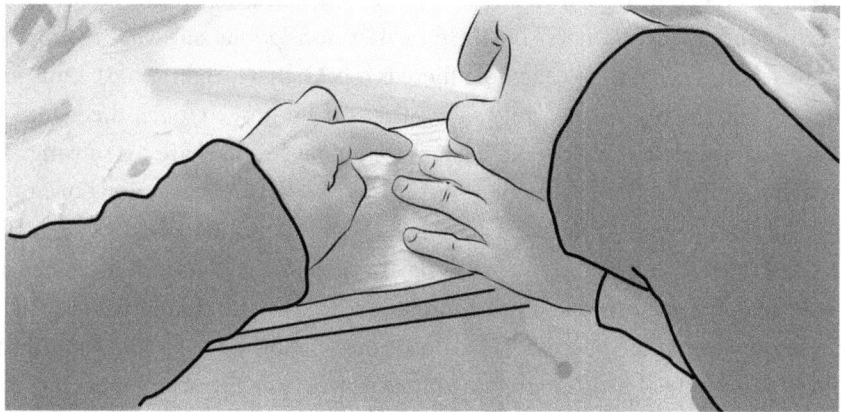

09 S—Yes
10 T—So just feel neatly and carefully so it is even, right?
   [Teacher feels the wooden surface with his own hand]
11 S—Yes

As the teacher senses the wood, he begins to develop a response to the student's question. The response is both explanatory—what he is doing when he is sensing—and instructive—what the student should do herself: "be a bit critical" (01), "feel a bit there where you have" (02). He suspends further explanations at the same time as he starts to feel a narrower area with his left hand (02). He then drops the tool on the bench and grabs the student's hand. He tells her to sense the wood like that, at the same time as he makes her fingers scroll the surface (03). He continues by telling her how this sensing should be executed, neatly and carefully (04). At the same time, we can observe that the teacher is very gentle when moving the student's fingertips on the surface of the wood.

At this point, we can conclude that as a response to the question of "what to do next" the teacher first of all takes a woodcarver's position as he grabs the carving tool with one hand and starts to sense the wood with the other. Before revealing his judgment about what to do next, he guides the student in a "critical" (01) sensing exploration of the piece of wood. He does this in a very direct way by grabbing her hand and moving her fingertips to feel the wooden surface. The student is at this moment also encouraged to move carefully in her body–material–tool transactions (04). In this way he lets her share his reaching out technique, which then makes it possible for her to have an immediate experience of the material. The student also confirms these instructive actions by saying "yes" (05). The teacher then moves the student's fingers toward another spot, "and then you feel bit here" (06). He furthermore points out what is supposed to be felt at this spot, "for example there is a peak there, right?" (06). Our point here is that the teacher not only shows the student how to touch the wood, but also what to sense in the wood. That is, he guides her to share his sensing. The student confirms this instruction with "mm" (07). The instructions of how to sense (reaching out) and what to sense (taking data) are verbally agreed on by the student and become something that is known in common. When the peak and the proper sensing technique are known in common, the teacher finally answers the student's "what to do next" question: "so just smooth out those kinds" (08). This emerges as an objective; not because the teacher tells the student about his personal judgment, but rather because they are able to act in a shared context of use. If only a short verbal response about what to do had been given, the student might not have been able to develop an expanded usage of felt qualities but may rather have developed an expanded need for the teacher to explore any remaining peaks in the wood. The creation of the objective (iii) "smooth out those kinds" thus emerges as a desired action on the basis of a shared engagement in actions of reaching out (i) and taking data (ii).

Phases of actions in which data is taken are typically challenged by the "overflow" of qualities. It is therefore important for students to be alert to the right ways of discerning felt qualities. The different examples shown in extracts 2–5 point to very brief situations in which the teacher instructs and guides the student in *how* to sense (i) and *what* to sense (ii).

Extract 2, Those sharp

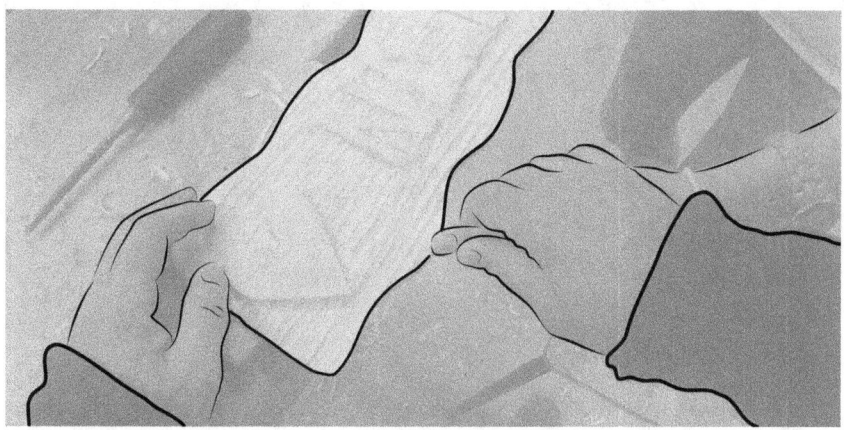

01 T—So just here, so you just sense
02 T—So that you round off those sharp
03 S—Yes

Extract 3, It's choppy

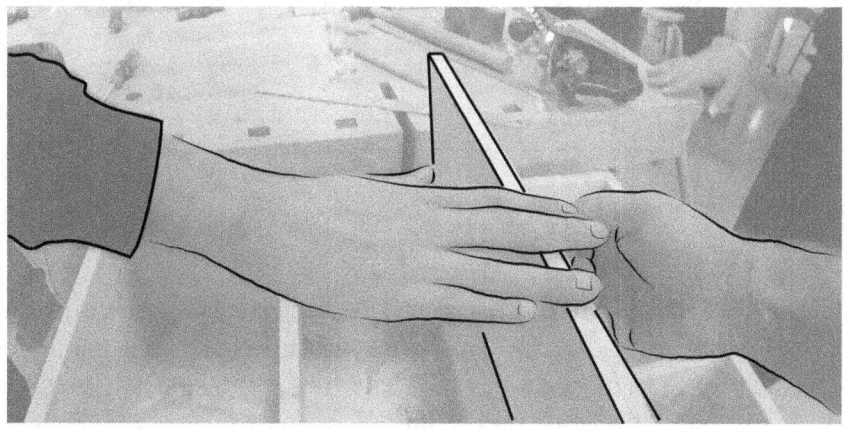

01 T—Feel there, it's choppy
02 S—Yes

Extract 4, It's smooth

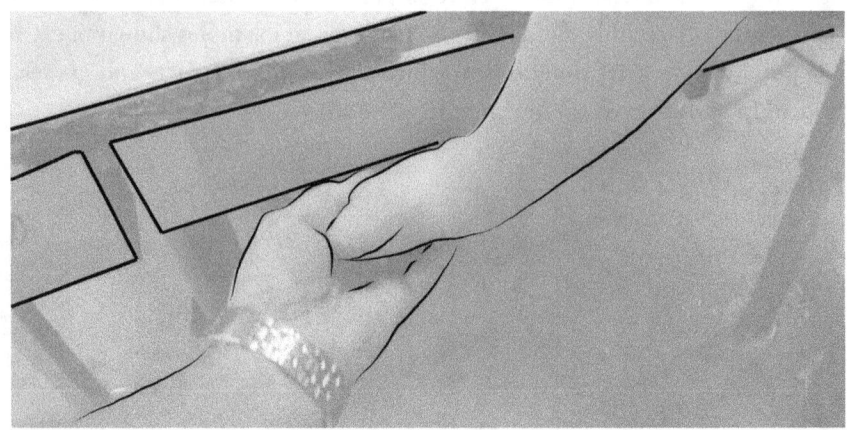

01 T—Feel there, it's smooth and there it goes up
02 S—mm

Extract 5, There's a slope

01 T—If you sense there, there's a slope there
02 T—Can you feel that?

In these brief situations, the teacher guides the student in *how* to sense (reaching out) and *what* to sense (taking data); using their hands and point out to them the "sharp" (Extract 2), "choppy" (Extract 3), "smooth" (Extract 4), and "slope" (Extract 5). Shared engagement like this has the capacity to reach beyond the particular situation and also account for a cultural knowledge through which the overarching task can be carried out; carving a texted sign out of a piece of wood, etc.

Zooming In on What Is Sensed

Each aspect of the various actions (reaching out, taking data, creating objectives) can, of course, include different disruptions. To further illustrate the purposeful character of taking data, and how it is connected to the crafting process the students are involved in, we present two extracts as examples of how disruptions can emerge. The encounter in extract 6 is initialized by a student who seeks the teacher's attention after drilling holes in steel plate pieces that are to be assembled into a figure. At the bench the teacher picks one of the steel plates up and touches and feels the drilled holes. At the same time, he explains to the student that there are still some burrs. The teacher then batches three file-stop-sense sequences, after which he instructs the student to feel the material for herself, "if you feel there now, like that" (01).

Extract 6, Getting warm

> 01 T—If you feel there now, <u>like that</u>
> [Teacher feels both sides of the plate with his thumb on top and his index finger underneath]
> [Student touches the plate with her fingers in a similar way]
> [Student instantly withdraws her hand, and shakes it]
> 02 S—My <u>god</u>, it's getting <u>warm</u>
> 03 T—<u>Nnooyeahh</u>, but it is completely <u>smooth</u>
> [Teacher touches the plate]
> 04 S—Yes
> 05 T—Because then, when we assemble the pieces, it would not be possible to …
> [Teacher picks up two plate pieces and demonstrates how burrs prevent the plates from sitting tight when assembled]

The student mimics the teacher's way of touching the filed steel plate (reaching out). In contrast to extracts 1 to 5, the teacher does not point out what to sense (i.e., taking data). Touching the steel plate, the student reacts instantly withdrawing her hand while expressing a mild surprise, "my god, it's getting warm" (02). The data taken by the student is brought forward as something unexpected. Even though such experience is plausible (based on the intense filing sequence), the teacher starts to reject such judgment (03). Even though the rejection ends up as an acceptance "Nnoyeaaah" (03), he points out that this is not the kind of data that is supposed to be taken. Instead, they search for "smoothness": "but it is completely smooth" (03). So, even if the plate is warm, that meaning is taught as invalid in regard to the overarching task. At this point of a disruption such background is also brought to the front by the teacher: "Because then, when we assemble the pieces … " (05). Again, reaching out and taking data are taught as sensing for something in particular, and should be understood as a purposeful act in relation to an aim. What we take from a situation and secure for further use is always relative to the problem that is defined (burrs) in the crafting process (assembling pieces). It is not any sensory stimuli (heat) that is at stake; it is *that* sensed experience (smoothness).

In our final extract we describe a disruption connected to creating objectives. Below, in extract 7, the student calls for the teacher after cutting a steel plate according to the measurements provided in the assignment. Arriving at the bench, the teacher picks up the plate and senses the edges with his finger. He then grabs the student's hand and scrolls the end of the steel plate (reaching out) and suggests that the sharp edges need to be filed down (creating objective). The student indicates that she recognizes all these actions and confirms this by saying "yes" (02). So far, the teacher and the student proceed by reaching out and taking data without any great disruption. However, when the student suggests using "ordinary sandpaper" (03), such tool is rejected by the teacher, "N-no" (04).

Extract 7, With ordinary sandpaper

01 T—… and file those edges
[Grabs the student's hand, unfolds the index finger and scrolls it in a similar way]
02 S—yes …
03 S—with ordinary sandpaper
04 T—N-no, take …
[Teacher walks over to another bench to get a file and returns to the student]
06 T—One like this, a metal file
07 S—yes

Even though the proposed action of "file those edges" (1) could be said to index a certain tool (file), the student suggests using sandpaper. Rejected as a proper tool (04), the teacher then picks up the right tool, a metal file. This demonstrates that creating objectives cannot only be understood as a final step in a linear relationship between reaching out and taking data. Instead, all these actions must come together in further direction. Creating objectives refers to how students learn to use the data they take as a means for the further direction of their actions. But even though they take the right things (sharp edges) they may use them in incorrect ways. To realize objectives, you also need to know about the usage of cultural tools. In the wood crafting process, they have previously sensed (reached out) sharp edges (taking data) and arrived at the insight that the correct tool for future action would be sandpaper. This last extract exemplifies that what is crucial for satisfactory outcomes of creating objectives is that students relate their sensing to the cultural use of tools. Sharp edges are not merely sharp edges. They can be sharp wooden edges (processed by sandpaper) or sharp steel edges (processed by filing).

Discussion

At the most general level, sensing together can be conceived of as the shared embodied language of inquiry in sloyd education, where certain cultural aspects of the world are brought to the front. That is, crafting sloyd products using materials like wood and steel is a meaning-making process that relies on ways of sensing and culturally specific ways of valuing and judging the experiences and outcomes of that process. In this regard, sensing together refers to both the tactile technique through which teachers and students encounter materials jointly (using their hands, experiencing materials immediately) and their ability to sense together what novices might regard as separate parts (i.e., a warm piece instead of a sharp edge that should be smoothed out). In their crafting, "The senses are the organs through which [they] … participates directly in the ongoings of the world about [them]. In this participation the varied wonder and splendor of this world are made actual for [them] in the qualities [they] experiences" (Dewey 1934/2005: 22).

Teaching students how to judge work processes using craft specific terms and tactical-aesthetic awareness requires the teacher to meet them in the "overflow" of impressions and expressions. To empirically describe and conceptually explain this process, we have identified three characteristic aspects of actions. *Reaching out* refers to how students are taught to relate in a tactile way to objects, *taking data* refers to how students are taught to probe for and secure the right characteristics, while *creating objectives* refers to what to secure for the further direction of actions. From the perspective of an experienced and reflective practitioner, like the teacher, actions like these often emerge as one sensed situation. By reaching out and touching the material, the teacher's judgment is made and his vision cleared in an instant. Though, as Dewey writes in *Art as Experience*, such recognitions of objects "is not itself a mere point in time. It is the focal culmination of long, slow processes of maturation. It is the manifestation of the continuity of an ordered temporal experience in a sudden discrete instant of climax" (1934/2005: 23–4).

In this chapter we have shown how such transactions of instant recognition are unpacked by the teacher and reinforced as learning content. For the purpose of describing the educational essentials of these craft-specific judgments, we have shown how the teacher responds to the students' "what to do next" questions by first positioning himself in the situation before giving an answer. From a zoomed-out perspective, the teaching events illustrated in extracts 1–7 can be summarized in the following way: (a) the students reach out for the teacher, (b) the teacher reaches out for the material and (c) together they seek to experience a sensed quality of a situation. Taken together, these focused encounters are illustrative examples of how learning not always begins with conscious problems but starts with sensory experiences. Although these are often vague and inexact (and as yet unknown), they can be taught as valid experiences.

Asking what to do next is also deeply connected to the learning technique of experiencing what is immediately there. Following the teacher's actions in these situations it is evident that he teaches the students that "what is next" depends on "what is at hand." To know what is at hand, we need to busy our hands. In the extracts the teacher grabs, touches, and feels the materials while talking about what he is experiencing. Expressed differently, he recognizes experiences of what is immediately sensed. He goes on to include the students in this sensing technique and encourages them to judge their own immediate experience of the material. Thus, the teacher and the students can sense the quality of the material jointly. In the first section we highlighted that "that peak" can finally present itself as that thing due to the sensory efforts that the teacher and the student invest together to realize what it is. This empirically demonstrates how attention is directed to reaching out for the material directly, and how objects are taken and transformed into objectives of practical inquiry. In the second section, we show how disruption occurs in different phases of sensing together and that students need to make judgments in a specific cultural context (e.g., it is not "warm" but "smooth," even though it is warm).

To conclude, rather than illustrating how knowledge is used to interpret materials and objects, our examples describe and explain how actions of sensing gradually change the material, objects and/or relations that are attended to. In the extended transactional event of taking part in sloyd education, the consequences of these focused encounters are connected to how teachers navigate in the transactional midland of teaching. If the teacher leaves the students more or less alone in the crafting process, they may have to coordinate a scope of experience that is too wide. Thus, they will encounter problems in singling out the right moments of sensed qualities. On the other hand, if the teacher guides them too much in the process, they may never meet the material through their own sensory work, but instead only experience sensed qualities through the teacher, or even worse, the teacher's sensed qualities. Both these problems can arise in any sensing together phase and require the teacher to inhabit the transactional midland by sensing along with the students, rather than simply teaching various concepts and techniques.

Finally, students may also experience different outcomes in their problem-solving activities with regard to language use. One way of thinking is that the materialistic world assists language by providing raw sensory experiences that students learn to point to in words as they progress in the practice. If this is the case, their learning could be described as progressing toward a more verbal practice. Another way of thinking of the crafting process is that students already are active language users, but by learning to talk through habits of sensing together they can progress toward a more concise and embodied practice. A transactional perspective on handicraft education regards those different descriptions of learning as specific results of investigations of teacher–student–material–body–tool encounters, rather than starting points for inquiry.

12

The Museum as Exploration

Petra Hansson and Johan Öhman

Introduction

This chapter presents Louise Rosenblatt's (b. 1904–d. 2005) contribution to a transactional perspective on education. Rosenblatt was an American professor in English Education and a highly influential thinker in literary, critical theory, and reading pedagogy. Her theories are widely spread within the realm of teaching, learning languages, and literature, but we regard her ideas to have wider implications. According to Rosenblatt, the meaning of a text emerges transactionally in a given context wherein the reader and the text are inseparable. Here we first present her transactional theory of reading and writing with a particular focus on the reading process and the aesthetic dimension of the transaction. Next, we take Rosenblatt's theorizing with us into the Nobel Prize Museum in Stockholm and the exhibition *A Right to Freedom-Martin Luther King Jr.* We use empirical data from student's documented experiences of documentary photographs to illustrate the processes of transaction. We argue that a museum education that draws on a transactional understanding of the integration of object, visitor, and museum context can give students opportunities to explore both themselves and the encountered objects.

Background

The title of this chapter, "The Museum as Exploration," is a rewording of the title of Louise Rosenblatt's first book, *Literature as Exploration* (1995), first published in 1938; the same year as John Dewey's *Experience and Education* (1938) and four years after the publication of *Art as Experience* (1934). In the last chapter "Retrospect and Prospect" of the fifth edition of *Literature as*

Exploration Rosenblatt describes how her experiences of conventional methods of teaching which ignored the perspective of the readers motivated her to develop an approach to reading which took both text and reader into account. Her experiences of having explored students' responses to literature inspired her to write a book that presents "a philosophic or theoretical foundation for revising the teaching of literature, a foundation for setting up a process that would make personal response the basis for growth toward more and more balanced, self-critical, knowledgeable interpretation" (286). Rosenblatt proposes an interdisciplinary approach to teaching literature that encourages readers to focus on "social, psychological, and aesthetic assumptions implied by the literary work and by their own and others' responses" (286). From such a starting point, the reading of literature becomes something more than just interpreting and understanding a literary text. Rosenblatt's intention is mirrored in the slogan "Reading is a journey," in other words, she puts forward a "living-through approach" to reading. Inspired by Dewey's concept of transaction Rosenblatt develops a theory that aims to explain the reciprocal integration of reader and text where "[t]he transactional phrasing places the stress on each reading as a particular event involving a particular reader and a particular text recursively influencing each other under particular circumstances" (Rosenblatt 1995: 292). Furthermore, Rosenblatt situates her contribution in the field of teaching literature in the present state of the world and claims that "in our tumultuous, changing world, beset by poverty, pollution, and war, unthinking ready-made responses are dangerous" (Rosenblatt 2005: ix). Thus, she contextualizes her theory of reading in a wider societal context implying that reading literature can be key for sharpening our abilities to develop new ways of seeing and being in the world. However, she claims, for this to happen, equal attention needs to be paid to both reader and text.

A Triadic Relation: Reader, Text, and Literary Work

Rosenblatt's work has been widely discussed within the context of literary studies and the teaching of literature but also with regard to how pragmatic philosophy has influenced her work (Connell 2008). Rosenblatt takes Dewey and Bentley's transactional understanding of the knower and known as a starting point for developing a transactional theory that involves a mutual relation between reader and text. In a transactional approach, humans are viewed as being in constant motion and action, which means that "[h]uman beings are always in …

a reciprocal relationship with an environment, a context, a total situation" (Rosenblatt 2005: 26). Rosenblatt's transactional approach to texts rejects the view of texts as having meaning "independently" of both authors and readers. Therefore, both writing processes and reading processes consist of various encounters. The author's writing process includes encounters between the author's previous experiences and the actual writing of the text, and potential encounters between the text and its future readers. The reader's reading process involves encounters with the author's experiences as expressed in the text as well as the reader's previous and present experiences. Thus, Rosenblatt regards the interactional model as being too mechanical and argues that it constitutes reading processes as comprising "separate elements or entities acting on one another" (1985: 98). In order to get away from the interactional view of readers and texts, she suggests a "triadic relationship" which in addition to the *reader* and the *text* also encompasses the evocation of a *literary work of art* which is what the reader evokes while reading a text. Thus, "the literary work or the evocation corresponding to the text" (1985: 103) together with the reader and the text are all involved in crafting a reader's response. Accordingly, she considers the meaning of a text to be "evoked" in the encounter between reader and text: "A story or poem or play is merely ink-spots on paper until a reader transforms them into a set of meaningful symbols. When these symbols lead us to live through some moment of feeling, to enter into some human personality, or to participate imaginatively in some situation or event, we have evoked a work of literary art" (Rosenblatt 2005: 62–3). The meaning of the concept "evocation" refers "to the lived-through process of building up the work under the guidance of the text" (Rosenblatt 1994: 69). Thus Rosenblatt distinguishes between an "evocation" and the interpretation of this evocation; the evocation produces its own "ideas" or work. During the reader-text transaction a new text is born. This is the lived-through work, the literary work. The evocation of a text is the first encounter and the spontaneous reactions that occur when transacting the text, which can later be reflected upon and interpreted. Evocations are effortless, focusing on what is noticed and perceived—the literary work in becoming.

However, every reading does not necessarily lead to a literary work. This depends on how the texts are approached and read. At times, when readers, for example, read a recipe or an instruction for how to use a new toaster, they are not as personally involved as when they are reading a novel by their favorite author. In these kinds of readings when we do not primarily read to be engaged or personally involved we take what Rosenblatt calls a non-aesthetic mode of reading or an *Efferent stance*. This means that the focus is primarily on what will be "extracted and retained after the reading event" (Rosenblatt 2005: 11)—for example, understanding how to bake the cake or what to do to in order to get the toaster up and going. If we take an *Aesthetic stance* on the other hand, our reading is directed to what happens during the reading-event, which means that we pay attention to personal associations, feelings, and ideas and "on what is being lived through during the reading event" (11). In such readings readers' personal feelings and opinions are merging with the content of texts while reading and evoking the *literary work*. Thus, for a literary work to happen, an aesthetic reading is essential. This means that the reader is involved in a spiraling process integrating the text with the reader, requiring an openness for what the text says as well as being open to personal reactions. Rosenblatt clearly states that it is important to realize these two stances are not completely separated but lie on a continuum. In most readings these two stances are combined. Rosenblatt argues, nonetheless, that efferent stances have dominated in the history of literature teaching in schools where the focus is on extracting information from literary texts. It is still common either for the purpose of passing a test or for reaching the supposedly one "correct" interpretation of a text.

Thus, the outcome of a reading is geared by the stance of the reader. Will it be a literary work? Or will it be a rational conclusion? Additionally, the triadic transactional relationship of the reader, the text, and the literary work raises questions of what readers do while reading and what such transactional processes look like. We will now take these questions and Rosenblatt's transactional perspective on reading into the context of museum education: what do objects and visitors do to each other while visiting a museum exhibition? We start with a short review of how the relation between museum visitors, exhibitions, and their objects has been discussed within museum education research.

The Efferent Aesthetic Continuum in Museums

Historically, art and aesthetics as something separate from everyday experiences has mostly defined museum practices. Art was located in museums for the purpose of being observed and admired rather than for the purpose of enhancing museum visitors' experiences or learning. Knowledge was viewed as "inherent in objects; visitors did not require additional interpretation since they, like curators, were assumed to be able to read the record inscribed within the objects" (Bedford 2014: 23). Thus, the function of museums was to transfer knowledge through valuable historical, natural, and cultural objects. In the 1980s, ignoring museum visitors' experiences, needs, or preferences was challenged by the "arrival" of the "new museology." The new museology movement involved a shift from discussions of knowledge as inherent in objects that can be transferred to the visitors to visitors' experiences and meaning-making (Falk & Dierking 2012). Thus, attention turned to how museums might promote visitors' learning and experiences as well as cultivating their emotions and imaginations (Hooper-Greenhill 2007; Hein 1998, 2006, 2012).

Shifting from knowledge transfer to visitor experience changes the role of museums in society as well as the epistemological and aesthetical premises of museums (Hein 1998; Ljung 2009; Latham 2013). It also initiated a new interest in how to organize museum education and efficient learning in museums. This implies that the traditional pedagogical role of museums to deliver knowledge shifted into discussions of how to develop interactive and participatory museum education practices (Ljung 2009), how to enhance museum visitors' learning (Illeris 2006; Hooper-Greenhill 2007; Hein 2012), and how museums with their exhibitions and objects can and do offer visitors "deep" and meaningful experiences (Latham 2007).

Museum education research has much focused on either how to design and organize exhibitions to achieve purposive experiences for the visitors or how the visitors' experienced the museum visit. However, less attention has been payed to the relation between exhibitions and visitors, what happens when museum visitors experience museum objects, and how they respond to museum objects in practice. We believe Dewey's transactional perspective in general and Rosenblatt's reading theory specifically have much to offer here. Already in *Art as Experience* (1934/2005) Dewey opposes the traditional image of artworks as objects envisaged in museums as something separate from everyday experiences. Dewey discusses how aesthetic experiences diverge from ordinary experiences by a sense of wholeness and unity, and are differentiated by feelings of enjoyment and fulfillment. He calls such experiences "*an* experience" and argues that they are distinct from the flow of ordinary experience: "We have an experience when the material experienced runs its course to fulfilment. Then and then only is it integrated within and demarcated in the general stream of experience from other experiences" (36–7). Such experiences are inherently meaningful and emotionally engaging and therefore particularly memorable. Dewey argues that experiences with art objects best illustrate what it means to have "an experience" and that art has a specific potential of generating imaginative responses. Rosenblatt's theory on the reciprocal integration of the reader and the text can offer a more detailed understanding of the process where the meaning of museum objects is "evoked" in visitor–exhibition encounters. In Rosenblatt's terms this process can be understood as a combination of taking efferent and aesthetic stances to exhibitions and their objects, which to different degrees leaves the visitor with a sense of having learned something useful from the exhibition or with the sense of having "lived-through" something which deeply affects them. The next section takes Rosenblatt's theorizing into the realm of museums and in particular to the Nobel Prize Museum in Stockholm.

The Nobel Prize MLK Exhibition

At the core of the Nobel Prize Museum are the Nobel Prize laureates and according to the museum's website, the museum's focus is "the great issues of our time and shows how we can respond to them through science, humanism and cooperation" (https://nobelprizemuseum.se/en/cultures-of-creativity). The museum displays one permanent exhibition, Cultures of Creativity, which shows presentations of the work of the laureates circling around innovations, creative environments, and the characteristics of creativity departing from the history of Nobel Prizes of the laureates. Alongside the permanent exhibition, the museum shows temporary exhibitions. For this study, we engaged in research over a sixteen-month period and worked closely together with one of the museum educators regarding the temporary exhibition *A Right to Freedom-Martin Luther King Jr* displayed from September 2018 to 2019. The exhibit was produced in collaboration between the Nobel Prize Museum, Nobel Media, and the King Estate. According to curator Ashley Woods, the aim of the exhibition was to "bring attention to the importance and necessity of basic human rights; promoting Martin Luther King, Jr.'s vision of equality and justice for all through nonviolence, and providing a common forum where people, have the opportunity to learn and share their ideas and experiences with others" (https://nobelprizemuseum.se/en/new-exhibition-about-martin-luther-king-jr-opens-this-autumn/). The exhibition displayed photographs, films, newspaper articles, collages, and digital media to tell stories of Martin Luther King's life and work.

In the context of our study, Rosenblatt's "texts" are switched to "museum objects" and the "readers" to students who visited the museum to participate in an educational program connected to the exhibition. Their visit was part of their ordinary education which implies that it had a pedagogical purpose. Thus, our empirical data is collected within the context of the museum education program connected to the exhibition.

The educational program consisted of four connected activities: (1). Introduction to Martin Luther King and the exhibition. (2). Guided tour in the exhibition led by the museum educator. (3). Aesthetic reading of documentary photographs. And (4). writing and performing *I have a dream* speeches in groups. The aim of the aesthetic reading activity was to let the students spontaneously explore and experience the exhibition through an aesthetic reading. In Rosenblatt's words, the aim of the activity was to encourage the students to create "object works." They were asked to choose one photograph that for some reason caught their attention and write down their own "evocations" of the displayed documentary photographs in the exhibition. The students were asked to walk around in the exhibition space, select one photograph, and write down their spontaneous emotions and feelings while encountering the selected photograph. Accordingly, the students were encouraged to start writing instantly in dialogue with the photograph rather than to first look at it, interpret it, and then write down their concluding remarks. These quick and tentative notes provided us with insights in the early stage of the processes by which the museum visitors were evoking "object works."

The photographs displayed in the context of the exhibition consisted of both private and public photographs ranging from family images of Martin Luther King's childhood to famous images such as of Rosa Parks sitting on the bus during the Montgomery bus boycott, Sit ins, and the "Little Rock nine." Thus, many of the photographs are informative portraying historical events. The students' texts were produced in place of the museum and collected directly after being written. Accordingly, these evocations of the photographs were produced in the situation of the museum education program. Our ambition in the next section is to capture the transactional process through which the students engaged with the exhibited museum objects in an "interpretive act." We will follow three students' evocations of two different documentary photographs and their processes of crafting "object works."

Three Evocations

In the following, notes written by the three students are used to illustrate the students' ongoing evocations while exploring the photographs at the MLK exhibition. These tentative notes provide insights of what is going on in visitor–object encounters and as such what transactional processes may involve. Since these notes are written quickly they can be viewed as snapshots in the students'

172 Deweyan Transactionalism in Education

journeys of making meaning with the photographs. Thus, they are not final interpretations but beginnings of continuous transactional processes. From this it follows that we do not intend to evaluate or analyze the students' evocations but rather to illustrate the transactional processes taking "reader," photograph, and the situation of the museum visit into account.

The *carte de visite* photograph below portrays the scars on the back of an enslaved African American named Gordon, or "Whipped Peter" (Figure 12.1). Gordon escaped from a Louisiana plantation and joined the Union army. The photographs of him and the damage from the whippings were published and provided evidence of the brutality of slavery and the treatment of slaves.

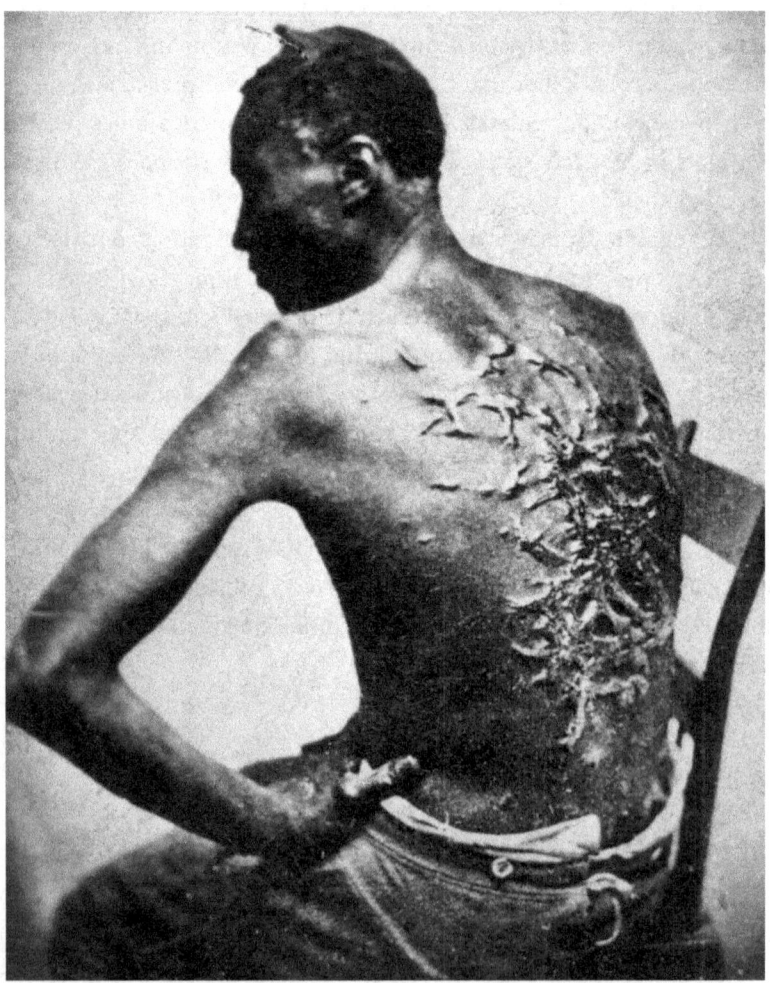

Figure 12.1 Whipped Peter.

One student writes:

> I am choosing the picture of "Whipped Peter". This picture immediately caught my attention, and I did not manage to let it out of my mind. It is extremely powerful and terrifying, almost haunting. It feels like one of the most tangible proofs of the cruelty that existed (and still exists) during this time. It also stands out and is effective because it is found among "milder" images. The scar looks a bit like blood vessels, or like the tree of life, or a map. Mainly the map. The scar makes him look barely human, but that was exactly what the racists/slaveholders wanted you to believe. "All men are created equal!" Whipped Peter was created like everyone else, but was shaped by slavery into something different.

This student note reflects a continuous dialogue with the photograph. The lines "It immediately caught my attention and I did not manage to let it out of my mind" reveals that this photograph has lingered and stayed with the student. The selection is made due to a poignant experience and the student also comments on the fact that this image stood out in the context of the exhibition. By encountering the image of "Whipped Peter," the student becomes an emotional and moral subject who reacts and objects to the cruelties of slavery and injustice. Also, the transaction leads the student to conduct a poetic interpretation of the photograph, paying detailed attention to the pattern of the back depicted in the photograph: "The scar looks a bit like blood vessels, or like the tree of life, or a map. Mainly the map." Here we can see that the student shifts perspectives starting from the exhibition and the context in which the photograph is noticed. The photograph is selected in relation to the surrounding other displayed "milder" objects by being "powerful" and "terrifying" to the student. Through the analysis of the details of the back the student is coming to the conclusion of the slave being dehumanized as a consequence of the system of slavery. In Rosenblatt's terminology, the note illustrates how the student is crafting the "work" in a nonlinear way as an event in the particular place of the Nobel Prize Museum in the context of the museum education program. Also, the photograph and its qualities are guiding the student's journey toward making meaning of both the photograph per se in the context of the exhibition and the historical context of the photograph. As such the student is actively participating not only in the educational activity within the context of the museum but also "in the photograph".

In contrast, another student writes the following while encountering the same photograph:

I think the picture shows how the slaves were treated and how they are abused in their daily lives. It is a very old picture that shows what the slaves' backs can look like. The man in the picture is perhaps 35-40 years so it shows how a slave is beaten for over 30 years.

Here, the student is not as personally involved as in the previous example. Instead this student is trying to come to a conclusion, to an understanding of what it is that is there. This student is not using personal thoughts, ideas, and feelings to make meaning of what is encountered. Thus, the photograph is not transformed into an "object work" and as such it does not cease to be an exhibition object.

Figure 12.2 Black Students Integrate Little Rock's Central High School (Bettman via Getty Images).

The iconic image above portrays Elisabeth Eckford on her way to her first school day in Little Rock Central High School, Little Rock, Arkansas, in 1957 (Figure 12. 2). Following the *Brown v. Board of Education,* racial segregation in public schools was declared unconstitutional. However, segregation did not disappear and it took a long time until African American students could safely attend previously segregated schools. Elizabeth Eckford was one of nine African American students, later known as the Little Rock Nine, who tried to enter the school that day. In this image we can see how Elizabeth Eckford is followed by a white mob protesting against her as she enters the school building.

One student writes:

My attention was caught by an image of a dark-skinned woman on her way to school being persecuted by adult white people. I feel sad that the world once looked this way. I feel equally grateful that I did not grow up in such a climate. But I also feel grateful for the way we learn from history. That I get to learn from this, everything that has happened, to be able to see how far the world has come today. That we do not repress history but can learn and grow based on our mistakes. Become stronger as the human race. The picture evokes emotions in me. This visit today has also given me a deeper understanding of the sick racism that was and the importance of not letting it happen again and the importance of the equal value of all people. And my own role in it today when exclusion and racism actually exist.

This note reflects dialogue between the student and what is portrayed in the photograph which goes even further than the first student above. The beginning: "My attention was caught by … " implies an active choice and selection within the context of the museum exhibition. By encountering Elisabeth Eckford and the surrounding mob of people, the student draws on personal experiences and feelings ("I feel sad," "I feel … grateful") to make meaning of both the past, him- or herself, and the present world, still marked by "exclusion" and "racism." Accordingly, the student is elaborating and expanding on personal feelings to create relations between feelings about the past and feelings about the present. As such, this particular photograph sparks the student to take a route that is not directly related to the event illustrated in the selected photograph but to more general and broad considerations. Quite early on the student expresses gratitude for being given the opportunity to "learn from history." The emotional starting point of the transaction is moving into a reflection of having gained "deeper understanding" during the museum visit which leads to a personal reflection on the student's own role in present-day society.

These are just three illustrations of the transactional process by which the museum visitors engaged with the exhibited museum objects. As we have seen these processes take different routes—the evocations differ in stance, to use Rosenblatt's words. In the second example above the student's focus is on describing the photograph. This is what Rosenblatt (1994) defines as a more efferent stance to the reading of the photograph: "The reading which results in the literary work of art requires something more than an ordinary putting-together of clues"(51). The two other examples represent evocations of a more aesthetic character: "The aesthetic stance provides the differentiating factor as the reader builds up and contemplates a unique synthesis of his responses which is for him the poem" (51). The first student goes deep into the image to create a relation between the image and the past, while the third student is creating a relation between the event portrayed in the image and the student's own life. However, both these evocations are built on engagement and emotional involvement. The students were not given much time for reading and commenting on the photographs and it was not possible for them develop the texts further during the museum visit. However, these short spontaneous evocations tell us something about what the exhibition means for the students and how aesthetic readings within the museum education program give the students the opportunity to explore both the museum objects and themselves.

The Museum as Exploration

In this section, we elaborate a view of the museum as exploration based on the triadic relationship of museum visitor, exhibition object, and "object work." Recall, Louise Rosenblatt's transactional theory of reading and writing highlights the idea that the meaning of a text emerges transactionally. This means that we cannot leave out the reader, the text, or the situation to understand meaning-making. They are mutually interconnected. Transferred to museums this means that meaning is not inherent in exhibitions or in displayed objects but is constituted in transactions of museum visitors, museum exhibitions, their exhibited objects, and the specific situation of the museum visit. Much research within the field of museum studies has concerned the visitors on the one hand and the design of exhibitions and museum objects on the other. The importance of designing engaging museum exhibitions can, if transferred to the realm of literature, be compared to the role the author has in writing an engaging novel. However, from a transactional point of view, no matter how well written a novel is or how creative and welcoming a museum exhibition is, their meaning cannot be clarified without taking the readers or visitors into account.

According to Rosenblatt, a text does not mean anything in itself but when encountered by a reader the text is transformed into the "literary work" which consists of the meshing of the text and the reader. Drawing on this line of thought, museum objects displayed in exhibitions need to be encountered and evoked to be transformed into what we call "object work." For this evocation to take place, museum objects need to be encountered and transactionally meshed together with the visitor's previous experiences and whatever occupy the "reader" of the object at the time of the encounter. Considering this from a pedagogical point of view, it becomes important to stage encounters among exhibited objects and visitors that encourages them to explore both the objects and themselves, that is encourage them to take an aesthetic stance. In the illustrations envisaged in this chapter, we have seen how students actively engage in crafting their own meaning of the displayed photographs. However, their routes vary and so do their "object works." Some of the students adopt a predominantly efferent stance while others adopt a more aesthetic stance. To conclude, through a transactional perspective we can understand the museum as exploration in which museum objects and exhibitions become important and valuable in relation to how they are encountered, evoked, worked upon, and crafted into personal object works in museum education practice.

13

Aesthetic Experiences and Artistic Creation: A Transactional Analysis of Learning in Computer Programming

Michael Håkansson, Lennart Rolandsson and Leif Östman

Introduction

This chapter presents and illustrates a model for exploring the artistic dimension of teaching and learning and creating knowledge about it. We are motivated by Dewey's claim that artistic expressions and aesthetic experiences are found in the work of both artists and scientists (Dewey 1925/1981: 268). We especially draw on the works of Garrison (1996, 2015) and Andersson, Garrison, & Östman (2018). The latter work presents systematic analyses of the artistic expressions and aesthetic experiences that occur when teaching and learning the school subject of sloyd. In this chapter we expand this work by focusing on the practice of programming in the school subject of mathematics.

In developing the model, we use a transactional methodology, built on Dewey's understanding that we constantly coordinate with the environment in order to maintain transactional harmony with it (Östman & Öhman 2021). For example, if it is raining, we may put on a hat or use an umbrella, if it is too bright, we might wear sunglasses. Whatever the nature of the harmony we are striving for, whether physical, practical, social, and intellectual, etc., both we and the environment are reciprocally and simultaneously co-present in the coordination. Stated differently, the participants in the transaction will find meaning reciprocally and simultaneously.

From a first-person perspective, a transaction consists of a doing and undergoing. A doing is present and becomes meaningful when the person staging the action experiences the consequences of it. The other participant(s) taking part in the doing—for example a stone or a human being—will also acquire meaning and become present in a specific way simultaneously as the doing of the person becomes meaningful. In this sense, the doing and undergoing constitute a unity (Dewey 1934/1987: 54).

When we make ourselves, our actions, and the rest of the world intelligible—in and through transactions—we, as the experiencing subject, will make use of our earlier experiences, and the kind of consequences that we imagine will result from the doing. Dewey explains it like this: "What the live creature retains from the past and what it expects from the future operate as direction in the present" (1934/1987: 24). This means that learning should be understood as making new experiences out of past experiences in a purpose-driven coordinative process consisting of alternating doings and undergoings.

In the following, we first describe the trajectory of learning that takes its departure in Dewey's (1949/1989a) work on the disturbance of habit, inquiry, and experience. In *Art as Experience*, Dewey emphasizes the process of doing and making which we interpret that learning is about doing and making an inquiry. The trajectory of learning begins in a disturbance of habit which require an inquiry; a making to adjust the habit. Dewey distinguishes between two processes of doing and making an inquiry. The first is a creative-artistic inquiry, where the transaction with the material and medium is in core of the process. In our empirical illustration the codes are the material and programming the medium. According to Dewey (1934/1987), a contrasting inquiry is instrumental or mechanical: "a display of technical virtuosity ... and repeats some old model fixed like a blue print in his mind" (57). Then, there is a brief presentation of the analytical method used—practical epistemology analysis (PEA)—in analyzing the empirical illustration of learning the artistic dimension that transpires. We end the chapter with a discussion about the model and the consequences of perceiving learning from a transactional perspective when taking aesthetic experiences and artistic expressions into consideration.

The Trajectory of Learning

We take departure in a model of the trajectory of learning based on Dewey's work on inquiry developed by Östman, Van Poeck, and Öhman (2019a). Here, we develop the model further by identifying the different phases of an inquiry. Figure 1 shows a cut-out, built on Dewey's understanding that life consists of the rhythm of tranquility and disturbance. Consequently, the basic trajectory of learning is as follows: a disturbance of our habitual ways of acting leads to a

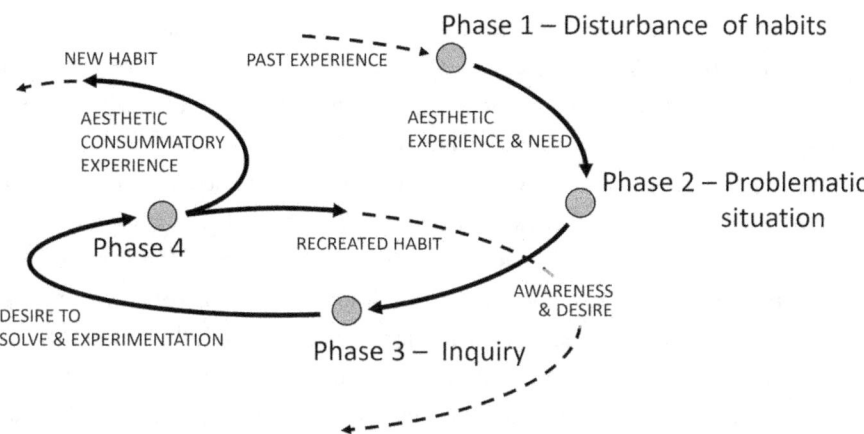

Figure 13.1 The trajectory of learning with four phases.

so-called problematic situation that we as individuals want to understand and solve. We therefore start an inquiry. If the inquiry is successful, learning has occurred and either our old habits are enriched or a new habit develops and thereby, new knowledge, skills, values, and so on are learned. In our explanation of the model we also highlight the transactions that occur in the different phases of the trajectory. We use this model, together with the analytical method of PEA, in our empirical analysis.

Phase 1: An Anoetic Experience of a Disturbance of Habits

The first phase in the trajectory of learning is a non-cognitive immediate aesthetic experience of a disturbance of the students' repertoire of habits. This means that the activity in which they are involved cannot be continued.

Dewey (1925/1981) calls immediate, anoetic (non-cognitive) felt qualities aesthetic experiences, where aesthetics has a meaning close to *aisthetikos*, the old Greek term referring to sentient, feeling, sensitivity, etc. Aesthetic experience occurs through transactions involving the sensory system and the world (Andersson, Garrison, & Östman 2018: 74). What is crucial to notice is that no subjects or objects are established in the transaction: what is established is the qualitativeness of a qualitative whole—what Dewey calls an anoetic experience. It is a pre-subjective experience. Thereby, the anoetic experience makes up the non-cognitive condition (background) for the subsequent reflections and intentional experimentation (phases 2–3) that take place in the trajectory of learning: the cognitive phase of the inquiry remains perpetually *qualified* by the non-cognitive background, or what Dewey also called "the context of thought" (Garrison 2010: 87). According to Dewey (1925/1981), to make the phenomenon of anoetic experience part of our scientific vocabulary we linguistically capture quality from its "immediate qualitativeness" (82).

Consequently, an anoetic experience has to be expressed in terms as, for instance, frustration-ness. For example, when we are frustrated we are not aware of the frustration, but only physically recognize the *quality* of the situation we are involved in, thereby had and felt, but not known. In other words, we feel the "frustration-ness" before we know it. Similar remarks would hold for "fondness" and "disappointment-ness," mentioned below. Thus, we notice the qualitativeness as a bodily (physical) change which, in itself is a discrimination, albeit a physical one, of the anoetic experience of a quality. Therefore, the anoetic experience is the bodily "signal" of a disturbance (Dewey 1934/1987: 20). Consequently, it is only when we know it that we can specify the qualitativeness of it.

Additionally, the qualitativeness of tension is accompanied by a need. This need is an immediate biological response to the tensional situation; there is a need to transformatively restore a fruitful coordination in and with an environment. This can permeate the subsequent phases of the learning trajectory, for example when the need invokes desire and selective interests (Garrison 2010: 92). If we choose to continue the trajectory of learning, the attentiveness to the qualitativeness (phase 1) is transformed into: "caring *for* in the sense of fondness, and through being deeply stirred, over to caring *for* in the sense of *taking* care, looking after, paying attention systematically, or *minding*" (Dewey & Bentley 1949/1989a: 247). Thus, every step of the learning trajectory implies some kind of specific care and concern on the part of the individual student.

Phase 2: A Feeling of the Quality of a Situation as Problematic

This phase is a "point of transition" between the non-cognitive phase and the subsequent cognitive phases (Garrison 1996). The most important characteristic of this phase is that people become aware of the quality of the anoetic experience. In other words, the qualitativeness of tension is transformed into a situation that is cognitively experienced as a specific feeling, i.e., a feeling of the dominant quality. Thus, the need is transactional transformed into a desire to understand and solve.

Furthermore, as an effect of becoming part of the transaction, the quality of the anoetic experience becomes an object of thought. Dewey (1930/1984) expresses it a "the quality, although dumb, has as a part of its complex quality a movement or transition in some direction. It can, therefore, be intellectually symbolized and converted into an object of thought" (254). Here, the effect of the transaction is that a new object—feeling—is established for further transactions. The qualitativeness thus becomes a subject matter (a matter that concerns the subject) and subsequently turns into a feeling. The participants in the transactions are the bodily effects of the whole on the one hand, and the cognition on the other.

Dewey (1925/1981) makes us aware that the transition from non-cognitive (anoetic) to cognitive is transformational:

> Any quality as such is final; it is at once initial and terminal; just what it is as it exists. It may be referred to other things, it may be treated as an effect or as a sign. But this involves an extraneous extension and use. It takes us beyond quality in its immediate qualitativeness.
>
> (82)

Hence, this phase transforms the had and felt tension into something precognitive—in terms of experiencing the quality of the situation as a specific feeling. It is in the transition of becoming an object of thought that the qualitativeness—the had and felt quality—turns into a specific feeling. This is an important shift in the nature of transactions compared to the first stage. However, it is still precognitive because the feeling lacks a discriminatory reference while the direction for how to proceed is intuitive, rather than formulated as a clear end-in-view.

Phase 3: The Problematic Situation Turns into an Inquiry

The desire established in the previous phase can be seen as an engine for inquiry, while the feeling regulates the inquiry in the sense that subsequent cognitive discriminations are dependent on it: the feeling is a subject matter in this phase and acts as a control over ordering the means and ends-in-view. Many new disturbances and sub-inquiries may emerge in the inquiry and emanate from the participants' desires to cognitively understand the feeling. During the inquiry, intuition about how to tackle the problematic situation is developed first into an imagination and then an idea of how to achieve fulfillment. However, as Dewey (1938/1986) remarks, such an idea becomes increasingly precise and concrete as the inquiry continues:

> An idea is first of all an anticipation of something that may happen; it marks a possibility ... Because inquiry is a progressive determination of a problem and its possible solution, ideas differ in grade according to the stage of inquiry reached. At first, save in highly familiar matters, they are vague.
>
> (113)

It is only after the inquiry starts that ends-in-view are established, and it is in the process of inquiry that the problematic situation is eventually transformed into a well-defined problem. The inquiry may involve a number of different participants in the transactions that are staged, although what is characteristic in this phase is that previously acquired knowledge becomes crucial, as does the desire of coming to a closure.

Phase 4. The End of the Inquiry as a Fulfillment of the Problematic Situation

In this phase the inquiry comes to closure. It is accompanied by an aesthetic experience of fulfillment, which can be expressed in immediate expressions as "YES," or similar vocal utterance. Such aesthetical experiences are bodily affects that "marks the realized appreciation of a pervading quality that is now translated into a system of definite and coherent terms" (Dewey 1930/1984: 250). Experiences of fulfillment can also show as gestures, as we do when we score a goal by raising our arms (however, often accompanied with a guttural roar). Bodily affect also occurs if a fulfillment is not reached, but this often manifests as disappointment-ness, or a similar specific negative feeling but still lack a discriminatory reference, thereby require an inquiry. In addition, Dewey says that "[w]hether the necessary undergoing phase is itself pleasurable or painful is a matter of particular condition" (48). The aesthetic experience of fulfillment or non-fulfillment is an experience of the whole process, from desire to the end of the inquiry (Wickman 2006). If the inquiry is successful it is often a process that is something worth remembering—it constitutes *an* experience (Dewey 1934/1987).

The Artistic Inquiry and Other

In *Art as Experience* (1934/1987), Dewey distinguishes between skilled and artistic craftsmanship. However, in our empirical illustration, we find a third inquiry which have several similarities with an artistic inquiry, for instance a wholeheartedly aesthetical engagement in the educational activity. The difference lies mainly in the nature of the purpose and desire. In this third inquiry the purpose is induced by the teacher. Thus, we expand Dewey's two inquiries, by constructing a third inquiry between instrumental and artistic inquiry. We call it a creative inquiry. In creative inquiry engagement springs from a student's transaction in and with the purpose induced by the teacher while in an artistic inquiry the purpose springs from a students' transaction with the material and medium. In artistic inquiry the desire springs from an entirely personal orientation. Thereby, the personal vision becomes invested in the inquiry. This *personal* investment is not part of a creative inquiry to the same extent as in artistic inquiry since it is influenced by the teacher's purposes.

Above, we described how we construct a third category—a creative craftsmanship, by situating the skilled and artistic craftsmanship into the trajectory of learning above described. The three different inquiries—artistic, creative, and instrumental—are constructed regarding the nature of the purpose-driven coordination, i.e., the craftsperson's desire for doing the work. In other words, the need to adjust the disturbed habit emerges in three different desires for doing an inquiry. In order to get a sense of the different inquiries, an analogy is used.

Imagine three different potters are making a vase. An artistic potter makes the vase as an expression of a feeling when walking in a lava-landscape. The potter has a personal vision and a desire to express that feeling, thereby the inquiry includes artistic craftsmanship. The creative potter experiments with different clay, perhaps commissioned by a company, with a specific desire to create a more sustainable vase. The instrumental potter works in a kind of industrial production and makes vases in the way they have done hundreds of times before. The potter's desire is to finish and receive payment (award). If we analyze the three potters, we can say that the first makes use of a personal feeling as the vision expressed in the vase. This work involves artistic inquiry. The second potter tries to find a way to solve a practical issue; here the inquiry is creative but does not include any attempt to express a personal vision. In order to solve any issues that occur, the third potter makes use of a habitual inquiry to solve them. The inquiry will involve skilled craftsmanship, but does not have the purpose of creating something new or expressing a personal feeling or vision and is in this sense an instrumental inquiry. In the end, this third potter experiences the process of making as a blueprint of a vase, which has been created by someone else (e.g., a company), both regarding design and clay.

If we turn to the educational setting and the trajectory of learning, the third potter would translate into a student who takes on a task as instructed without having any desire to be creative or expressive themselves. The inquiry is done for external reasons, for example to get a good grade, although done in a skilled way. While experiencing a disturbance, the desire that is developed is institutionally driven (a student's desire to have a good grade). The relation to the subject matter—the feeling—is indirect because the relation is driven by an external force—the hope of getting a good grade—and not by caring about or having any concern for the subject matter. Dewey (1916/1980) clarifies:

> The [student's] problems are not his: or, rather, they are his only as a [student], not as a human being. … His problem becomes that of finding out what the teacher wants, what will satisfy the teacher in recitation and examination and outward deportment. Relationship to subject matter is no longer direct.
>
> (163)

In artistic inquiry there is direct care for the subject matter, and the desire involves a personal vision grounded in an experienced feeling. An artistic inquiry is "dependent on our affective, caring, and concerned involvement in the antecedent qualitative situation" (Garrison 1996: 403). It is because of this personal trait that an artistic inquiry also involves "yourself": a personal vision to be expressed through the material being worked with. In an artistic inquiry, the inquirer cannot calculate in advance what kinds of effects will be produced and then produce them. If the inquirer could make such a calculation, there would be no need for an inquiry. In relation to artistic inquiry, Dewey (1934/1987) explains:

> The artist is compelled to be an experimenter, because he has to express an intensely individualized experience through means and materials that belong to the common and public world. This problem cannot be solved once for all. It is met in every new work undertaken. Otherwise, an artist repeat himself and becomes esthetically dead.
>
> (149–50)

A creative inquiry (the second potter in the example above) shares most of the traits of an artistic inquiry except for one—the desire to express a personal vision that is grounded in a feeling in the material being worked with. Thereby, the personal vision becomes invested in the inquiry. This investment is not part of a creative inquiry, at least not to the same extent.

Analytical Method

For the empirical examples in this chapter we use PEA as an analytical method. PEA was developed by Wickman and Östman (2002), inspired by the later work of Wittgenstein, and is well suited for delivering empirical findings for use in a transactional theory (Andersson, Garrison, & Östman 2018; Shilling 2018; Östman & Öhman *forthcoming*). The reason for this fit is Wittgenstein's first-person perspective on language, which makes it possible to identify what stands fast for people in a situation—previously acquired experiences, knowledge, skills, values, and so on. The focus in PEA is to concretely investigate how the world is made intelligible and meaningful in actions or in encounters with the world. The analytical procedure is to identify and describe the:

a) lingering *gaps* that occur when people encounter a world in an activity. Lingering gaps becomes visible when they hesitate, ask questions, or start to guess, thereby indicating that the activity can continue.
b) *encounters* that are staged in order to bridge a gap, for example encounters with a book, a teacher, a friend.
c) *relations* that are construed in the encounters that are staged (b). The relations that are construed relate to what stands fast (habits) for each person, and are described as relations construed to what stands fast in the environment that becomes present in the encounter.

The empirical material consists of video recordings of lessons in a computer programming course for beginners at an upper secondary school. The set task for the students was to make a digital version of "noughts and crosses." The game was constructed in eight steps, where each step took one lesson to complete. Between the different steps the teacher delivered a solution that helped the students stay on track. We use the fifth lesson for analysis, and the students work on a specific sub-task to create the code for a message dialog box (MDB) that would announce who won the game.

What is important to highlight is that when programming the result of each attempt to solve a task by entering codes is shown on the screen in terms of right and wrong. This often creates an anoetic—immediate aesthetic—experience, here shown by students using expressions of like and dislike. Due to limited space, we have chosen to use part of the analysis of the lesson to illustrate the results.

Analysis and Results

At the beginning of the assignment, three boys were engaged in an inquiry in which the disturbance of their habits was induced by the teacher. During the lesson, engagement was shown by many expressions of aesthetic experiences of fulfillment. During the inquiry, several sub-inquiries had to be staged when sub-problems, or lingering gaps, were encountered during the main inquiry. One example is shown in the following transcript, where the students are in the process of inserting a MDB (row 1). This involved inserting a code in the program so that when a player got three markers in a row the MDB displayed that this person had won.

1   Olle: I suggest that in our next step we add a message dialog box. Do you agree?
2   Jan: Yes, but we do all this first.
3   Olle: Ok, we'll put that on hold for a while.
4   Jan: Are you ready? Let's execute the code …

They agreed that they had to finish the sub-task that they were engaged in first, and that this was necessary before trying to bridge the gap by inserting a MDB. They struggled, experimented, and tested different ideas. Their failure was displayed on the screen, which made Harald (row 36) express a negative consummatory experience.

36   Harald: Come on! [when waiting for the result to come up on the screen] No! It failed.

They continued to experiment and then waited for the result to show on the screen. Olle (row 44), and perhaps also Harald (row 45), expressed an aesthetic experience of fulfillment—"perfect"—when the message on the screen showed that this time the code was correct. As they had achieved what they wanted to achieve, they could now focus on what came next, namely, bridging the gap of inserting a MDB (rows 46–8). Olle came up with an idea about where in the coding the MDB should be situated, which Harald agreed with (row 48).

44   Olle: No, it works! Yes, perfect. It works anyhow!
45   Harald: Yes.

46 Jan: Do we need some …
47 Olle: We need to create a message dialog box [simultaneously], but it has to be down there, doesn't it? [points to the screen and to a specific line of the code]
48 Harald: Yes, I agree!

In the above conversation we can see that many words and utterances stand fast for the students (such as getting a MDB to work properly). The technical vocabulary of programming is not shown here because a detailed explanation would be needed to make it intelligible to those unfamiliar with programming practice. What is important here is that bodily actions stand fast for them, such as how to use the keyboard, or where to look to find out whether the programming has been done correctly.

What we can see in rows 44 and 45 is that the encounters that occurred were between Olle and the screen and between Olle and Harald. When Olle encountered the screen and had an aesthetic consummatory experience, he construed a relation to what stood fast for him—a relation to the result shown on the screen: "Yes, perfect. It works anyhow!" Thus, in the transaction involving the result shown on the screen, a feeling of satisfaction—"perfect"—occurred with regard to the situation as a whole: "it works anyhow." This utterance refers to the entire process, from a problematic situation and the inquiry to the result of the inquiry, where "it" refers to the programming that is done and "it works" indicates that a problematic situation has been solved.

Jan's utterance (row 46) was vague, but in line 47, Olle transacted with the code on the screen, thereby constructing a relation between the MDB and its specific location in the code (on the screen). Also Harald constructed this specific relation by saying "yes."

During the lesson the inquiry and sub-inquiries were characterized by some of the participants coming up with ideas about how to proceed with the coding, agreeing to try it out, and waiting for the result on the screen to show whether the coding was correct or not. When it was indicated as correct, they expressed an aesthetic consummatory experience of successful closure.

In the following conversation (rows 49 and 50) we can see a shift in the inquiry from a creative to an artistic one. In the sub-inquiry of which this conversation is a part, the students suggested two different ways of inserting the code for a MDB in order to succeed. Olle had one idea and argued for it (row 49). Jan, on the other hand, did not agree with it (row 50).

In this conversation, and also for the remainder of the lesson, the efficiency of the coding became regulative. But this was not part of the task that the teacher

49 Olle: But I think that is the most efficient way of doing it.
50 Jan: That way is not efficient. It is better to work …

had set for the students. Thereby, the end-in-view became part as a personal vision, which occurred from Olle's transaction with the code. Efficiency also became a gap for the whole group that they then tried to bridge, at the same time as trying to solve the task set by the teacher. For them efficiency meant avoiding unnecessary codes, which Olle expressed in the following utterance:

178 Olle: … As it is, we are in a situation where we have to act in a way that we have tried to avoid, as we knew our goal in the first place. In short, we have to add an abundance of codes … in vain.

Interestingly, after a while efficiency became connected to an expression of the qualities of beautiful and ugly. The first time it appeared was when Jan commented on a coding that had been executed after trying one of the ideas out.

208 Jan: Damn how handsome!

After this utterance, the felt qualities of beautiful and ugly were collectively attended to in subsequent sub-inquiries, in that the students suggested ideas, tried them out, and evaluated the results in terms of these qualities. These qualities were part of a feeling connected to the amount of unnecessary code. In the end the students arrived at a solution to the teacher's task, which included inserting a MDB. When it was confirmed on the screen that they had completed the task of inserting the MDB in the right way, the following conversation took place:

351 Jan: shitty beautiful, shitty beautiful, I am amazed …
352 Olle: But it is only good enough as long as it works, but still not as beautiful! But could we be satisfied with the result so far?
353 Harald: I don't know
354 Jan: Ok, but I am satisfied

In the above, Jan (row 351) expressed a consummatory experience in relation to the message on the screen. Olle agreed that it was good but added that the code was still not beautiful and ended with a question to his colleagues about whether or not they were satisfied. Harald hesitated about making a judgment, whereas Jan confirmed that he was satisfied.

Olle continued to suggest how the coding could be made more beautiful. Harald (row 362) counteracted Olle's idea, but Jan (row 363) was quite happy with the already-existing code and made the judgment that "it's not that ugly." Olle (row 364) responded by agreeing with Jan that the structure of the coding was beautiful, but not all that beautiful because it contained too much code.

362 Harald: It will not be more beautiful
363 Jan: Listen, it's not that ugly [giggling] at all
364 Olle: It's not, it is beautifully indented, it looks like everything is indented. I don't like it as there is too much code [laughing]
365 Jan: Yes, there is too much code
366 Olle: yes!
367 Jan: It could be solved …
368 Olle: But how? That is my question … (silence for three seconds). How could it be solved? Harald?

They continued to suggest different ideas for a minute or two but as none were judged satisfactory, they were never tested. Thus, although the students never reached an aesthetic experience of fulfillment in the artistic inquiry, they did manage to solve the task given by the teacher.

In the last two sequences, the transaction that occurred involved students themselves, the code on the screen, as well as the keyboard. In the transactions many different relations were created to what stood fast for them. Those that we particularly want to highlight here are connected to their expressions of beauty and ugliness: code on the screen—shitty beautiful (row 362); it will not be more beautiful (row 365); code on the screen—too much code (row 368). These examples show that certain feelings and judgments were present in the transactions involving the actual codes on the screen, but also the ideas about a specific coding. In this way, the feeling of beauty or ugliness was regulatory for the experimentation and the discriminations (certain signs were used in the coding and others were not) made in the inquiry.

Conclusion

Above we illustrate a transactional methodology designed for systematic, transparent, and high-resolution analyses of the artistic dimension of teaching and learning based on the philosophical works of Dewey and Wittgenstein. The analysis illustrates that such a methodology delivers empirically grounded insights into the importance of aesthetic experiences and artistic expressions for students' inquiries and learning. By situating an artistic dimension of doing inquiry into the trajectory of learning we constructed an inquiry which is similar to an artistic inquiry but differs regarding the nature of the purpose-driven coordination. By encouraging artistic inquiries means that students develop as humans when they become increasingly interested in and care about the subject matter in terms of material and medium. Hence, we argue that the artistic dimension transforms the inquiry from caring for the subject matter to a caring that also involves caring for the human subject. At the same time, the students learn important basic knowledge and skills. What is perhaps even more impressive, they successively develop a highly crucial skill in programming—making judgments about what is beautiful and ugly in coding. In addition, a crucial challenge, in terms of teaching, is that what is knowledgeable, skilled, creative, and artistic expression in a practice is not always a matter of a sequential development, but instead appears to develop, as our analysis shows, as companions.

14

A Transactional Perspective on Ethics and Morals

Louise Sund and Johan Öhman

Introduction

This chapter explores John Dewey's transactional perspective on ethics and morals as a situated practice. We take a closer look at Dewey's critique of traditional morality where moral standards and fixed ethical principles form the fundamental bases for morality, and his commitment to reflective morality, the experimental method, and the importance of engaging moments of resistance in our experiences to confront a morally problematic situation. From a transactional viewpoint moral habits are shaped in transaction with our natural, social, and cultural environment. The transactional perspective implies that morality is a learning process and we make moral progress by reflectively revising our moral habits. This is illustrated by the aid of empirical material where a teacher experiences a moral situation, inquires intelligently into the problematic situation she faces, considers consequences, and comes to value what proves to be valuable by the end of the inquiry.

Dewey's Criticism of Traditional Ethical Theories

This section addresses some of John Dewey's criticism of the reductive nature of traditional ethical theories and shows how his criticism stems from a naturalistic and pluralistic approach to philosophy and ethical theory.

In the 1930 essay *Three Independent Factors in Morals* (Dewey 1930/1984) and in *Ethics* (Dewey 1932/1985), Dewey elaborates on his critique on approaches relying upon non-empirical, a priori claims for determining moral issues and argues that normative ethical theory falls short in the task of doing justice to moral experience. The issue of what ends an individual should live for does not arise as a *general problem* in morality but is affected by an individual's habits and social context (Dewey 1932/1985: 183–4). Dewey claims that different ethical theories only emphasize *one* factor which produces a one-sided view (based on principles of the good, the right, *or* the virtuous). Instead Dewey argues that these principles should rather be used as tools or hypotheses to be tried. Dewey (1932/1985) writes: "No theory can operate in a vacuum. Moral as well as physical theory requires a body of dependable data, and a set of intelligible working hypotheses" (178). We need, Dewey holds "the presence of moral perplexity, of doubt as to what is right or best to do" for a systematic raising of an issue (1932/1985: 164). As Dewey (1938) sees it, "to set up a problem that does not grow out of an actual situation is to start on a course of dead work" and he explains that the way the problem is seen decides what ought to be done among alternative ways of acting (108). As each case is unique and conditions are constantly changing Dewey rejects the idea that universal moral rights and rules can determine the right choice. A fixation of morality would deprive us of the ability of judging any value and will eventually face moral chaos.

Dewey's Alternative: Reflective Morality

The starting point of Dewey's reflective morality is practical—moral problems cannot be solved solely on the basis of ethical principles. In the preface of *Ethics*, Dewey (1932/1985) and Tufts state that the true significance of their work lays "in its efforts to awaken a vital conviction of the genuine reality of moral problems and the value of reflective thought in dealing with them" (5). So, one could say that Dewey's focus is on what the individual might "do of" ethical theory in terms of giving (philosophical) answers to concrete moral problems, or to give attention to both the philosophical theorizing and the practical character of moral reflection itself. Pappas (2019) explains that from the pragmatic pluralist approach there are as many problems of injustice as there are morally problematic situations suffered in a particular way (245). Thus, as a strong pluralist, Dewey proposes a shift to a non-ideal starting point for moral and social inquiry where values have to be judged based on the particular purposes and contexts that generated them.

Dewey holds that "an alternative to fixity in habits and principles is change and continuity of growth" (Pappas 2008: 50). Dewey is an *experimentalist* and a *pluralist* and claims that moral theory can only emerge through *reflective morality*, that is the "conscious and systematic raising of the question which occupies the mind of any one who in the face of moral conflict and doubt seeks a way out through reflection" (1932/1985: 164).

Dewey (1932/1985) subscribes to a situational, contextual, and consequential ethics and points out that "reflective morality demands observation of particular situations, rather than fixed adherence to a priori principles" (329). Consequently, Dewey believes that experience and inquiry should influence morality. In this way morality can be continuously evolving as we are constantly exposed to situations of insecurity and conflict where we are forced to reflect on our choices. Following Dewey, we cannot identify an ultimate end or supreme principle that can serve as a criterion for ethical evaluation in all situations as this would hinder this development and we would become insensitive to the circumstances of the *particular* situation. Thus, morality is about meaningful reflections on specific situations and consequently something we need to *learn*. The self can change itself by reflecting on and altering its own habits and that means we grow and adapt to new experiences. In this way can create a repertoire of *moral habits* (see below).

The relationship between the self and action Dewey understands by considering the nature of choice, e.g. when you weigh the values of various ends. The key to morality is "the essential unity of self and its acts" (Dewey 1932/1985: 288). In choosing to act, you are also choosing what kind of person (or self) you are going to be. This changes everything and not just in morality. In this unity of self (character) and action the environment plays an important role (see Alexander 1993). Dewey sees ethics as existing in and through our actions, as interconnected with everyday life and as always situated in the interface of person and context (Dewey 1922; Pappas 2008). In this way Dewey challenges the idea that morals are something that we have and are hidden in the minds of human beings. In Dewey's words mind has the ability to think, adapt, and adjust to problems. Mind, or a self, "is an agency of novel reconstruction of a pre-existing order" (Dewey 1929/1958: 217). This view of mind as a *process* Dewey continued in *Art as Experience* (1934/1980) where mind "denotes every mode and variety of interest in, and concern for, things: practical, intellectual, and emotional. / ... / Mind is primarily a verb. It denotes all the ways in which we deal consciously and expressly with the situations in which we find ourselves" (263).

Thus, from a transactional perspective morality is a continuous process and a matter of how we, in everyday lived experience, coordinate or (re)direct our actions with other people. The essence of this process is our systematic and critical reflection of the consequences of our actions on other humans, nonhumans, and environmental systems in various situations in life.

Moral Experience

For Dewey (1930/1984), a problematic situation, or a *moral experience*, contains elements "of uncertainty and of conflict" where we are ambiguous about how to value our possible actions or our actions yield unsatisfactory consequences (279). When our functioning is disrupted it often takes a great deal of inquiry to actually determine the "problem." A moral experience is accordingly described as one in which the individual "is ignorant of the end and of the good consequences, of the right and just approach, of the direction of virtuous conduct, and that one must search for them" (280). Thus, it is the *search* for the right and the just that gives reflective morality its meaning.

Dewey holds that uncertainty and conflict arise because of the complexity of discovering what is good, right, or virtuous. For Dewey, the more care an individual expends on "the moral quality" of her moral acts, the more "aware of the complexity of this problem of discovering what is good" she will have. Dewey goes on to say that "he [sic] hesitates among ends, all of which are good in some measure, among duties which obligate him [sic] for some reason. Only after the event, and then by chance, does one of the alternatives seem simply good morally or bad morally" (1930/1984: 279). Since what is regarded as the good or bad aspects of a *particular* situation depend on which alternatives arise, Dewey's moral conception brings a situated, contextual dimension into view.

When we deal with moral situations, we relate action and consequence to our earlier experience; it is a trans-action. Dewey referred to the role of continuity of experience in determining the value of an experience. He contended that "from this point of view, the principle of continuity of experience means that every experience both takes up something from those which have gone before and modifies in some way the quality of those which come after" (Dewey 1938/1997: 35). This means that not only do we recall our earlier experiences to (re)solve a moral dilemma, but that these habits and experiences are also crucial for how we recognize the dilemma in the first place (see Sund & Öhman 2014).

Re-actualizing our *moral habits* allows us to recognize and deal with moral situations. Habits as understood by Dewey goes deeper than the ordinary idea of habits as more or less fixed ways of doing things: "It covers the formation of attitudes, attitudes that are emotional and intellectual; it covers our basic sensitivities and ways of meeting and responding to all the conditions which we meet in living" (Dewey 1938/1997: 35). Our habits form our character, or rather we are structured and characterized by our habits. For Dewey (1922), habits have the power to override "our formal resolutions, our conscious decisions" because habits are so "intimately a part of ourselves" and have a hold upon us "because we are the habit" (21). Thus, from a Deweyan perspective our moral habits are basically the same as our *moral beliefs*. Our moral habits, or the way we (trans)act, are the best representation of our morality (what we value and believe is right and wrong).

When we find ourselves in a moral situation where our habits cannot guide us and we are torn between opposed courses of action based on previous experience, we have to reflect on the consequences of our actions. In such a situation where our habits meet resistance from our environment and are challenged, we are forced to reflect on our primary (embodied, emotional) moral experiences. Resistance brings us into a state of doubt which "open us up to questioning our taken-for-granted ideas and habitual ways of being" (English 2016: 1048). In other words, doubt and uncertainty can spark the drive to resolve problems and initiate a moral situation.

But, as argued by Ryan (2003), directionless doubt "gains no traction in a transactional world" (26). And when doubt sticks and evokes inquiry in order to determine what I ought to do in a particular situation, moral deliberation is necessary: "I must ask myself whether what I like, desire, or value *really is* likeable, desirable, or valuable" (Ryan 2011: 66). Pappas (2008) describes moral deliberation as "*a phase in a process of transforming* a morally problematic situation into a determined one" (94, our italics). However, it is worth pointing out, as Ryan (2011) does, that systematic thinking/inquiry is only intermittent as the default mode of everyday experience is more nonreflective than reflective. It is only in response to a problem "that nonreflective experience is shocked into cognitive awareness" (41).

The ability to reflect on why and what one does is vital to intelligent practice. Dewey (1910/1991) believes that such processes are necessitated in and by any problematic situation, or what he refers to as "a forked-road situation, a situation which is ambiguous, which presents a dilemma, which proposes alternatives" (11). Thus, a state of doubt and perplexity is crucial and fosters reflective thinking. We here find it important to make a distinction between a moral problem and a moral dilemma. A moral problem denotes any situation where we are uncertain about what constitutes the right and just response. A moral dilemma is a situation where two or more exclusive alternatives immediately appear, and we are in doubt about which one to choose. Thus, a dilemma is a problem in which a difficult choice has to be made where there is no clear solution. The reason for our doubt can be that there exist either several good alternatives or several bad alternatives (see Rhees 1970/1996).

In situations of uncertainty and conflict, Dewey draws attention to our *imaginative* capacity to reflect, and how we can imagine ourselves doing something and still understand the consequences of different actions and ends (Alexander 1993; Fesmire 2003). In *Ethics* (Dewey 1932/1985), Dewey remarks that in "imaginative rehearsal" it is possible to try different outcomes, "in our mind" that can illuminate and open up a situation so that it is seen in a new light: "Through various steps, we find ourselves in imagination in the presences of the consequences that would follow" (275). Like Dewey's call to imagine ourselves doing and trying out different things, Peirce stresses the element of surprise which is essential to his notion of experience and to think otherwise, according to Pollard (2008). Peirce describes experience as a conversation with the self and what is not yet known, accelerated by surprise as that which forces changes to habits, "thus making the study of surprise a central feature of reflective practice" (Pollard 2008: 399). Also drawing on Dewey's account of our imaginative capacity to reflect, English (2016) underlines how imagination helps us reflectively engage moments of resistance in our experiences.

Moral inquiry processes can have several different outcomes (see Van Poeck, Östman, & Öhman 2019). If the situation experienced reveals aspects that we have never approached or thought of before, the ethical reflection may result in an adjustment, nuancing, or enrichment of our previous moral habits. If we repeatedly meet these new aspects, we could even form new moral habits. But it might also be the case that although we discover new aspects of moral life—we are unable to find a morally proper/right response and thus the problem lingers and "the experience had is inchoate" (Dewey, 1934/1980: 17).

Person–Environment Transactions

For Dewey, experience is what it is because of a transaction involving an individual and what constitutes its specific environment. In other words, the environment is "whatever conditions interact with personal needs, desires, purposes, and capacities to create the experience which is had" (Dewey 1938/1997: 43–4).

Thus, Dewey uses transaction to theorize the complex integration of self and environment (including the natural, social, and cultural environment).

Dewey (1916) draws a distinction between environment and what he calls surroundings. According to Dewey, environment denotes something more than surroundings. The environment pertains to "the specific *continuity* of the surroundings with his [*sic*] own active tendencies" (15). It is not everything that surrounds us, but rather the things with which a person "varies," that are one's "genuine environment" (ibid.): "In brief, the environment consists of those conditions that promote or hinder, stimulate or inhibit, the characteristic activities of a living being" (ibid.). In Dewey's view environment is a *process* where we actively can co-create and reorganize ourselves through our actions and "environing conditions" (Dewey 1934/1980: 35; Dewey 1938/1997: 44). Thus, as human beings we are deeply interconnected with the world in processes which consist of interrelated aspects (ways) where we in a literal sense become what we do and feel: "Life activities flourish and fail only in connection with changes of the environment. They are literally bound up with these changes; our desires, emotions, and affections are but various ways in which our doings are tied up with the doings of things and persons about us" (Dewey 1916: 132).

The situational orientation of moral problem-solving refers to a transformation of both person and environment. Ryan (2011) describes transaction as an entire (organism–environment) system where the individual is *transactionally* interrelated with environment and formed within a set of relations, rather than an external environment (34–5).

Dewey (1922) found that we develop our habits by transactionally integrating them with "the support of environing conditions" (17). Our moral habits Dewey describes as "working adaptations of personal capacities with environing forces" (16), which means that we dynamically reconstruct our habits through an environing process (Cf. Van Poeck 2019).

It is important to keep in mind that moral habits are inevitably social (Dewey 1932/1985: 316). They are shaped biologically and socio-culturally and reconstructed and reformed within the environment as a result of transaction *in* and *through* the exchange with others.

The Value of Ethical Theory

As we have seen, Dewey is critical of the idea of universal moral principles. However, this does not mean that he totally rejects the value of ethical theory.

Dewey (1932/1985) means that each type of theory has a unique and permanent value which contributes to the "clarification and direction of reflective morality" (183):

> A genuinely reflective morals will look upon all the codes as possible *data*; it will consider the conditions under which they arose; the methods which consciously or unconsciously determined their formation and acceptance; it will inquire into their applicability in present conditions. It will neither insist dogmatically upon some of them, nor idly throw them all away as of no significance. It will treat them as a storehouse of information and possible indications of what is now right and good.
>
> (179)

Thus, the moral framework Dewey provides is *non-reductive* (to one single end and universal good, right, or virtue) and treats ethical theories as *resources* for moral reflection on problematic issues.

Dewey pointed to the need of moving away from ethical theories that normatively prescribe what is right or wrong, and instead deepening our understanding of how humans in their everyday experience try to coordinate their actions with other people. Ethical theory cannot make personal reflective choices *for us*, but it can function as "an instrument for rendering deliberation more effective and hence choice more intelligent" (316).

Dewey rejection of fixed and universal ethical principles should not be perceived as an "anything-goes," relativist perspective. As argued by Hickman (2007), it is reasonable to conclude that it is the pragmatic method, the *experimentalism* of pragmatism, not the scepticism of cognitive relativism, "that provides the better grounds for resolving differences that are rooted in conflicting cultural practices" (45). On the same note, López (2018) argues that Dewey's position on ethics must be understood as a *political* project and for the use of a *scientifically* informed ethical deliberation when people face and handle ethical problems. He concludes that the use of scientific knowledge when dealing with ethics is not only possible but also the best way to address ethical problems—and a project in which education is the key.

Summary: The Circle of Moral Doubt-Belief

From a transactional perspective morality can be seen as a problem-solving activity where our principles and values are tested by experience through an open-ended experimental process of inquiry which has the potential to reveal new challenges and generate new possibilities of human experience. Moral deliberation (and imagination), as a part of that process of forming a judgment and arriving at a choice, is decisive for the chosen/reached disposition or character. Our habits are the tools that guide and help us to define problems. This process of inquiry and its mutually dependent stages in which morals take form can be summarized and illustrated by a revised version of Peirce's circle of doubt-belief (Ryan 2011: 21) (Figure 14.1).

The central concepts of inquiry and experience link to the situating context, that is, the surroundings that give rise to problems. However, it is not everything surrounding us that forms our moral environment. Our moral environment takes shape in the "environing" process where we, as explained by Van Poeck and Östman (this volume), co-create an environment out of the surroundings. The moral environment in this case features the activities that engage our immediate and direct concern or our essential moral interest. Since we are always already transactionally integrated alongside the moral environment, we regularly meet resistance which sometimes makes us doubt our previous habits and open us up to questioning taken-for-granted ideas, habitual ways of being and making sense of the world. Thus, doubts (perplexity, surprise) call forth and spark inquiry, which drives a systematic ethical reflection that might resolve the moral problem. This is a qualitative, ever-changing transformation and a process

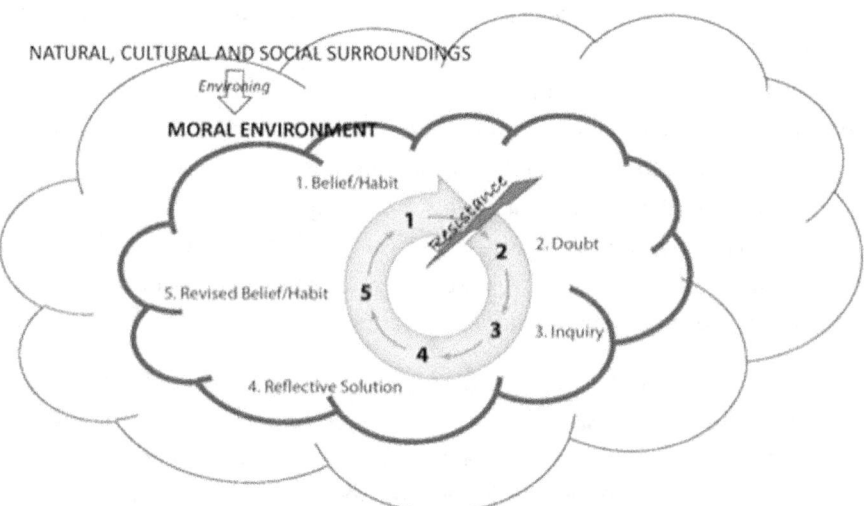

Figure 14.1 The circle of moral doubt-belief (adapted from Ryan 2011: 21).

where principles and values are reached, or where we *try to* reach a useful or satisfactory resolution to our moral problems. At every stage of the inquiry process an individual–environment transaction is taking place. The means that the resolution of a moral problem always emerge as an individual–environment relationship (rather than a resolution existing either in an inner mind or in the outer environment). When the problem is managed and a solution is achieved this solution becomes part of a renewed background of habits.

In its wider sense this process shows, in Dewey's (1902–1903/1976) words, that the "ultimate value of the logic of experience" is resolution of social and moral problems (313).

Engaging Morality from the Transactional View: An Illustration

In the following we will use an authentic event to illustrate how ethical reflections can arise from environment transactions that disturb our accustomed moral habits. The specific example involves a Swedish teacher, Marcia, who took part in a three-week study visit (with a total of 22 teachers) to a country in Central America (Sund & Öhman 2014). Before arriving, the teachers were made aware of the contrast between poor indigenous villagers in the rural highlands and the wealthier, urbanized mestizo population. During the study visit, the teachers lived with rural host families in one of the indigenous communities in the highlands. They took part in local excursions and seminars and conducted field studies on attitudes and values. They were also informed about the villagers' everyday problems and how marginalization and social and economic exclusion contribute to the community's limited opportunities to participate in political processes. Clearly, this is a moral environment very different from the teacher's ordinary life and that is also what sparks moral inquiry.

In the following, Marcia reflects on the values of education and information that she received from the village study centre, namely, that educated young women often leave the village and do not return:

> Well, it is easy to say that women should be educated and so on ... but it impacts their society ... and is that good? Of course this might be good in some respects ... but on the other hand ... you have to consider all that ... things aren't just black or white or yes or no ... it is not only good ... / ... /I mean, I haven't yet seen anyone who is suffering, who suffers or is badly treated, they are confident,

quite happy, very close to their children, if you think of the women that is ... kind of plodding along ... is that wrong ... can we say that is wrong?

(Marcia)

The starting point for moral inquiry is thus a range of conditions and relations enmeshed in the particular context and the actual situation which also forms Marcia's moral environment. From a transactional perspective it is possible to discern how morality arises *in* the moral environment in which the experience is had and *through* transaction between Marcia, people in the village, and the surroundings (the highlands, the study centre, cultural traditions, etc.), and how this interplay leads to a specific way of making meaning of the moral problem.

The conflicting principles in the actual situation are two good values: achieving elementary education for girls and preserving the indigenous way of life in the village.

Although Marcia is not the moral agent who has to make an active decision and solve the situation, she reflects on the complexity of the particular situation and when her moral habits are disrupted she ends up in a situation in which she is able to question one of her own standpoints, that of education as a universal "good," due to the supposed loss of another good—the value of preserving the traditional way of life.

It also becomes visible that it is a specific experience/environment that moves moral inquiry and makes Marcia consider the moral qualities of conflicting values. Marcia's reflection exemplifies Dewey's description of ethics as procedural, pluralistic, and imaginative. When faced with a moral issue we have to reflect on a variety of alternatives. In this case Marcia reflects on a moral experience that does not have any ethically correct or obvious answers with regard to the conflicting values. Marcia uses her capacity to imaginatively deliberate when "things aren't just black or white" and she inquiries into whether the life that the village people lead can be questioned (is that good? "can we say that is wrong?"). In this reflective solution she reaches the position that we do not discover (universal) values outside context and experience. On the contrary, we construct and recreate values *within* experience and the moral environment. Doubt is here an occasion for moral deliberation, and it becomes evident that our moral habits are flexible and open to revision as we face a specific situation. Seeing these questions through the lens of only one perspective would have made Marcia's moral response context insensitive, static, and condemnatory. Understood transactionally, this cultural encounter disrupts Marcia's moral habits and the reflective solution here represents her learning. The example illustrates the importance of taking a critical stance towards universal aspects and concepts and not to marginalize other approaches. The interview with Marcia indicates that the study visit gave rise to comprehensive and varying reflections on moral issues and situations where she was able to recreate personal values and goods through an inquiry.

Consequences for Education

Seeing individuals and environments transactionally is to see them as dynamically interdependent and mutually constitutive. In other words, they are what they are because of their conjoint *relation*. We believe that a transactional perspective on morality can be helpful for teachers in their understanding of ethics and morals in educational practice. An important consequence that can be drawn from a transactional perspective is that value judgments cannot be made in general; you can only make them in particular, by ways of acting and putting them *into* practice. It is, therefore, crucial that value education relates to moral experiences in students' daily lives and uses these as opportunities for further ethical reflection and to discuss the moral consequences of potential actions.

As one's morality is reshaped and adapts to changes in the surrounding world, students can develop new ways to deal with unprecedented challenges (such as cultural loss among indigenous peoples, climate change, and forced migration) if they are allowed to engage in critical ethical reflections, that is, to formulate arguments for their standpoints and moral actions and consider other people's arguments. Thus, it is vital to support students' reflection on (the nature of) their values and relate them to changing cultural and socio-political contexts. This requires a moral sensitivity for the particular context instead of holding on to abstract fixed moral principles. The teacher has an essential role here, namely, to choose and present possible alternatives, clarify purposes in view of what the learning process is expected to pursue, and highlight subject matters and perspectives that may be uncomfortable for the student (Biesta 2013).

The circle of moral doubt-belief (Figure 14.1) can here be useful as a didactical tool for teachers' systematic planning and reflective teaching when engaging in value education. The model suggests that an important starting point is students' environing process where the natural, social, and cultural surroundings become their moral environment. Teachers need to support and facilitate such a process by clarifying and directing students' concern to essential moral issues in their surroundings. The teacher can also provide the resistance that challenges students' moral habits, e.g., by questioning arguments or moral principles and thus facilitate critical modes of reflection. In the further process, teachers can support students in every step—when experiencing *doubt*, structuring *inquiry*, trying out and reflecting on possible *solutions*, and finally, reaching a satisfactory and sound solution and *revised* beliefs/habits to the moral problem or problematic situation.

As noted by Dewey, ethical theory has a unique and situational value when we reflect and deliberate on problematic situations. A vital part of teachers' professional task is therefore to connect students' moral experiences with ethical theories that challenge students' moral thoughts rather than just confirming or rejecting them. And to provide students with an ethical language to create a conversation that way enables students to go from primary moral experiences to a reflective morality (see Öhman & Kronlid 2019).

In this way value education can function as a crucial part of the curriculum where students learn from moral experiences that make them reflect on values that they have previously taken for granted. A transactional perspective on morality also points to the need for creating space for and illuminating the idea that there are multiple perspectives on a given issue—there are different ways of understanding and experiencing the world.

15

Transactional Analyses of the Entanglement of the Aesthetical, Moral and Political in Learning Processes

Michael Håkansson and Leif Östman

Introduction

This chapter presents and illustrates a model for learning moral and political *concerns for* in educational settings. By introducing two analytical principles, it is possible to explore and create knowledge about what and how *concerns for* can become part of educational activities. At the core of this model, we find poignant aesthetic experiences, quality, habit, inquiry, and a transactional approach of understanding experience and learning. The model derives from previous educational research on moral reaction (Öhman & Östman 2008), the political moment (Håkansson & Östman 2019), trajectory of learning (Östman, Van Poeck, & Öhman 2019a), and the role of aesthetical experience in learning (Wickman 2006; Andersson, Garrison, & Östman 2018).

By moral and political concerns for, we mean *something* that is strongly valued and *something* that we care passionately about, i.e., something that is a guiding force for our feeling and believing, thus part of personality. We analytically differentiate between a moral concern for, in terms of an individual dimension of proper conduct regarding a person's concern for "things," such as human beings, other animals, etc., and a political concern for, which refers to a public and political dimension, such as organizing a society, political communities, etc. In the chapter we show how a "concern for" can spring from a poignant aesthetic experience and be important moment to manifest relations between the learner and the moral or political realm (Gould 2011).

The chapter begins with a brief presentation of the model. Here, we elaborate on the learning trajectory, transactional processes of learning, aesthetic quality and experience, customs and habits, needs and desires, etc. The next section presents three empirical illustrations. In the conclusion, we discuss how the presented model and analytical principles can be used in educational settings. Here we take inspiration from the term "educative moment" (Garrison, Östman, & Håkansson 2015).

The Learning Trajectory and the Transactional Approach on Learning Processes

The learning trajectory model (Östman, Van Poeck, & Öhman 2019a) describes the various phases of learning and is inspired by Dewey's work on inquiry (Dewey 1938/1986). In Table 15.1, these phases are illustrated in relation to the topic of this chapter and make up the model we call "A Model of Transactional Learning Moral and Political Concerns *for*." Briefly, the learning trajectory can be described as follows. The first phase consists of an interruption of our habitual actions that gives rise to an affect, an experience that is felt as a physical change in the body, such as an increase in the heart rate. As this is a non-cognitive experience it is had and felt but not yet known. In the second phase, the unknown affect is transformed into a known feeling. This feeling and the situation to which the feeling is connected become the focus for the inquiry (phase 3). The inquiry ends in the fourth phase by creating an experience of fulfillment. If the learning trajectory is successful, it includes the learning of new knowledge, skills, values, etc.; the creation of a new relation to the environment, which means that our interrupted habit adjusts into a recreated or brand new habit.

The different phases of the model are presented below. The point of departure is a poignant experience that occurs when our repertoire of habits is interrupted.

First Phase: Interruption of Habits as a Bodily Aesthetical Experience

Pragmatists emphasize that our dominant way of everyday living is habitual and that thinking, reflecting, and so on are primarily for resolving problematic situations. The outcome of thought and reflection, if they are successful, is learning. From birth we are driven by so-called "first nature" (biological) impulses, instincts, etc. However, according to Dewey, human beings can also develop habits that operate as "second nature," which "under ordinary

Table 15.1 A Model of Transactional Learning Moral and Political Concerns *for*

Phases	Description
1: An interruption of habits – a state of disequilibrium	A poignant aesthetical experience: – an immediate affect that is intensive and deeply felt – the experience is anoetic – involves a need as a lack of equilibrium
2: Problematic situation	An awareness: – the aesthetical experience is transformed into a feeling of the interrupted situation – the need is transformed into a desire to restore the state of equilibrium
3: Inquiry	A cognitive process of analyses and experimentation: – the feeling of the interruption becomes an object for inquiry – The feeling gets a reference – Idea(s) for the restoration of the state of equilibrium is developed and tested
4: Closure	Consummatory experience: – an immediate aesthetical experience of fulfilment – concerns the whole process from phase 1-3 – constitutes an experience Learning: – (re)creation of habits – (re)discovery of a moral/political concern for

circumstances is as potent and urgent as first nature" (Dewey 1939/1988: 108). In many situations habits constitute our will, in that they determine how we feel, believe, and act in specific situations: "Concrete habits do all the perceiving, recognizing, imagining, recalling, judging, conceiving, and reasoning that is done. …. Yet, habit does not, of itself, know, for it does not of itself stop to think, observe or remember" (Dewey 1922/1983: 124). Another characteristic of pragmatism is the belief that what we value is mostly visible in our actions. We act on our habits, which largely determine who we are, what we believe in, and what we care about passionately. Therefore, moral and political concerns *for* are observable in individuals, or, as in our case, in students' actions as linguistic expressions: "[B]elieving is something we do, and what we do is premised on what we believe" (Festensteiner 1997: 6). We acquire our social habits by participating in customary social practices. Dewey (1922/1983) maintains that an individual's habits evolve in and with collective habits, i.e., customs, and states that "individuals form their personal habits under conditions set by prior customs" (21), and that customs "pre-exist individual habits" (44).

Life occurs as a rhythm between harmony and dissensus, or as a state of equilibrium and disequilibrium of being in the world; it is our way of coordinating with the world (Dewey 1938/1986). When our life is in a state of equilibrium, we are in harmony with the environment, whereas when our life is in a state of disequilibrium, we are in "tension" in and with the environment. Consequently, when our habits are interrupted, we enter into a state of disequilibrium: our habits fail to coordinate our actions, in that we do not know how to act in this situation. There is an interruption in our living in and with the environment which we register in the body as an effect of being affected by the world. From a transactional approach this means we reciprocally and simultaneously affect and are affected in and with the environment, where affect is something "unfixed, unstructured, and something we do not quite have a language for, something that we cannot fully grasp or express" (Gould 2010: 26–7).

Affect is an anoetic bodily experience that is given; something that we have before we do anything with it. In other words, it is only brutally there as a non-cognitive and non-linguistic experience. In this capacity, "It forms that to which all objects of thought refer" (Dewey 1930/1984: 254). It is an immediate experience, which James (2003) called pure experience. Dewey frames it in terms of an immediate anoetic or aesthetical experience of quality (1930/1984). In this context, aesthetical experience refers to the ancient Greek term *aisthetikos*, meaning sentient, sense, sensitivity (Andersson, Garrison, & Östman 2018: 29).

The bodily experience of this "affection" is had and felt but is not known. Two things are felt: the *intensity* and the *quality*. Intensity refers to the strength of the effect on our body (Massumi 1995). Here we focus on affect as having a powerful intensity, something that shakes us and that interrupts our habit. The affect is overwhelming, unutterable, heart rending, and strikes us unexpectedly—we call it *poignant aesthetic experience*. By focusing on poignant aesthetic experiences, we pay attention to existences that, in many cases, gives rise to the disruption of habitual activity that sometimes turns into an inquiry on moral and political doubts, conflicts, and struggles, which in turn may develop into a commitment. Notably, though, not all such experiences turn into a problematic situation and an inquiry.

For Dewey, qualities are a notification of immediate existence. He says that the "world in which we immediately live, that in which we strive, succeed, and are defeated is pre-eminently a qualitative world" (1930/1984:243). Color can function as an example to explain what quality refers to. Color is a quality that we experience with our bodily senses but it is only after inquiry that we can call it red, a color, etc. Of great importance for Dewey is that when we reflect on an affect, a "qualitativeness," we do something, and it becomes transformed:

> Any quality as such is final; it is at once initial and terminal; just what it is as it exists. It may be referred to other things, it may be treated as an effect or as a sign. But this involves an extraneous extension and use. It takes us beyond quality in its immediate qualitativeness. If experienced things are valid evidence, then nature in having qualities within itself has what in the literal sense must be called ends, terminals, arrests, enclosures.
>
> (1925/1981: 82)

If we want to communicate the non-cognitive and non-linguistic ("dumb") bodily experience of a quality, we need to use *abstract* terms that express "qualitativeness," such as red-ness or, of relevance for our topic, cruelty-ness, hatred-ness, love-ness, caring-ness. A poignant aesthetic experience connected to the situated interruption is not just any tension, but one that can be described afterwards as a dismantling experience, i.e., an experience that stirs and jolt us deeply.

From the perspective of the experiencer, the experience concerns the durational–extensional quality of the situation as a whole. Although this aesthetic experience originates in our transaction in and with the world, the experience is non-cognitive in that it is precedes any intellectual discrimination. The transaction is sense-ational. Notably as human beings we are non-rational without being irrational.

People often use "dumb" words or sounds, such as ugh, shit, nooo, when struck by such an aesthetical experience. These utterances are not part of any intellectual endeavor but are reactions accompanying the immediate bodily experience of a durational–extensional quality. Utterances or other types of bodily actions are immediate reactions and as such automatic. They can be compared to when a doctor checks our reflexes by hitting our knee softly with a tool so that the leg, in most cases, jerks automatically when hit and not by us consciously thinking that we should move our leg.

As we will show later (phase 3), the physical change that we experience in our bodies has crucial consequences for our minding (thinking), since "the immediate existence of quality, and of dominant and pervasive quality, is the background, the point of departure, and the regulative principle of all thinking" (Dewey 1930/1984:261). In our exploration of a poignant aesthetic experience, we follow Dewey in that such experience carries *need*, which is directly connected to the lack of equilibrium. Dewey (1938/1986) states that "living may be regarded as a continual rhythm of disequilibrium and recoveries of equilibrium … the state of disturbed equilibrium constitutes need. The movement towards its restoration is search and exploration. The recovery is fulfillment or satisfaction" (34). Every need, such as a hunger for fresh air or food, is a lack that denotes at least a temporary absence of an adequate adjustment with surroundings (1934/1987: 19).

Second Phase: An Awareness of a Problematic Situation

If the first phase is a fully bodily non-cognitive reaction, the second phase represents a preparatory inquiry phase, where the intense fuzzy qualitativeness turns into a feeling of the dominant quality of the situation; the bodily non-cognitive affection turns into a conscious awareness of a discriminated specific feeling, such as turning cruelty-ness into cruel. The feeling of cruel is the feeling that there is a problem, although still not yet any reference or cognitive discrimination of what the cruel or the problem is about. As James (1890/1950) explains, we can have a feeling for relations: "We ought to say a feeling of and, a feeling of *if*, a feeling of *but*, and a feeling of *by*, quite as readily as we say a feeling of blue or a feeling of cold" (245–6). Feelings may involve primordial connections among the otherwise diverse aspects of immediate qualitativeness.

The "awareness turn" in this phase means that the flow of transactions involving the poignant aesthetic experience (the anoetic bodily felt qualitativeness and intensity of the interruptive situation) and our cognition (our previously acquired habits consisting of knowledge, skills, feelings, values, desires, etc.) has been initiated and in the subsequent phase turns into cognition. What is important to recognize is that the interruptive situation (the "whole") is complex. This means that different affects can be the effect of the same interruptive situation, but also that the complexity implies that more than one affect can occur in the same situation. Due to this, the feelings that arise in this phase can vary "in quality and intensity" (Dewey 1925/1981: 198; see also Johnson 2015: 33).

However, it is not only the feeling referred to above that becomes the "product" of the transformation in the transactional awareness turn. The need, established in the first phase transforms, into a desire—a desire to restore the disequilibrium to become equilibrium again (Dewey 1934/1987: 20). Additionally, we can also decide to ignore to act upon the need, thereby no desire emerge to deal with the problem; instead we escape from the situation.

Notably, the intensity and quality of the feeling connected to the tensional and interruptive situation on one hand and the intensity and the quality of the desire on the other, is one experience, not two separate experiences. Thereby making the quality and intensity of the feeling a *subject-matter*—something that requires attention (of different intensity and quality) and that we should take care of. Implicated in the learning trajectory in general is the notion of care and concern for subject-matter. Though, here the focus is on poignant aesthetic experiences, which means that this care and concern can be very strong and described as "caring *for* in the sense of *taking* care of, looking after, paying attention systematically, or *minding*" (Dewey & Bentley 1949/1989a: 247).

Third Phase: Inquiry

The third phase of resolving the interruptive qualitative situation is mainly cognitive, although it may also involve sub-phases of transactionally arising new aesthetic poignant experiences within the inquiry. By cognitive we mean that the transactions that occur are undertaken with the aim of discriminating, understanding, creating meaning, solving problems, and such; for instance, identify a reference of the feeling of cruel. The participants in the transactions can be the physical surroundings, the social surroundings, our bodily habits, etc. However, what is important is that the subject-matter has a regulatory function for our endeavors (Garrison 2010), it gives us direction in terms of the selectivity of our attention and action.

The cognitive discrimination of the problematic situation turns into an imagination of a cognitive resolution. Imagination involves experimentally staged transactions that connect our earlier experiences with the present subject-matter and then turn into an idea about how to reach restoration and an adjustment of the interrupted habit. According to Garrison (2010), imagining and coming up with an idea means arriving at something that mediates "between the actual and the possible, between ignorance and wisdom" (97).

Some ideas may become ends-in-view that help to guide our actions. The same applies to our acquired customs and habits and the phenomena and processes with which we transact, including the subject-matter. The influence of these different participants in a transaction is reciprocal and simultaneous, in that the participants become present at the same time and relationally. This means that our feelings, habits, and beliefs become part of our selective interest and determine which phenomena and processes we will pay attention to and what we do with them (Andersson, Garrison, & Östman 2018, Ch. 3). But in accordance with the transactional perspective on influence in encounters in and with the world, our selective interest is also affected by the subject-matter, other phenomena, and processes that take part in the transaction that we will either stage or become part of.

In the inquiry the subject-matter becomes clearer as the feelings connected to the tensional situation as well as the interrupted habits are analyzed and given meaning. Questions become answered, such as what habit must be changed to dissolve the interruption, what gave rise to the feeling, what the feeling consists of, why the feeling has this or that intensity and why I have never felt like this before in connection to other situated interruption of my habits. In addition, to making the subject-matter intelligible, we use the past (our experiences) to perhaps come up with an imaginative idea, which is part of the future and therefore still non-existing, of how to handle the present problem. If we take the starting point for this chapter into account, that the aesthetical experience and the feelings have a high intensity, then the qualitativeness can be described as poignant. In this case, the outcome of the inquiry concerns the (re)discovery of what it is in the world that concerns us deeply and existentially, i.e., a (re)discovery of what defines us as the specific person we are or have become in relation to the world, including what we deeply concern for and want to take care of.

The Fourth Phase: Consummatory Experience

When an inquiry settles, the participants often have an aesthetical experience (Dewey 1930/1984), i.e., a bodily reaction of fulfilment that can be a joyful expression such as "YES" or a disappointed expression such as "DAMN" (Wickman 2006). Regardless, such expressions "mark[s] the realized appreciation of a pervading quality that is now translated into a system of definite and coherent terms" (Dewey 1930/1984:250). The aesthetic experience of fulfillment is an experience of all four phases—from that of the qualitativeness to the consummation of the inquiry. If the inquiry is successful, it is often a process that is long remembered and constitutes what Dewey calls "an experience" (Dewey 1934/1987). "An experience" is an experience that stands out in the flow of experiences and is remembered as extraordinary. Below we illustrate three students' inquiries of poignant aesthetic experience which ends in aesthetic fulfillment.

Empirical Illustration

In this illustration we will reuse empirical examples from previous studies of moral reaction (Öhman & Östman 2008; Andersson & Öhman 2015) and political moment (Håkansson & Östman 2019). Our illustration consists of two examples of moral concern and one of political concern.

The illustration is based on two crucial analytical principles. The first principle is that poignant aesthetic experiences connect to a situated interruption, which can often be directly visible in a person's verbal and/or bodily reactions. What characterizes such a reaction is that it is immediate, unexpected, and strongly expressive. For example, sudden, almost automatic, jerky movements and/or sudden and strongly expressive sounds (vocals, words, etc.). We illustrate one such example below.

The second principle is that poignant aesthetical experiences can emerge in persons' reflections, conclusions, and so on as expressive bodily gestures and/or words or utterances. We offer two such examples below: One connected to an educational activity observed by researchers and the other a student reflecting in retrospect by "pointing to" the experienced educational activity. What is important to recognize is the transformation that occurs between the first and second phases when a dumb aesthetical experience starts to become cognitive. Due to this transformation, Dewey (1925/1981) emphasizes that cognition can only point to primary aesthetical experience (74–5) because it can never be fully described or defined. Cognition "takes us beyond quality in its immediate qualitativeness" (82). What "the pointing to" can lead to is a careful exploration of the denoted experience, which often includes a bodily reconnaissance of qualitativeness.

The first example is an educational activity at a Swedish university in which the students are collecting creatures on the shore in order to put them in an aquarium for ecological studies. The following conversation occurs between two of the students:

1   Karin: Hell, for crying out loud. It feels awful when you pull them loose.
2   Ellen: So what is it?
3   Karin: A sea urchin.
4   Ellen: It's stuck.
5   Karin: I don't know. It seems weird. We've got to learn to pick them off with our hands.

This transcript exemplifies our first analytical principle, namely, that a poignant aesthetical experience of a situated transaction is directly visible in a person's reaction. Here the utterance in line 1, "Hell, for crying out loud," reflects an immediate and unexpected bodily reaction to an interruption: an interruption of the activity to collect animals. Furthermore, the immediate reaction is expressive in both content and intensity. The direct reflection on the dumb aesthetical experience is uttered in the same line. Here the feeling is defined as "awful" and the feeling has a reference; "to pull them loose." The feeling of awful-ness is a feeling of a relation (cf. James above). The continued reflection includes a judgment—"weird"—and covers the activity as a whole, which is learning to pick animals with their hands. The story does not end there, though, because Karin voices her concern about the need to pick animals with hands with the teacher, i.e., she questions the custom. Thus, the poignant aesthetic experience that is connected to the disturbing situation is transformed into a moral concern: a concern for the activities in which the relation to animals becomes problematic. Here the learning involves a (re)discovery of an object that one has a deep "concern for."

The second example is when pupils aged 8–9 years were collecting creatures in a stream and putting them into containers for further studies. We enter the conversation when the students have already experienced the disturbance of the activity and discovered that a salamander was dying and a rescue activity had to be started. They collectively gathered their efforts to release the salamander back to the stream (lines 1–5). It is obvious that solving the problematic situation is emotionally charged and a strong concern for the salamander is expressed (see lines 6–13), in that the pupils' voices are high pitched and excited. The inquiry

1   Olle: Now we hold it [the jar].
2   Max: Everybody?
3   Linus: No wait, you too.
4   Max: Careful.
5   Nellie: Bye-bye. [They pour the water and the salamander back into the lake.]
6   Linus: Is he out (of the jar)?
7   Max and Olle: Yes!
8   Olle: I cannot see it! There (pointing at the water).
9   Nellie: No, it does not live.
10 Olle: Yes, it makes it, it makes it, it is swimming!!
11 Max: No
12 Olle: Yes.
13 Linus: Yes, it swims.
14 Nellie: This is almost cruelty to animals.
15 Anton: He did like this [raises his hands in the air]. He is dead scared.
16 Viktor: It survives!

is successful and is accompanied with consummatory experiences which is illustrated by Victor in line 16 and Nellie in line 14.

Although the poignant aesthetical experience is not visible, as was the case in the first example, by concentrating on the pupils' ways of reacting and acting during the inquiry and its fulfillment, we can draw the conclusion that the learning event concerns a (re)discovery of a strong moral concern. Thus, the conversation exemplifies our second analytical principle. What is of additional interest is Nellie's utterance (line 14). Here she extends the inquiry and makes a judgment about the activity, in much the same way as Karin did above: "This is almost cruelty to animals," where the cruelty refers to the quality of the customized activity in which she is involved.

The third example is a debate in an upper secondary school class about how to accomplish an ecologically, economically, and socially sustainable society. Among the students who expressed their beliefs (some students did not say anything) there was a consensus that one obstacle to reaching a sustainable society was that citizens had too much freedom of choice. Directly after the lesson, the students were asked to describe their experience of it. The empirical material exemplifies the second analytical strategy in much the same way as the second transcript. The difference is that we do not get access to the poignant aesthetical experience or the inquiry. The only thing that we have access to is the students' retrospective written reflections of—their pointing to—their experience from the lesson. Their reflections do not reveal any consensus, rather the opposite. One student answered:

> At the same time, my classmates' contributions sometimes make me worry about different worldviews and, consequently, how differently my own worldview could run our world.

The student expresses a strong feeling—a worry—which has a concrete reference and thereby the poignant aesthetic experience is cognitivized. The experience of worldviews revealed by her classmates changed the student's relation to the classmates, thereby manifesting "we" and "them." Further, there is an imagination regarding how differently the student's own worldview could run the world. This can be seen as a political "concern for" different worldviews in terms of how to organize a political community, including inclusion and exclusion, when there is a plurality of worldviews. Notably, even that there is a consummatory experience of both feeling and the reference of the feeling, obviously there is a requirement of new inquiry testing ideas how to solve the problematic situation of organizing a political community of a plurality of worldviews. But the poignant aesthetic experience shows that there is something that attached the student, why we argue that the student's political reflection may emerge into a political concern for or maybe against a plurality of worldviews.

Conclusion

By taking a transactional approach we developed a model on how poignant aesthetic experiences emerge into an inquiry and ends in a consummatory experience. In order to be able to use the model successfully, we briefly presented two important analytical principles, both of which are exemplified in the analyses. In line with this exemplification, we argue that the model and the two analytical principles can be used to analyze different kinds of empirical materials containing: (i) a poignant aesthetic experience and inquiry, (ii) an inquiry settled in an expression of fulfillment, and (iii) the result of an inquiry. In these different kinds of empirical materials, the model can be used to describe and explain the learning of moral and political concern for which may turn into a commitment.

In relation to the chapter's topic, the examples show that the learning that takes place can be formulated as a (re)discovery of deep "concerns for." We can of course not draw any conclusions as to how these moral and political "concerns for" will be taken forward.

What this model and our illustrative analyses show is the entanglement of poignant aesthetic experiences and strong and deep moral and political "concerns for." This entanglement, we argue, occurs through the learning trajectory. Dewey (1934/1987) states that "esthetic cannot be sharply marked off from intellectual experience since the latter must bear an esthetic stamp to be itself complete" (45). In addition, the experience of the feeling and the felt object that is referred to is one transactional unified experience, not two. Further, caring for something inevitably includes being affected by it, thereby when we transact within a situation in which our interrupted habits fail us, the affection is strong, but has no determined direction. The affection is had and felt but is not known.

These kinds of poignant aesthetic experiences can be crucial in students' development of moral and political commitments. From a transactional point of view, there is a change of the moral and political relation in the students' transaction with the environment. In both Karin's and Nellie's cases it is a moral concern for the activity of not exposing the sea urchin or salamander in an educational activity. The third example is a student's reflection on the classmates' different worldviews. Here a poignant aesthetic experience evolves from the subject of "running the world." Even there is no obvious political concern *for* in the student's reflection, we argue that the intensity in the reflection may be the beginning of a development of a concern for, a concern for how to organize a society including a plurality of worldviews.

We end the chapter by arguing that students' poignant aesthetic experiences are "educative moments" (Garrison, Östman, & Håkansson 2015). The similarities between a poignant aesthetic experience and an educative moment are the sudden and unexpected occurrence, which for a teacher involves opportunities for educative use. To take advantage of these experiences requires reflection, creatively changing old habit or develop commitment. Thereby, this "time pause" is crucial for developing moral and political concern for.

However, they are also accompanied by risks and dangers, because a need to change old habits can be a dismantling experience. Thereby, changing habit can be seen as replacing a habit, a kind of re-birth of the relation to the world— which may be painful. For instance, experiencing a conflict with customized educational activity or changing a social relation with your classmates into "we" and "them," which may turn into an antagonistic or violent relation regarding which worldview should run the world. Obviously, to be able to use educative moments regarding the development of moral and political concern requires a teacher being able to take educative use of the unexpected.

16

Links between Pandemics, Politics, and People

Ninitha Maivorsdotter and Joacim Andersson

Introduction

John Dewey and Arthur F. Bentley (1949/1989a) stressed that the behavioral sciences lagged behind the natural sciences in the transition from interaction to transaction because the relationships they explored were comparatively complex. Frank X. Ryan (2011) put it like this: "Human behavior is less predictable than the activity of water molecules or a colony of ants. It is thus not surprising that psychology, sociology, and political science have lagged behind physics and chemistry, both in terms of discoveries made and the methods used to attain them" (69). In this chapter we seek to describe and explain a method that has evolved from the concepts of environing and body pedagogy and was developed in a series of articles designed to address the complexity of people's embodied experiences (Andersson, Östman, & Öhman 2015; Andersson & Maivorsdotter 2017; Andersson, Garrison, & Östman 2018; Maivorsdotter & Andersson 2020). The method can be understood as a transactional salutogenic approach focused on health behavior in specific sociocultural settings. Our case in this illustration is the global Covid-19 pandemic that erupted in 2020. A pandemic affects individual human behavior as well as that of populations. Traditionally, pandemics have been studied as biological events (McNeill 1976). However, we argue that a transactional approach, with a focus on environing and body pedagogy, can show how pandemics, politics, and people are parts determined by the whole. The case outlined here show how the Covid-19 pandemic was addressed differently in Denmark and Sweden. We show this by identifying public narratives in speeches to the nation. The overall aim is to describe how Dewey's concept of experiences and habits, combined with Aaron Antonovsky's salutogenic approach to health, can help us to explore public narratives in ways that deepen our knowledge about the links between pandemics, politics, and people.

Transactional Perspective on Pandemic, Politics, and People

To understand how the coronavirus infects populations in different countries, and why disparate political strategies are used to combat the virus, we need to explore how pandemics, politics, and people transform and are transformed by each other. This question goes beyond self-action and inter-action while involving education and public health.

The Danish and Swedish governments' recommendations about how to behave during the pandemic are very simple: keep your distance, wash your hands regularly, and meet as few people as possible. On the other hand, adapting to and adopting these new habits requires an enormous engagement with what sociological and educational researchers have identified as body pedagogics. Body pedagogics seek to study how bodies are fostered and focus on "the relationship between those social, technological, and material means through which institutionalized cultures are transmitted, the experiences of those involved in this learning, and the embodied outcomes of this process" (Shilling 2017: 1205). Starting in the context of disparate political strategies (Denmark and Sweden) for tackling Covid-19, we follow the body pedagogic tradition and approach health arguments and social regulation norms as constitutive for certain educational settings in which individuals, families/cultures, and societies need to engage in ways of re-inhabiting their familiar environments. The reason speeches to the nation are of empirical interest is that analyzing the public narratives of these speeches enables us to identify health arguments and social regulation norms linked to the collective memories and shared experiences of an entire population. In other words, the speeches are seen as connected to the body pedagogics of the whole population.

To explore how public narratives can deepen our knowledge about the links between pandemics and people, our body pedagogic perspective combines Antonovsky's salutogenic approach to health with Dewey's concept of experience and habits. In this context, experience and habits contribute to people's abilities to create environments in which they are capable of realizing collective interests. In the active process of environing, people incorporate some surrounding conditions and disregard others (Andersson, Garrison, & Östman 2018). Hence, health can be understood as a transaction integrating internal and external environments, in which each is connected to the other in reciprocally transformative ways. Just as individual organisms take the external environment into their internal being through processes of breathing, eating, and drinking, people also take a particular public narrative into their orientations and habits

(Shilling 2018). When official authorities make speeches to the nation during an influenza pandemic, the speakers and the audiences take particular aspects of the virus into account.

Antonovsky (1979) stresses that health is a process that stretches along the continuum from health ease to health dis-ease. A salutogenic approach implies that everyone is in some way always healthy, in contrast to the pathogenic paradigm in which people are healthy or unhealthy. This rejection of a healthy–unhealthy dualism is in line with Dewey's transactional view of experience and habit. For example, the transactional view allows us to recognize health behavior as not only a chain of activities (e.g., adhering to health arguments and social regulations) but also analyses that seek to depict the transactional relationships between internal and external environments for people, governments, and societies. In the field of public health, the World Health Organization (WHO) seminars are of great importance, and the seminar in 1992 is of particular interest for this chapter. Here, Antonovsky presents the river metaphor to illustrate his vision of salutogenesis as an approach to guide health promotion. McCuaig and Quennerstedt (2018: 2) summarize the seminal presentation as follows:

> Antonovsky (1996) considers curative medicine's preoccupation with saving swimmers from drowning downstream, and preventive medicine's concern with preventing people from falling or being pushed into the river upstream. Antonovsky argued, however, that from a salutogenic perspective, nobody is actually on the shore, "we are all, always, in the dangerous river of life. The twin question is: How dangerous is our river? How well can we swim?"
> (Antonovsky 1996: 14)

From this perspective health should always be attended to as a dynamic, ever-present, swimmer–water relationship. In connection to this, Dewey suggests that we should always start with the empirical situation of an already-active participant and pursue inquiries that focus on organism–environment transactions (Ryan 2011). In the context of a population's body pedagogic work of inhabiting its environment in new ways, we might fare better if we reconsider Antonovsky's river metaphor and instead use the landlubber perspective of walking.

The body pedagogic work that the practice of social distancing requires can be exemplified by the basal and everyday habit of walking. In environing processes, we get much of our sense of attunement from walking. Just think back to what it was like to walk in an urban environment before Covid-19 and how we moved, stopped, met, started, gave room, squeezed through, hurried past, caught up, decided whose path to cross, when to display, and when to hide, etc. In this way, walking rhythm as a social behavior continuously adapts to particular circumstances in public spaces (e.g., Edensor 2010). Or, in other words, walking rhythm is the habitual way of transactionally coordinating (including environing) our moves with the material and sociocultural world. Considering urban life's complex polyrhythmic patterns, there is also a certain body pedagogic associated with the transformation of everyday life in a pandemic, e.g. how walking rhythms are interwoven with daily practices of staying healthy. Rhythms of urban walking are not merely routinized social behavior but can also be understood as situations that in their specific outcomes can hinder or enable health interventions.

Using "speeches to the nation" as an empirical case makes it possible to show what might become educational settings for citizens when such speeches are transactionally integrated into such body pedagogic processes. The qualitative data of public narratives can, for example, be used to analyze the spatial and temporal pattern of how people, cultures, and societies tune into public narratives by means of different body techniques and the norms and values connected to them. It is in this context that a transactional and salutogenic perspective suggests that we should not exclusively focus on people's individual behavior (how they march to their own beat) or on health as a chain of actions (whether or not they adhere to social regulations). Instead, we should focus on the dynamics of organism-in-environment (walker and place, swimmer and river) and ask empirical questions about the transactional relationships that people and state engage in through their body pedagogics.

Dewey (1922/1983: 16) explains that "all virtues and vices are habits which incorporate objective forces." Walking consists of a number of habits that incorporate the conditions of a place, although no habit can incorporate the entire conditions of that same place. This means that walkers need to discriminate and selectively attend to some feelings, interests, and problems while disregarding others. Antonovsky (1996) provides a similar description when explaining that the sense of coherence (SOC) construct refers to a position in which "the stimuli bombarding one from the inner and outer environments were perceived as information rather than as noise" (5). In this chapter, the difference between "information" and "noise" is an important analytical distinction between environment and surrounding, as noted by Andersson, Garrison, and Östman (2018), i.e., that anything surrounding an organism that does not enter into its functioning is not part of its environment. We, therefore, seek to understand a heightened regulation of social behavior as not just particular rules that citizens need to adhere to, but as a certain body pedagogic that also extends to the everyday realm and the practice of social distancing.

Influenza Pandemic: An Educational Setting

Decades after historian William McNeill's publication *Plagues and Peoples* (1976) examined the impact of infectious diseases throughout the ages, it is clear that such threats to people's health are still present and, furthermore, are increasing at an alarming rate. There is reason to conclude that plagues and people are, and remain, inextricably linked (Sommerfeld 2003).

Today, in order to understand how the coronavirus infects populations in different countries and the kinds of disparate political strategies that are used to combat the virus, we not only need to use a biomedical lens, but other approaches as well. In the past influenza pandemics were studied in isolation, but social, economic, cultural, and political factors are now emerging as major contributors to their spread. Drawing on the work of McNeill (1976), among others, it is now acceptable to argue that diverse events like ecosystem change, urbanization, poverty, inequality, and many other issues are decisive in the transmission of infectious diseases, and that pandemics are both social and biological events (Sommerfeld 2003). Furthermore, this chapter argues that pandemics are educational events and elaborates on the dynamic relations between pandemics, politics, and people by using a transactional approach outlined by Garrison (2001, 2003), with a focus on education and embodied experience (Andersson et al. 2018). The key point here, in relation to body pedagogics, is that humans do not transact with their environment as separate beings, but engage in a constant process of environing the conditions of social action (Shilling 2017). The political strategies that are used and the public health arguments underpinning them are here seen as educational settings for individuals and societies. In this view, the outcome of the pandemic—how the virus is spread and how well the population can adapt to the new situation—is dependent on the transformation of people's means, experiences, and habits (Dewey 1920/1986, 1922/1983, 1925/1981).

Taking embodied experience and the body–environment transaction as starting points, public pandemic narratives are seen to promote certain norms, behavior, and values that require individuals and populations to (re)inhabit their familiar environments in new ways. Everyday life in a pandemic can, thus, be conceived of as an educational situation where habits are challenged and it is impossible to maintain a "business as usual" approach to life.

Drawing on two examples of "speeches to the nation" that were broadcast in Denmark and Sweden—two similar Nordic countries employing different strategies to limit the effects of the Covid-19 pandemic—we utilize a theoretical framework informed by the works of John Dewey and Aaron Antonovsky (see Maivorsdotter & Andersson 2020). To identify the public narratives in these speeches we use analytical questions such as: How do representatives of the state present "a good life" in the Covid-19 crisis? How can people stay healthy and protect each other? What do representatives of the state suggest in order to engage people in particular practices or life activities? The identification of public narratives enables further investigations of how the pandemic, state, and citizens transactionally transform each other.

Pandemics and Public Narratives

The conceptualization of a historical and societal trauma—like an influenza pandemic—as a public narrative helps us focus on narrative accounts linking a group or community's past experiences of traumatization to health over time (Mohatt et al. 2014). Narratives about past traumas and group health can be identified throughout the globe and refer to a wide diversity of mass-experienced trauma, from a single event like a natural disaster to the SARS outbreak in 2002–4. Narratives are stories that string events together to construct meaning and establish discourse. By shaping past experiences into coherent stories, narratives are the primary ways in which people convey contemporary interpretations and aspirations (Mohatt et al. 2014). In particular, people employ narratives to express individual and collective identities and to situate themselves in their social contexts (Wertsch 2008). Personal narratives are stories told by an individual and are unique to that person (Rappaport 2000), such as a personal account of surviving a car accident. Public narratives differ from personal narratives in that they are expressed in public discourses (Ganz 2011), are indicative of intersubjective understanding (O'Donnell & Tharp 2012), and are common to a group of people (Rappaport 2000). Thus, public narratives are stories that potentially shape collective memory by relying on narrative elements such as characters, actions, places, and time (Wertsch 2008). The creation of public narratives is also a durational process and not simply "a fixed moment in time." For example, when a head of state or monarch—or someone in a responsible position—makes a "speech to the nation" this is part of a public narrative that influences public discourse.

The speeches we refer to here are those given by the heads of state and monarchs in Denmark and Sweden. Denmark and Sweden are Nordic countries with similarities as well as differences in history, society, and culture. Crawford (2014) suggests that strong cultural identity may be emblematic of public resilience in the face of national trauma. Taylor and Usborne (2010) argue that the reconstruction of a strong cultural identity following a collective trauma, such as war or disaster, is critical for individual and community well-being. Hence, the chapter also discusses the relation between public norms and individual habits in terms of transactions that foreground well-being, possibilities, and risks during an influenza pandemic. The public narratives that are identified in the two nations' speeches show the kinds of health arguments and social regulation norms at stake for individuals and populations when adjusting to the new circumstances of a pandemic in their everyday lives. Viewed this way, public narratives seek to transfer the population from an environment in which everyday habits—such as going to work, going to school, or socialize with friends—are usually taken for granted to one in which habits must be problematized.

An Illustration

The method is grounded in Andersson and Maivorsdotter (2017) and Maivorsdotter and Andersson (2020) and consists of analytical steps proven to be effective in conjunction with Dewey's transactional theory of learning. To elicit how public narratives dictate some of the conditions for environing (Andersson et al. 2018) during a pandemic, we pose the following analytical questions:

A. How do representatives of the state present "a good life" in the Covid-19 pandemic in terms of promoting health and avoiding illness?
B. What are the major concerns expressed in the speeches to the nation in terms of promoting health and avoiding illness?
C. What do representatives of the state suggest in order to engage people in particular practices or life activities?
D. What kind of health resources do representatives of the state refer to in order to secure a good life for people and address their daily life challenges during the pandemic?

All the analytical questions take the dynamic relations between individuals/cultures and pandemic health narratives as a starting point and align well with Dewey's transactional approach to experience, habit, and meaning-making. The analytical questions were used by the authors independently. In every step, each author formulated main themes, sub-themes and narratives ("public narratives") that then became the basis for deliberations about whether the themes/narratives had anything "in common." The public narratives that are provided below are the authors' common statements based on the actual speeches that were given at the time.

Denmark

In Denmark, both the prime minister's and the queen's speech had a main theme, namely, *to combat Covid-19 with force and with every available means*. The two speeches were broadcast on March 11 and 17, 2020, respectively and were also available on the internet. Prime Minister Mette Frederiksen, the leader of the Danish Social Democrats, came to power in 2019. Queen Margrethe II has ruled Denmark since 1972.

Combat Covid-19 with Force and with Every Available Means

Yesterday the number of people in Denmark affected by Covid-19 was 157. Today it is 514. This shows how quickly the virus can spread. Experiences from other countries show how difficult things can be if we don't react quickly and with force and take all the necessary precautions to combat the virus. At this moment in time we have no idea how this can best be done, but not reacting, or not reacting forcefully enough, is a bigger mistake than not reacting at all. We need to react in order reduce social contacts and thereby stop the virus spreading. Those citizens who do not respect the lockdown—with the exception of life-sustaining functions—are both thoughtless and reckless. The government's ability to make these forceful and important decisions, which limit citizens' freedom of movement, is an important resource in the fight against the virus. Likewise, that there is political unity on the restrictions that are imposed. Agencies like the armed forces and the police play an important role in the enforcement of these measures. Central resources are also the medical and nursing staff who care for those who are affected, despite the risks to their own lives and health. That citizens follow the decisions that are taken and help each other to act in the right way are also resources in the efforts to contain the virus. The government needs, in agreement with other parties and based on experts' knowledge about the spread of infection, to make essential and long-term decisions that citizens must respect. This means staying at home and avoiding social contacts outside the family. Even those with important social functions—such as the prime minister and other members of the government, but also medical and nursing staff, drivers and shop workers—need to be extremely vigilant in their occupations. The good life during the pandemic is about accepting and welcoming the limitations that are introduced in order to ensure the greatest possible safety for everyone living in Denmark. By acting resolutely, forcefully and collectively we will prevent people dying from Covid-19.

The focus of the public narrative in Denmark during the early phase of the Covid-19 pandemic was on the control of infection; a body pedagogy in the logic of biomedicine in which the transmission of infection is at the center of attention. In handling the threat of the transmission of the virus, actions like closing schools, avoiding public transport, and staying at home were regarded as reasonable and became the environing element of when trying to keep distance. Speed and force were also reasonable in the face of an enemy where the only protection was to stay away from each other. In this narrative, the pandemic became a well-identified and very deadly threat. The government and the monarchical head of state became leaders in a "war zone," where forcefulness and the courage to mobilize all the available means were prioritized. In turn, the population became law-abiding citizens in a situation in which public laws seemed to be negotiable for reasons that could be seen as being for the "public good."

Sweden

The main theme in Sweden's public narrative differed from that in Denmark. In Sweden, the theme *to activate the competent and responsible citizen* played a crucial role in the public narrative created by the Swedish prime minister, Stefan Löfven, and the king, Carl XVI Gustav. The two speeches that created the narrative were given on March 22 and April 5, respectively. Löfven, the leader of the Swedish Social Democratic Party, became prime minister in 2014. Carl XVI Gustav acceded as king in 1973. Both these men's speeches were broadcast and made available on the internet.

Activate the Competent and Responsible Citizen

> Sweden is faced with a new situation—a global threat that we have never before encountered in modern time. The Coronavirus is a deadly virus that threatens life, health and work. The threat is already amongst us. We have a general spread of the virus in Sweden and it is inevitable that people will die. Therefore, we

must do all we can to keep the death toll down and prevent the virus spreading, so that the health service can take care of those who are worst affected. The most important resource if Sweden is to overcome the crisis is the civil society. Primarily the health service, but also other parts of society such as schools, care homes for the elderly and public transport. All these workers, who are also at risk of being infected, are vital for ensuring that society continues to function, despite the restrictions and difficulties. Combatting the crisis also requires courage, solidarity and perseverance, being careful about your own health, other people's health and your country, following the authorities' advice and directives and avoid spreading disinformation and panic. Every citizen has a great responsibility here. We'll face the threat to our country together, by every one of us taking responsibility for our own actions. We'll do this knowing that the crisis will be lengthy, but also knowing that Sweden has successfully come through difficult times in the past. Regardless of place or position in society, we will all be able to look back on this time and be proud of how we acted, that we dealt with the situation together, with care and in solidarity.

Sweden's public narrative had a broader focus on health promotion—a body pedagogy associated with public health—than Denmark's. A broader scope than the transmission of infection was environed into the public narrative. This meant that environing factors influenced the adoption of health at the community level and, in particular, the possibility to adopt and sustain new health behavior for a long period of time. In the Swedish narrative, the pandemic became a threat with widespread consequences that could not easily be grasped and explained in the short term. In Sweden's case, the monarch and the government communicated the expert advice from the public health authorities. This public narrative regarded the population as competent and responsible. Regardless of differences in ability and motivation, the population in Sweden was expected to be well informed and competent in terms of adopting new behavior in a society in which everything—at a first glance—seemed to be very much the same, for example, with schools, restaurants, and shops remaining open.

Concluding Remarks

In relation to understanding how the coronavirus infects populations in different countries and which disparate political strategies are used to combat the virus, the established ground in the field of public health encourages us to comprehend it both as a biological and social event. We have tried to illustrate this by adopting a transactional view, i.e., that such events also emerge as truly educational at an individual and a public or population level. The public narratives outlined in this chapter are not *the* answer but *an* answer to what "the whole" that determines the pandemic, politics, and people in Denmark and Sweden might look like. By rethinking Antonovsky's salutogenic construct in terms of how individuals and societies engage in certain body pedagogics (e.g., walking), we have pointed to the connection between state and citizens as an ongoing engagement with aligning the body, the mind, and the environment. An illustrative analysis of the characteristics of the public narratives identified in two countries' speeches to the nation has shown that our methodological approach can create qualitative data that complies with a transactional study of the dynamic relations between pandemics, politics, and people.

Public narratives about Covid-19 seek to transfer the population from a situation in which everyday habits are usually taken for granted to one in which habits must be problematized. To facilitate for individuals how to respond to this interruption of routine involves encouraging them to foreground and respond to certain relevant conditions, regarding others as irrelevant, if they are to stay "afloat." Identifying and analyzing public narratives with analytical spotlight on processes of environing, can then tell us something about the contrasting environments in which cultural body pedagogics place individuals and the practical meanings these promote (Shilling 2018). Thus, we can raise important questions about complementarity, overlap, and potential dissonance among how states and nations seek to shape people's embodied being.

Our approach suggests that it is possible to determine some of the body pedagogic conditions of individuals', groups', and societies' environing processes by identifying public narratives, i.e., how people take a particular public narrative into their orientations and habits. For example, how health arguments and social regulation norms connect to certain means, experiences, and outcomes of pandemic habits. In learning when and how to socialize and when and how not to, individuals, families/cultures, and societies continuously sustain a functional alignment with body, mind, and environment. In the extended transactional event of being a coronavirus-infected population, a new culture or identity could also be shared. By identifying public narratives at different levels and points in time throughout a pandemic one can thereby facilitate analyses of certain dynamics between a state and its citizens in times of crisis. For example, analyses of how we are dealing with loneliness among certain groups in society, study of how family relations are inflicted by the lockdown of public institutions, or how elderly people are experiencing online technology.

Conducting large-scale, qualitative, empirical research on public health with our transactional salutogenic approach requires further descriptions of the kinds of health experiences that certain social, technological, and embodied material means connect to, as well as discussions about, what the pedagogic outcomes of public narratives are for individuals, families/cultures, and societies. Internalizing certain "modes of work," such as the washing of hands, distance learning and how to move/walk in public, also means that individuals, cultures, and societies continuously transform the environment in which they act. Hence, governments who seek to support their citizens through crises also need to continuously adjust their health arguments and social regulation norms to these transformed environments. Analyzing public narratives from a transactional salutogenic perspective at different levels and different points in time during pandemics can therefore support qualitative data that helps is to study how state–citizen relationships transform during crises.

Notes

Chapter 1

1. Nowhere in this introduction has emphasis been added to any citation.
2. In organism–environment transaction the environment is often other people, but of course the environment has many nonhuman components as well. Hofverberg shows how to empirically investigate the nonhuman components.
3. See Andersson, Garrison, and Östman (2018, 110–11).
4. See Hickman (1992, 220). The subject–predicate nature of Western language makes it difficult to speak or even think transactionally.
5. Rosenblatt dedicates the book to her husband Sidney Ratner. Ratner and Altman (1964) co-edited the correspondence of Dewey and Bentley.

Chapter 2

1. For an early analysis of some of these views, see my "Primary Experience as Settled Meaning," which I'm extending and updating for a forthcoming work.
2. For example, Garrison (2001: 294) describes semiotic activity as the coordination of (1) a natural biological being, (2) an object referred to, and (3) the sign used to refer.
3. Even in empirical description, I avoid any suggestion of containment or interaction; and with Andy Clark prefer "situated" to "embodied" cognition—stressing, first and foremost, *situation* as the *problematic situation* for which the attained objective marks closure (Clark 2008:107).

Chapter 3

1. Ryan worries that embodiment "flirts with the quagmire of containment" (this volume). However, he refers to this passage from Dewey, "The epidermis is only in the most superficial way an indication of where an organism ends and its environment begins" (Dewey 1934/1987: 64). Meanwhile, Dewey and Bentley (1949/1989a) remark: "Organisms do not live without air and water, nor without

food ingestion and radiation. They live, that is, as much in processes across and 'through' skins as in processes 'within' skins" (119–20).

2   It must also have a chrome grill, a flying Goddess hood ornament, and a custom interior.
3   Einstein's theory of the relativity of simultaneity provides an example. Since light propagates at a fixed speed, simultaneity depends on the observer's position (i.e., perspective) relative to the event. What is past for one observer may be in the future for another. Hans Joas (1985) put it this way: "All scientific measurement rests upon practical activities of cognizing subjects: all scientific cognition must self-reflectively include considerations of the location and the perspective of the cognizing subject" (173). The same holds for social practices involving language learning.
4   See Dewey's *Logic*, chapter 12, "Judgment as Spatial-Temporal Determination: Narration-Description."
5   The "dating" of the location of suspects is imperative to the formation of judgment in criminal investigations.

Chapter 5

1   It is important to notice here that un-healthy play, according to Dewey, is not fruitful for human development, although it might be perhaps considered in a transactional perspective to distinguish, for instance, when a game is gambling, or a player becomes a spoilsport.
2   For Dewey, "aesthetic" referred to a wider, deeper, richer, and more intense way to experience the world, while "artistic" is included in that notion and it is specifically referred to the production of art and works of art. Both terms are strongly interdependent and highlight the continuity of art and life (1934/1987: 9).
3   Dewey defines (sound) emotion as a whole of experience, resulting from the coordination of sensory-motor, ideo-motor, and vegetative-motor activities, and involving a cognitive evaluation of the emotional object, a disposition to action, and a diffusive wave reverberating in the consciousness (1895/1971: 180–1). Both the aesthetic and the artistic emotion are synonymous and allow one to experience the world in a deeper more integrated way (1934/1987: 75).
4   Although regulated due to player's disposition to spontaneously submit her/his behavior to rules arising in transactionally integrated play.
5   The Dutch historian Johan Huizinga (1872–1945) is well known for *The Autumn of the Middle Ages* (first published 1919), while *Homo Ludens* is his book devoted to play. Thomas S. Henricks (1950) is a renowned American sociologist, whose interest has been focused on play in contemporary society.
6   Michael Rosen (1946) is an English writer, poet, and author of children's books.

Chapter 7

1. Students start Grade 6 at the age of twelve in the Swedish school system.

Chapter 8

1. This example is collected from Klaar and Öhman (2012).

Chapter 9

1. Facilitation of learning has much in common with teaching but focusing on non-formal learning in this chapter we use a different vocabulary.
2. Learning facilitators outside formal education do not consider themselves as teachers, hence the term "facilitators." However, didactical theories on teaching in formal education settings can be employed/developed to investigate their work.
3. We use the term "didactical" here in line with the Continental, Northern European tradition where "Didaktik" is closely related to the reflexive pedagogic idea of "Bildung." This differs considerably from the more narrow/instrumental Anglo-Saxon focus on methods, instruction, and learning outcomes.
4. Different authors use different terms for the same or overlapping phenomena, e.g., Burke and Hajer respectively use "act" versus "performance," and "scene" versus "setting." As explained below, we draw from Hajer's terminology—particularly his concepts of "scripting," "staging," and "performance"—and understand the staging of a "setting" as a process that also contains the staging of a "scene."

Chapter 10

1. Two of the examples in this chapter have been used in earlier studies. The first with Paul was used in Hofverberg and Maivorsdotter (2018). The second has not been published before and the third transcript has been used in Hofverberg (2020).

Chapter 11

1. The transcript preceding each figure serves as the figure's caption.

References

Alexander, T. M. (1993), "John Dewey and the Moral Imagination: Beyond Putnam and Rorty toward a Postmodern Ethics," *Transactions of the Charles S. Peirce Society*, 29 (3): 369–400.

Andersson, J. and N. Maivorsdotter (2017), "The 'Body Pedagogics' of an Elite Footballer's Career Path – Analyzing Zlatan Ibrahimovic's Biography," *Physical Education and Sport Pedagogy*, 22 (5): 502–17.

Andersson, J. and Risberg, J. (2018), "Embodying Teaching: A Body Pedagogic Study of a Teacher's Movement Rhythm in the 'Sloyd' Classroom," *Interchange*, 49 (2): 179–204.

Andersson, J., Garrison, J. and Östman, L. (2018), *Empirical Philosophical Investigations in Education and Embodied Experience*, New York, NY: Palgrave.

Andersson, J., Östman, L. and Öhman, M. (2015), "I Am Sailing – Towards a Transactional Analysis of 'Body Techniques,'" *Sport, Education and Society*, 20 (6): 722–40.

Andersson, K. and Öhman, J. (2015), "Moral Relations in Encounters with Nature," *Journal of Adventure Education and Outdoor Learning*, 15 (4): 310–29.

Andersson, P. (2018), "Business as Un-Usual through Dislocatory Moments – Change for Sustainability and Scope for Subjectivity in Classroom Practice," *Environmental Education Research*, 24 (5): 648–62.

Andersson, P. (2019), *Transaktionella analyser av undervisning och lärande: SMED-studier 2006–2018*. [Transactional Analyses of Teaching and Learning – SMED-Studies 2006–2018], Rapporter i pedagogik 22 [Reports in pedagogy 22], Örebro University, Sweden.

Antonovsky, A. (1979), *Health, Stress, and Coping*, San Francisco: Jossey-Bass.

Antonovsky, A. (1996), "The Salutogenic Model as a Theory to Guide Health Promotion," *Health Promotion International*, 11 (1): 11–18.

Bedford, L. (2014), *The Art of Museum Exhibitions: How Story and Imagination Create Aesthetic Experiences*, Walnut Creek: Taylor & Francis Group.

Bennett, J. (2010), *Vibrant Matter: A Political Ecology of Things*, Durham, NC: Duke University Press.

Bennett, J. (2013), "Eco-sensibilities: An Interview with Jane Bennett," Watson, J. *The Minnesota Review*, 81, 147–58.

Bernstein, R. (1961), "John Dewey's Metaphysics of Experience," *Journal of Philosophy*, 57 (1): 5–14.

Biesta, G. (2013), *The Beautiful Risk of Education*, Boulder: Paradigm Publishers.

Biesta, G. and Burbules, N. (2003), *Pragmatism and Educational Research*, Lanham, MD: Rowman & Littlefield.

Boisvert, R. (1988), *Dewey's Metaphysics*, New York: Fordham University Press.
Burke, K. (1945/1969), *A Grammar of Motives*, New York: Prentice-Hall.
Clancey, W. J. (2006), "Observations of Work Practices in Natural Settings," in A. Ericsson, N. Charness, P. Feltovich and R. Hoffman (eds.), *Cambridge Handbook on Expertise and Expert Performance*, 127–45, New York: Cambridge University Press.
Clancey, W. J. (2012), *Working on Mars: Voyages of Scientific Discovery with the Mars Exploration Rovers*, Cambridge, MA: MIT Press.
Clark, A. (2008), *Supersizing the Mind: Embodiment, Action, and Cognitive Extension*, Cambridge: Cambridge University Press.
Coenders, F., Terlouw, C. and Dijkstra, S. (2008), "Assessing Teachers' Beliefs to Facilitate the Transition to a New Chemistry Curriculum: What Do the Teachers Want?," *Journal of Science Teacher Education*, 19 (4): 317–35.
Connell, J. M. (2008), "The Emergence of Pragmatic Philosophy's Influence on Literary Theory: Making Meaning with Texts from a Transactional Perspective," *Educational Theory*, 58: 103–22.
Cotton, D. R. E. (2006), "Implementing Curriculum Guidance on Environmental Education: The Importance of Teachers' Beliefs," *Journal of Curriculum Studies*, 38 (1): 67–83.
Crawford, A. (2014), "'The Trauma Experienced by Generations Past Having an Effect in Their Descendants': Narrative and Historical Trauma among Inuit in Nunavut, Canada," *Transcultural Psychiatry*, 51 (3): 339–69.
Dewey, J. (1888/1969), "The Ethics of Democracy," in J. A. Boydston (ed.), *John Dewey: The Early Works, Volume 1*, 227–49, Carbondale: Southern Illinois University Press.
Dewey, J. (1895/1971), "The Theory of Emotion," in J. A. Boydston (ed.), *John Dewey: The Early Works, Volume 4*, 152–88, Carbondale: Southern Illinois University Press.
Dewey, J. (1896/1972), "The Reflex Arc Concept in Psychology," in J. A. Boydston (ed.), *John Dewey: The Early Works, Volume 5*, 96–109, Carbondale: Southern Illinois University Press.
Dewey J. (1902–1903/1976), "Studies in Logical Theory," in. J. A. Boydston (ed.), *The Middle Works of John Dewey, 1899–1924, Volume 2*, 293–378, Carbondale and Edwardsville: Southern Illinois University Press.
Dewey, J. (1903/1977a).,"Belief and Existence," in J. A. Boydston (ed.), *John Dewey: The Middle Works, Volume 3*, 83–99, Carbondale: Southern Illinois University Press.
Dewey, J. (1903/1977b), "The Postulate of Immediate Empiricism," in J. A. Boydston (ed.), *John Dewey: The Middle Works, Volume 3*, 158–67, Carbondale: Southern Illinois University Press.
Dewey, J. (1910/1991), *How We Think*, Amherst, NY: Prometheus Books.
Dewey, J. (1916/1980), "Democracy and Education," in J. A. Boydston (ed.), *John Dewey: The Middle Works, Volume 9*, Carbondale: Southern Illinois University Press.

Dewey, J. (1917/1980), "The Need for a Recovery of Philosophy," in J. A. Boydston (ed.), *John Dewey: The Middle Works, Volume 10*, 3–48, Carbondale: Southern Illinois University Press.

Dewey, J. (1920/1983), "Realism without Monism or Dualism," in J. A. Boydston (ed.), *John Dewey: The Middle Works, Volume 13*, 40–60, Carbondale: Southern Illinois University Press.

Dewey, J. (1920/1986), "Reconstruction in Philosophy," in J. A. Boydston (ed.), *The Middle Works: 1899–1924, Volume 12*, 71–201, Carbondale: Southern Illinois University Press.

Dewey, J. (1922), *Human Nature and Conduct An introduction to social psychology*, New York: Henry Holt.

Dewey, J. (1922/1983), "Human Nature and Conduct," in J. A Boydston (ed.), *John Dewey: The Middle Works, Volume 14*, Carbondale: Southern Illinois University Press.

Dewey, J. (1924/1988), "Some Comments on Philosophical Discussion," in J. A. Boydston (ed.), *John Dewey: The Middle Works, Volume 15*, 29–41, Carbondale: Southern Illinois University Press.

Dewey, J. (1925/1981), "Experience and Nature," in J. A. Boydston (ed.), *The Later Works: 1925–1953, Volume 1*, 1–409, Carbondale: Southern Illinois University Press.

Dewey, J. (1926/1984), "Affective Thought," in J. A. Boydston (ed.), *John Dewey: The Later Works, Volume 2*, 104–15, Carbondale: Southern Illinois University Press.

Dewey, J. (1928/1984), "The Inclusive Philosophic Idea," in J. A. Boydston (ed.), *John Dewey: The Later Works, Volume 3*, 40–54, Carbondale: Southern Illinois University Press.

Dewey, J. (1929/1958), *Experience and Nature*, New York, NY: Dover Publications.

Dewey, J. (1929/1984), "The Quest for Certainty," in J. A. Boydston (ed.), *John Dewey: The Later Works, Volume 4*, Carbondale: Southern Illinois University Press.

Dewey, J. (1930/1984), "Three Independent Factors in Morals," in J. A. Boydston (ed.), *The Later Works of John Dewey, 1925–1953, Volume 5*, 279–88, Carbondale and Edwardsville: Southern Illinois University Press.

Dewey, J. (1930/1984), "Conduct and Experience," in J. A. Boydston (ed.), *John Dewey: The Later Works, Volume 5*, 218–31, Carbondale: Southern Illinois University Press.

Dewey, J. (1930/1984). "Qualitative Thought," in J. A. Boydston (ed.), *John Dewey: The Later Works, Volume 5*, 243–62, Carbondale: Southern Illinois University Press.

Dewey, J. (1931/1985), "Context and Thought," In J. A. Boydston (ed.), *John Dewey: The Later Works, Volume 6*, 3–21, Carbondale: Southern Illinois University Press.

Dewey, J. (1932/1985), "Ethics," in J. A. Boydston (ed.), *The Later Works of John Dewey, 1925–1953, Volume 7*, 1–536, Carbondale and Edwardsville: Southern Illinois University Press.

Dewey, J. (1933/1986). "How We Think," in J. A. Boydston (ed.), *John Dewey: The Later Works, Volume 7*, 105–352, Carbondale: Southern Illinois University Press.

Dewey, J. (1934/1980), *Art as Experience*, New York: Perigee.
Dewey, J. (1934/1987), "Art as Experience," in J. A. Boydston (ed.), *John Dewey: The Later Works, Volume 10*, Carbondale: Southern Illinois University Press.
Dewey, J. (1934/2005), *Art as Experience*, New York: Perigee.
Dewey, J. (1938), *Logic: The Theory of Inquiry*, New York: Henry Holt and Company.
Dewey, J. (1938/1986), "Logic: The Theory of Inquiry," in J. A. Boydston (ed.), *John Dewey: The Later Works, Volume 12*, Carbondale: Southern Illinois University Press.
Dewey, J. (1938/1997), *Experience and Education*, New York: Touchstone.
Dewey, J. (1938/1988), Experience and Education, in J. A. Boydston (ed.), *John Dewey: The Later Works, Volume 13*, 1–62. Carbondale: Southern Illinois University Press.
Dewey, J. (1939/1991), "Experience, Knowledge and Value: A Rejoinder," in J. A. Boydston (ed.), *John Dewey: The Later Works, Volume 14*, 3–90, Carbondale: Southern Illinois University Press.
Dewey, J. (1939/1988). "Freedom and Culture," in J. A. Boydston (ed.), *John Dewey: The Later Works, Vol. 13*, 63–188, Carbondale: Southern Illinois University Press.
Dewey, J. (1946/1989), "Peirce's Theory of Linguistic Signs, Thought, and Meaning," in J. A. Boydston (ed.), *John Dewey: The Later Works, Volume 15*, 142–52, Carbondale: Southern Illinois University Press.
Dewey, J. and Bentley, A. (1949), *Knowing and the Known*, Boston: The Beacon Press.
Dewey, J. and Bentley, A. (1949/1989a), "Knowing and the Known," in J. A. Boydston (ed.), *John Dewey: The Later Works, Volume 16*, 1–279, Carbondale: Southern Illinois University Press.
Dewey, J. and Bentley, A. (1949/1989b), "Textual Commentary," in J. A. Boydston (ed.), *John Dewey: The Later Works, Volume 16*, 485–567, Carbondale: Southern Illinois University Press.
Dewey, J. and Bentley, A. (1964), *John Dewey and Arthur F. Bentley: A Philosophical Correspondence, 1932–1951* Sidney Ratner and Jules Altman (eds.), New Brunswick: Rutgers University Press.
Eberle, S. G. (2014), "The Elements of Play. Toward a Philosophy and a Definition of Play," *American Journal of Play*, 6 (2): 214–33.
Edensor, T. (2010), "Walking in Rhythms: Place, Regulation, Style and the Flow of Experience," *Visual Studies*, 25 (1): 69–79.
English, A. R. (2016), "John Dewey and the Role of the Teacher in a Globalized World: Imagination, Empathy, and 'Third Voice,'" *Educational Philosophy and Theory*, 48 (10): 1046–64.
Falk, J. H. and Dierking, L. D. (2012), *The Museum Experience Revisited*, Walnut Creek: Taylor & Francis Group. https://ebookcentral.proquest.com/lib/uu/detail.action?docID=1104662.
Feldman, M. S. (1995), *Strategies for Interpreting Qualitative Data*, Thousand Oaks: SAGE Publications.
Fenwick, T. (2015), "Sociomateriality and Learning: A Critical Approach," in D. Scott and E. Hargreaves (eds.), *The SAGE Handbook of Learning*, 83–93. DOI:10.4135/9781473915213.n8.

Fesmire, J. (2003), *John Dewey and Moral Imagination: Pragmatism in Ethics*, Bloomington: Indiana University Press.

Festenstein, M. (1997), *Pragmatism and Political Theory*, Cambridge: Polity Press.

Gale, R. (2010), "The Naturalism of John Dewey," in M. Cochran (ed.), *The Cambridge Companion to Dewey*, 55–79, Cambridge: Cambridge University Press.

Ganz, M. (2011), "Public Narrative, Collective Action, and Power," in S. Odugbemi and T. Lee (eds.), *Accountability through Public Opinion: From Inertia to Public Action*, 273–89, Washington, DC: The World Bank.

Garrison, J. (1996), "Dewey, Qualitative Thought, and Context," *International Journal of Qualitative Studies in Education*, 9 (4): 391–410.

Garrison, J. (2001), "An Introduction to Dewey's Theory of Functional 'Trans-Action': An Alternative Paradigm for Activity Theory," *Mind, Culture, and Activity*, 8 (4): 275–96.

Garrison, J. (2003), "Dewey's Theory of Emotions: The Unity of Thought and Emotion in Naturalistic Functional 'Co-ordination' of Behavior," *Transactions of the Charles S. Peirce Society*, 39 (3): 405–43.

Garrison, J. (2006), "The 'Permanent Deposit' of Hegelian Thought in Dewey's Theory of Inquiry," *Educational Theory*, 56 (1): 1–37.

Garrison, J. (2010), *Dewey and Eros: Wisdom and Desire in the Art of Teaching*, Charlotte, NC: Information Age Publishing.

Garrison, J. (2011), "Transacting with Clancey's 'Transactional Perspective on the Practice-Based Science of Teaching and Learning,'" in T. Koschmann (ed.), *Theories of Learning and Studies of Instructional Practice*, 307–21, New York: Springer.

Garrison J. (2015), "Dewey's Aesthetics of Body–Mind Functioning," in A. Scarinzi (ed.), *Aesthetics and the Embodied Mind: Beyond Art Theory and the Cartesian Mind–Body Dichotomy*, 39–53, Dordrecht: Springer.

Garrison, J. (2019), "The Myth That Dewey Accepts 'The Myth of the Given,'" *Transactions of the Charles S. Peirce Society*, 55 (3): 305–25.

Garrison, J., Östman, L. and Håkansson, M. (2015), "The Creative Use of Companion Values in Environmental Education and Education for Sustainable Development: Exploring the Educative Moment," *Environmental Education Research*, 21 (2): 183–204.

Goffman, E. (1956), *The Presentation of Self in Everyday Life*, Edinburgh: University of Edinburgh.

Gould, D. (2010), "On Affect and Protest," in J. Staiger, A. Cvetkovich and A. Reynolds (eds.), *Political Emotions: New Agendas in Communication*, 18–44, New York: Routledge.

Gould, D. (2011), "Desiring Politics," in M. Engelken-Jorge, P. I. Güell and C. M. Del Río (eds.), *Politics and Emotions*, 155–88, Springer: VS Verlag für Sozialwissenschaften.

Graham, B. and Kirby, C. C. (2016), "Gadamer, Dewey, and the Importance of Play in Philosophical Inquiry," *Reason Papers*, 38 (1): 8–20.

Greco, J. (2008), "Skepticism about the External World," in J. Greco (ed.), *The Oxford Handbook of Skepticism*, 108–28, Oxford: Oxford University Press.

Hajer, M. (2005), "Setting the Stage. A Dramaturgy of Policy Deliberation," *Administration & Society*, 36 (6): 624–47.

Håkansson, M. and Östman, L. (2019), "The Political Dimension in ESE: The Construction of a Political Moment Model for Analyzing Bodily Anchored Political Emotions in Teaching and Learning of the Political Dimension," *Environmental Education Research*, 25 (4): 585–600.

Håkansson, M., Van Poeck, K. and Östman, L. (2019), "The Political Tendency Typology: Different Ways in Which the Political Dimension of Sustainability Issues Appear in Educational Practice," in K. Van Poeck, L. Östman and J. Öhman (eds.), *Sustainable Development Teaching – Ethical and Political Challenges*, 70–82, Abingdon, Oxon; New York, NY: Routledge.

Hein, G. E. (1998), *Learning in the Museum*, London: Taylor & Francis Group. Available from: ProQuest Ebook Central. [September 18, 2020].

Hein, G. E. (2004), "John Dewey and Museum Education," *Curator: The Museum Journal*, 47: 413–27.

Hein, G. E. (2006), "John Dewey's 'Wholly Original Philosophy' and Its Significance for Museums," *Curator: The Museum Journal*, 49: 181–203.

Hein, George E. (2012), *Progressive Museum Pedagogy: John Dewey and Democracy*, Walnut Creek: Left Coast Press.

Henricks, T. S. (2015), *Play and the Human Condition*, Urbana, Chicago, and Springfield: University of Illinois Press.

Hickman, L. A. (1992), *John Dewey's Pragmatic Technology*, Bloomington: Indiana University Press.

Hickman, L. A. (2007), *Pragmatism as Post-Postmodernism: Lessons from John Dewey*, New York: Fordham University Press.

Hodkinson, P., Biesta, G. and James, D. (2007), "Understanding Learning Culturally: Overcoming the Dualism between Social and Individual Views of Learning," *Vocations and Learning*, 1: 27–47.

Hofverberg, H. (2019), *Crafting Sustainable Development. Studies of Teaching and Learning Craft in Environmental and Sustainability Education*. Diss., Uppsala: Uppsala University.

Hofverberg, H. (2020), "Entangled Threads and Crafted Meanings – Students' Learning for Sustainability in Remake Activities," *Environmental Education Research*, 26: 9–10, 1281–93.

Hofverberg, H. and Maivorsdotter, N. (2018), "Recycling, Crafting and Learning – An Empirical Analysis of How Students Learn with Garments and Textile Refuse in a School Remake Project," *Environmental Education Research*, 24 (6): 775–90.

Hofverberg, H. and Westerlund, S. (2021), "Among Facilitators, Instructors, Advisors and Educators – How Teachers Educate for Sustainability in Design and Craft Education," *International Journal of Art and Design Education*. https://doi.org/10.1111/jade.12366.

Huizinga, J. (1938/2014), *Homo ludens. A Study of the Play-Element in Culture*, Mansfield Centre: Martino Publishing.

Hume, D. (1748/1977), *An Enquiry Concerning Human Understanding*, Indianapolis: Hackett.

Hutchins, E. (1991), "The Social Organization of Distributed Cognition," in L. B. Resnick, J. M. Levine and S. D. Teasley (eds.), *Perspectives on Socially Shared Cognition*, 283–307, Washington, DC: American Psychological Association Press.

Illeris, H. (2006), "Museums and Galleries as Performative Sites for Lifelong Learning: Constructions, Deconstructions and Reconstructions of Audience Positions in Museum and Gallery Education," *Museum and Society*, 4: 15–26.

Ingold, T. (2011), *Being Alive – Essays on Movement, Knowledge and Description*, London: Routledge Taylor and Francis Group.

Ingold, T. (2013), *Making – Anthropology, Archaeology, Art and Architecture*, London: Routledge Taylor and Francis Group.

James, W. (1890/1950), *The Principles of Psychology*, Volume 1 New York: Dover Publications.

James, W. (1912/1976), *Essays in Radical Empiricism*, Cambridge: Harvard University Press.

James, W. (2003), *Essays in Radical Empiricism*, New York: Dover Publications.

Joas, H. (1985), *G. H. Mead: A Contemporary Re-examination of His Thought*, Cambridge, MA: The MIT Press.

Johnson, M. (2007), *The Meaning of the Body: Aesthetics of Human Understanding*, Chicago: University of Chicago Press.

Johnson, M. (2015), "The Aesthetics of Embodied Life," in A. Scarinzi (ed.), *Aesthetics and the Embodied Mind: Beyond Art Theory and the Cartesian Mind-Body Dichotomy*, New York; London: Springer, 23–38.

Klaar, S. and Öhman, J. (2012), "Action with Friction: A Transactional Approach to Toddlers' Physical Meaning Making of Natural Phenomena and Processes in Preschool," *European Early Childhood Education Research Journal*, 20 (3): 439–54.

Klaar, S. and Öhman, J. (2014), "Doing, Knowing, Caring and Feeling: Exploring Relations between Nature-Oriented Teaching and Preschool Children's Learning," *International Journal of Early Years Education*, 22 (1): 37–58.

Klafki, W. (1995), "Didactic Analysis as the Core of Preparation of Instruction" [Didaktische Analyse als Kern der Unterrichtsvorbereitung], *Journal of Curriculum Studies*, 27 (1): 13–30.

Latham, K. F. (2007), "The Poetry of the Museum: A Holistic Model of Numinous Museum Experiences," *Museum Management and Curatorship*, 22: 247–63.

Latham, K. F. (2013), "Numinous Experiences with Museum Objects," *Visitor Studies*, 16: 3–20.

Latour, B. (1996), On Actor-Network Theory: A Few Clarifications," *Soziale Welt*, 47 (4): 369–81.

Lidar, M., Almqvist, J. and Östman, L. (2010), "A Pragmatist Approach to Meaning Making in Children's Discussions about Gravity and the Shape of the Earth," *Science Education*, 94 (4): 689–709.

Lidar, M., Lundqvist, E. and Östman, L. (2006), "Teaching and Learning in the Science Classroom: The Interplay between Teachers' Epistemological Moves and Students' Practical Epistemology," *Science Education*, 90 (1): 148–63.

Lidar, M., Lundqvist, E., Ryder, J. and Östman, L. (2020), "The Transformation of Teaching Habits in Relation to the Introduction of Grading and National Testing in Science Education in Sweden," *Research in Science Education*, 50, 151–73.

Ljung, B. (2009), *Museipedagogik och erfarande*. PhD Thesis, University of Stockholm, Sweden. Available online: http://urn.kb.se/resolve?urn=urn:nbn:se:su:diva-28755 (accessed February 1, 2021).

López, F. (2018), The Place of Biology and Anthropology in Dewey's Ethical Project, *Cognitio: Revista de Filosofia*, 19 (2): 270–81.

Lovejoy, A. (1920/1983), "Pragmatism *Versus* the Pragmatist," in J. A. Boydston (ed.), *John Dewey: The Middle Works, Volume 13*, 443–81, Carbondale: Southern Illinois University Press.

Lumpe, A.T., Haney, J. J. and Czerniak, C. M. (2000), "Assessing Teachers' Beliefs about Their Science Teaching Context," *Journal of Research in Science Teaching*, 37 (3): 275–92.

Lundqvist, E. and Lidar, M. (2020), "Functional Coordination between Present Teaching and Policy Reform in Swedish Science Education," *Education Inquiry*. Available online: doi: 10.1080/20004508.2020.1823132 (accessed December 18, 2020).

Lundqvist, E., Almqvist, J. and Östman, L. (2009), "Epistemological Norms and Companion Meanings in Science Classroom Communication," *Science Education*, 93 (5): 859–74.

Lundqvist, E., Almqvist, J. and Östman, L. (2012), "Institutional Traditions in Teachers' Manners of Teaching," *Cultural Studies of Science Education*, 7 (1): 111–27.

Maivorsdotter, N. and J. Andersson (2020), "Health as Experience: Exploring Health in Daily Life Drawing from the Work of Aaron Antonovsky and John Dewey," *Qualitative Health Research*, 30 (7): 1004–18.

Maivorsdotter, N. and Wickman, P. -O. (2011), "Skating in a Life Context: Examining the Significance of Aesthetic Experience in Sport Using Practical Epistemology Analysis," *Sport, Education & Society*, 16 (5): 613–28.

Massumi, B. (1995), "The Autonomy of Affect," *Cultural Critique*, 31: 83–109.

McCuaig, L. and M. Quennerstedt (2018), "Health by Stealth — Exploring the Sociocultural Dimensions of Salutogenesis for Sport, Health and Physical Education Research," *Sport, Education and Society*, 23 (2): 111–22.

McNeill, W. H. (1976), *Plagues and Peoples*, New York: Anchor Books.

Mead, G. H. (1913/1964), "The Social Self," in A. J. Reck (ed.), *Selected Writings: George Herbert Mead*, 142–9, Chicago: The University of Chicago Press.

Mead, G. H. (1922/1964), "A Behavioristic Account of The Significant Symbol," in A. J. Reck (ed.), *Selected Writings: George Herbert Mead*, 240–7, Chicago: The University of Chicago Press.

Mead, G. H. (1932/1959), *The Philosophy of the Present*, LaSalle Illinois: The Open Court Publishing Company.

Mead, G. H. (1934/1967), *Mind, Self, and Society: From the Standpoint of a Social Behaviorist*, C. W. Morris (ed.), Chicago: The University of Chicago Press.

Medina, M. (2004), "In Defense of Pragmatic Contextualism: Wittgenstein and Dewey on Meaning and Agreement," *The Philosophical Forum*, 35 (3): 341–69.

Mindell, D. (2015), *Our Robots, Ourselves: Robotics and the Myth of Autonomy*, Cambridge, MA: MIT Press.

Mohatt, N. V., Thompson, A. B., Thai, N. D. and Tebes, J. K. (2014), "Historical Trauma as Public Narrative: A Conceptual Review of How History Impacts Present-Day Health," *Social Science and Medicine*, 106: 128–36.

Morris, C. (1938), "Foundations on the Theory of Signs," in O. Neurath and R. Carnap (eds.), *Foundations of the Unity of Science, Volume 1*, Chicago: University of Chicago Press.

Morris, C. (1946), *Signs, Language, and Behavior*, New York: Prentice Hall.

Morse, D. J. (2010), "Dewey on the Emotions," *Human Affairs*, 20 (3): 224–31.

Nahuis, R. (2009), *The Politics of Displacement. Towards a Framework for Democratic Evaluation*, Innovation Studies Utrecht Working Paper Series, ISU Working Paper #08.09, Utrecht: Universiteit Utrecht.

Nelsen, P. J. (2014), "Intelligent Dispositions: Dewey, Habits and Inquiry in Teacher Education," *Journal of Teacher Education*, 6 (1): 86–97.

Nussbaum, M. C. (2013), *Political Emotions: Why Love Matters for Justice*, Cambridge, MA: The Belknap Press of Harvard University Press.

O'Donnell, C. R. and Tharp, R. G. (2012), "Integrating Cultural Community Psychology: Activity Settings and the Shared Meanings of Intersubjectivity," *American Journal of Community Psychology*, 49 (1–2): 22–30.

Öhman, J. and Kronlid, D. O. (2019), "A Pragmatist Perspective on Value Education," in K. Van Poeck, L. Östman and J. Öhman (eds.), *Sustainable Development Teaching: Ethical and Political Challenges*, 93–102, Milton Park and New York: Routledge.

Öhman, J. and Öhman, M. (2013), "Participatory Approach in Practice: An Analysis of Student Discussions about Climate Change," *Environmental Education Research*, 19 (3): 324–41.

Öhman, J. and Östman, L. (2007), "Continuity and Change in Moral-Meaning Making: A Transactional Approach," *Journal of Moral Education*, 36 (2): 151–68.

Öhman, J. and L. Östman (2008), "Clarifying the Ethical Tendency in Education for Sustainable Development Practice: A Wittgenstein-Inspired Approach," *Canadian Journal of Environmental Education*, 13 (1), 57–72.

Östman, L. (2010), "Education for Sustainable Development and Normativity: A Transactional Analysis of Moral Meaning-Making and Companion Meanings in Classroom Communication," *Environmental Education Research*, 16 (1): 75–93.

Östman, L. and Öhman, J. (forthcoming), "A Transactional Methodology for Analysing Learning," *Mind, Culture, and Activity: An International Journal*.

Östman, L., Öhman, M., Lundqvist, E. and Lidar, M. (2015), "Teaching, Learning and Governance in Science Education and Physical Education: A Comparative Approach," *Interchange: A Quarterly Review of Education*, 46 (4): 369–86.

Östman, L., Van Poeck, K. and Öhman, J. (2019a), "A Transactional Theory on Sustainability Learning," in K. Van Poeck, L. Östman and J. Öhman (eds.), *Sustainable Development Teaching. Ethical and Political Challenges*, 127–38, Abington, Oxon; New York, NY: Routledge.

Östman, L., Van Poeck, K. and Öhman, J. (2019b), "Principles for Sustainable Development Teaching," in K. Van Poeck, L. Östman and J. Öhman (eds.), *Sustainable Development Teaching. Ethical and Political Challenges*, 40–54. Abington, Oxon; New York, NY: Routledge.

Pappas, G. F. (2019), "The Starting Point of Dewey's Ethics and Sociopolitical Philosophy," in S. Fesmire (ed.), *The Oxford Handbook of Dewey*, 235–53, Oxford and New York: Oxford University Press.

Pappas, G. F. (2008), *John Dewey's Ethics. Democracy as Experience*, Bloomington and Indianapolis: Indiana University Press.

Patton, R. M. (2014), "Games That Art Educators Play: Games in the Historical and Cultural Context of Art Education," *Studies in Art Education*, 55 (3): 241–52.

Peirce, C. S. (1960), *The Collected Papers of Charles Sanders Peirce, Volume V*, C. Hartshorne and P. Weiss (eds.), Cambridge: Harvard University Press.

Plummer, P. and Van Poeck, K. (2020), "Unpacking the Role of Learning in Sustainability Transitions: How Niche Actors 'Learn by Doing' to Challenge the Status Quo," *Environmental Education Research*, https://doi.org/10.1080/13504622.2020.1857703.

Pollard, V. (2008), "Ethics and Reflective Practice: Continuing the Conversation," *Reflective Practice*, 9 (4): 399–407.

Quennerstedt, M., Öhman, J. and Öhman, M. (2011), "Investigating Learning in Physical Education – A Transactional Approach," *Sports, Education and Society*, 16 (2):159–77.

Quine, W. V. (1969), "Ontological Relativity," in W. V. Quine (ed.), *Ontological Relativity and Other Essays*, 26–68, New York: Columbia University Press.

Rappaport, J. (2000), "Community Narratives: Tales of Terror and Joy," *American Journal of Community Psychology*, 28 (1): 1–24.

Ratner, S. (1964), "Introduction," in Ratner, S. and J. Altman (eds.). *John Dewey and Arthur F. Bentley: A Philosophical Correspondence, 1933–1951*, New Brunswick: Rutgers University Press.

Ratner, S. and Altman, J. (1964), *John Dewey and Arthur F. Bentley: A Philosophical Correspondence, 1933–1951*, New Brunswick: Rutgers University Press.

Rhees, R. (1970/1996), *Discussions of Wittgenstein*, Bristol: Thoemmes Press.

Rogers, D. R. (2016), "Deep Discoverer: ROV Connects Scientists and Citizens with the Deep Sea," *Robot Magazine*, November/December: 40–3.

Rogoff, B. (1995), 'Observing Sociocultural Activity on Three Planes: Participatory Appropriation, Guided Participation, and Apprenticeship', in J.V. Wertsch; P. Del Rio and A. Alvarez (eds.), *Sociocultural Studies of Mind*, 139–164, New York: Cambridge University Press.

Rømer, T. A. (2012), "Imagination and Judgment in John Dewey's Philosophy: Intelligent Transactions in a Democratic Context," *Educational Philosophy and Theory*, 44 (2): 133–50.

Rosen, M. (2019), *Michael Rosen's Book of Play*, London: Profile Books.

Rosenblatt, L. (1938/1995), *Literature as Exploration*, New York, NY: Modern Language Association.

Rosenblatt, L. (1978/1994). *The Reader, the Text, the Poem: The Transactional Theory of the Literary Work*, Carbondale and Edwardsville: Southern Illinois University Press.

Rosenblatt, L. M. (1985), "Viewpoints: Transaction Versus Interaction: A Terminological Rescue Operation," *Research in the Teaching of English*, 19 (1): 96–107.

Rosenblatt, L. M. (1994), *The Reader, the Text, the Poem: The Transactional Theory of the Literary Work*. Electronic resource, Carbondale: Southern Illinois University Press.

Rosenblatt, L. M. (1995), *Literature as Exploration*, New York: Modern Language Association of America.

Rosenblatt L. M. (2005), *Making Meaning with Texts: Selected Essays*, Portsmouth: Heinemann.

Rosenthal, S. (1985), *Speculative Pragmatism*, Amherst, MA: University of Massachusetts Press.

Rosenthal, S. (2001), "The Pragmatic Reconstruction of Realism: A Pathway for the Future," in J. Shook (ed.), *Pragmatic Naturalism and Realism*, Amherst, NY: Prometheus Books.

Rudsberg, K. and Öhman, J. (2010), "Pluralism in Practice – Experiences from Swedish Evaluation, School Development and Research," *Environmental Education Research*, 16 (1): 95–111.

Rudsberg, K. and Öhman, J. (2015), "The Role of Knowledge in Participatory and Pluralistic Approaches to ESE," *Environmental Education Research*, 21 (7): 955–74.

Rudsberg, K., Öhman, J. and Östman, L. (2013), "Analyzing Students' Learning in Classroom Discussions about Socioscientific Issues," *Science Education*, 97 (4): 594–620.

Ryan, F. X. (2016), "Rethinking the Human Condition: Skepticism, Realism, and Transactional Pragmatism," *Contemporary Pragmatism*, 13: 263–97.

Ryan, F. X. (2003), "Values as Consequences of Transaction: Commentary on 'Reconciling *Homo Economicus* and John Dewey's Ethics,'" *Journal of Economic Methodology*, 10 (2): 245–57.

Ryan, F. X. (2011), *Seeing Together. Mind, Matter, and the Experimental Outlook of John Dewey and Arthur F. Bentley*, Great Barrington, MA: American Institute for Economic Research.

Serres, M. (2007), *The Parasite*, Minneapolis: University of Minnesota Press.

Shilling, C. (2017), "Body Pedagogics: Embodiment, Cognition and Cultural Transmission," *Sociology*, 51 (6): 1205–21.

Shilling, C. (2018), "Embodying Culture: Body Pedagogics, Situated Encounters and Empirical Research," *The Sociological Review*, 66 (1): 75–90.

Shook, J. R. (ed.) (2011), *The Essential William James*, New York: Prometheus Books.

Showstack, R. (2019), "NOAA Budget Proposal Hits Rough Waters in Congress," *Eos*, 100. Available online: https://doi.org/10.1029/2019EO119557 (accessed October 22, 2019).

Skilbeck, A. (2017), "Dewey on Seriousness, Playfulness and the Role of the Teacher," *Education Sciences*, 7 (1), https://www.mdpi.com/2227-7102/7/1/16/htm (accessed April 2, 2020).

Skolverket (2011), *Curriculum for the Upper Secondary School 2011*. (Lgr11), Stockholm: Swedish National Agency of Education.

Sleeper, R. (1986), *The Necessity of Pragmatism: John Dewey's Conception of Philosophy*, New Haven: Yale University Press.

Sommerfeld, J. (2003), "Plagues and People Revisited," *EMBO Report*, Jun(4): S32–S34.

Stoller, A. (2018), "Dewey's Creative Ontology," *Journal of Thought*, 52 (3–4): 47–64.

Stroud, B. (1994/1999), "Scepticism, 'Externalist', and the Goal of Epistemology," in K. DeRose and T. Warfield (eds.), *Skepticism: A Contemporary Reader*, 292–304, New York: Oxford University Press.

Sund, L. and Öhman, J. (2014), "Swedish Teachers' Ethical Reflections on a Study Visit to Central America," *Journal of Moral Education*, 43 (3): 316–31.

Sund, P. and Wickman, P. O. (2011a), "Socialization Content in Schools and Education for Sustainable Development – I. A study of Teachers' Selective Traditions," *Environmental Education Research*, 17 (5): 599–624.

Sund, P. and Wickman, P. O. (2011b), "Socialization Content in Schools and Education for Sustainable Development – II. A Study of Students' Apprehension of Teachers' Companion Meanings in ESD," *Environmental Education Research*, 17 (5): 625–49.

Taylor, D. M. and E. Usborne (2010), "When I Know Who 'We' Are, I Can Be 'Me': The Primary Role of Cultural Identity Clarity for Psychological Well-being," *Transcultural Psychiatry*, 47 (1): 93–111.

Thayer, H. S. and Thayer, V. T. (1985), "Introduction," in J. A. Boydston (ed.), *John Dewey: The Middle Works, Volume 6*, Carbondale: Southern Illinois University Press.

Tiles, J. (1989), "Our Perception of the External World," in A. P. Griffiths (ed.), *Key Themes in Philosophy*, Cambridge: Cambridge University Press.

Tomasello, M. (1999), *The Cultural Origins of Human Cognition*, Cambridge: Harvard University Press.

Tomasello, M. (2008), *Origins of Human Communication*, Cambridge: The MIT Press.

Tomasello, M. (2019), *Becoming Human*, Cambridge: Harvard University Press.

Toulmin, S. (1984), "Introduction. The Quest for Certainty," in J. A. Boydston (ed.), *John Dewey: The Later Works, Volume 4*, Carbondale: Southern Illinois University Press.

Van Poeck, K. (2019), "Environmental and Sustainability Education in a Posttruth Era. An Exploration of Epistemology and Didactics beyond the Objectivism-Relativism Dualism," *Environmental Education Research*, 25 (4): 472–91.

Van Poeck, K. and L. Östman (2021), "Learning to Find a Way Out of Non-sustainable Systems," *Environmental Innovation and Societal Transitions*, 39: 155–72.

Van Poeck, K., Vandenabeele, J. and G. Goeminne (2017), "Making Climate Change Public? A Dramaturgically Inspired Case-study of Learning through Transition Management," *International Journal of Global Warming*, 12 (3–4): 366–85.

Vanderstraeten, R. (2002), "Dewey's Transactional Constructivism," *Journal of Philosophy of Education*, 36 (2): 233–45.

Wallace, C. and M. Priestley (2011), "Teacher Beliefs and the Mediation of Curriculum Innovation in Scotland: A Socio-cultural Perspective on Professional Development and Change," *Journal of Curriculum Studies*, 43 (3): 357–81.

Wals, A. E. J. (2010), "Between Knowing What Is Right and Knowing That Is It Wrong to Tell Others What Is Right: On Relativism, Uncertainty and Democracy in Environmental and Sustainability Education," *Environmental Education Research*, 16 (1): 143–51.

Wertsch, J. V. (1998), *Mind as Action*, New York: Oxford University Press.

Wertsch, J. V. (2008), "The Narrative Organization of Collective Memory," *Ethos*, 36 (1): 120–35.

Wickman, P. -O. (2006), *Aesthetic Experience in Science Education: Learning and Meaning-Making as Situated Talk and Action*, Mahwah, NJ: Lawrence Erlbaum Associates.

Wickman, P. -O. (2012), "Using Pragmatism to Develop Didactics in Sweden," *Zeitschrift für Erziehungswissenschaft*, 15 (3): 483–501.

Wickman, P. -O. and Östman, L. (2002), "Learning as Discourse Change: A Sociocultural Mechanism," *Science Education*, 86: 601–23.

Wikipedia (2019), "Transactionalism," *Wikipedia, The Free Encyclopedia*. Available online: https://en.wikipedia.org/w/index.php?title=Transactionalism&oldid=921501146 (accessed October 16, 2019).

Wilden, A. (1987), *The Rules Are No Game: The Strategy of Communication*, London: Routledge & Kegan Paul.

Wilden, A. ([1972] 1980), *System and Structure: Essays in Communication and Exchange*, Chapter 8: Epistemology and Ecology (Second edition), London: Tavistock.
Wittgenstein, L. (1953), *Philosophical Investigations*, New York: The Macmillian Company.
Wittgenstein, L. (1953/1997), *Philosophical Investigations*, Oxford: Blackwell.

Index

actants 11, 139–41, 146
action 2–4, 8–10, 16, 25, 40, 47, 95, 115, 195
    actants in 139–41
activity/category 6, 75–9, 81, 83, 85–6
actor network theory (ANT) 139–140
aesthetics 15, 76, 78–9, 168–9, 171, 179–92, 210, 215, 234 n.2
    bodily 208–12
    consummatory experience 189–90, 214
    of dramatization 84
    PEA of 187–91
    poignant 15, 207–18
    reading 168, 171, 176
affect 208, 210, 212
    bodily 15, 184
anoetic experience 181–2, 210
ANT. *See* actor network theory (ANT)
Antonovsky, A. 16, 221–4, 226, 231
    salutogenic approach 16, 221–3
arbitrary intellectualism 5
argumentation 91–2
Aristotle and play 79–80
art 6–7, 9–10, 13–14, 78–9, 85, 168–9
    literary work 166–8
artistic 9–10, 14, 76, 78, 83–4, 101, 179–92, 234 n.2
    craftsmanship 185
    inquiry 180, 184–6, 189, 191

Ballard, R. 53
behavior 3, 45–6, 76, 80–1, 83, 125, 221, 230
    conjoint 5, 41
    nonreflective 77
    sign-behavior 32–3
    social 81, 224
Bennet, J. 140
Bentley, A. F. 1, 3–4, 6, 9–11, 16, 25–7, 32, 34, 39–40, 42–3, 45, 70, 126, 150, 221
    action 2
    behavior 3, 76
    event 49

Knowing and the Known 1, 10, 12, 25–6, 32, 34, 39, 43, 76
    seeing together 69, 81
Bernstein, R. 26
Biesta, G. 120
bodily aesthetical experience 208–12
body 33, 40, 43, 68, 91–2, 117, 119, 121, 150–1, 153, 194, 208, 210, 224, 231
body pedagogy 16, 221–5, 229–31
Boisvert, R. 28–9
business as un-usual 93–4
business as usual 93, 225
business sustainability 93–4

children's learning transactions 9
circle of doubt-belief 200–2
circuit of inquiry 6, 15, 17, 21–4, 26, 76–7, 83
circularity 2–3
cognitive access 18–19, 24
commerce 28, 30
communal play 81
conjoint behavior 5, 41
containment 17, 23, 34
    within inference 21, 24
containment paradigm 4, 17, 22, 24, 26–7, 29, 34, 36, 40
    skepticism and 18–20
continuity, principle of 115, 127, 196
Covid-19 pandemic 15–16, 221
    body pedagogic and 223
    Denmark's public narrative 228–9
    politics/people and 222–5
    Sweden's public narrative 229–30
    walking rhythm 223–4
crafting activity 138–9
    sensing together (*see* sensing together)
    transactants and (*see* transactant)
Crawford, A. 227
creative craftsmanship 185
creative inquiry 180, 185–6, 189
cultivated naïve realism 23–4, 30

DA. *See* dramaturgical analysis (DA)
democracy, play and 82–3
dependent hierarchy 57–60, 70–2
    constraint in 71–2
    imaginary oppositions 68–70
Dewey, J. 69
    action 2, 25, 115
    aesthetic 78, 84, 181, 210
    "*an* experience" 169, 184, 214
    anoetic experience 181–2
    arbitrary intellectualism 5
    Art as Experience 13, 162, 165, 169, 180, 184, 195
    behavior 2
    conjoint behavior 5, 41
    context of thought 181–2
    cultivated naïve realism 23–4, 30
    democracy 82
    Democracy and Education 6, 12, 75–6, 79, 83
    doing *vs.* inquiry 180
    environment *vs.* surroundings 126, 199
    ethical theories, criticism of 193–4, 205
    Ethics 193–4, 198
    event 49
    experience 113–14, 169, 198
    Experience and Education 165
    Experience and Nature 30–1
    habits 8, 118, 197, 209
    How We Think 78
    Human Nature and Conduct 85
    imagination 84–5, 198
    Inclusive Philosophic Idea, The 41
    inquiry process 119
    intelligent/artistic habit 101
    intelligent observation 78–9
    Knowing and the Known 1, 10, 12, 25–6, 32, 34, 39, 43, 76
    knowledge 4
    Logic: The Theory of Inquiry 2, 39–40, 48–9
    moral experience 196–8
    philosophical system 18–20
    play 75–86
    postulate of immediate experience 22
    principle of continuity 115, 127, 196
    problematic situation 196
    Quest for Certainty, The 10
    radical empiricism 149, 151
    reflective morality 194–6
    Reflex Arc Concept in Psychology, The 1, 12
    seeing together 69
    skilled *vs.* artistic craftsmanship 184–5
    transactionalism 2
didactics 10, 87–8, 97, 124, 128, 204, 235 n.3
    gaze 87, 92
    research problems 90–8
    timing 10, 128–9
didaktik-tradition 7, 87, 235 n.3
dislocatory moments 93–4
dive 54
doing 12, 43, 76, 117, 121, 126–8, 179–80
dramatic rehearsal 85
dramaturgical analysis (DA) 123
    characteristic of 124
    learning, facilitation of 124–35
    performance 125
    scripting 125
    settings and actions 124–5
    staging 125
durational-extensional transactions 3–6, 10, 39, 42, 44–5, 47, 59–60

ECC. *See* Exploration Command Center (ECC)
education 12, 16, 75–6, 79–80, 83, 93–4
    activities 90
    child 75–6, 78
    emancipatory aspects of 93
    environment and sustainability 91, 93
    influenza pandemic and 225–6
    moral consequences for 204–5
    play and democratic 82–6
    sloyd 11, 137, 149–63
    value 204–5
embodiment 33–5, 40, 67
emotions 6–7, 76, 78, 83–5, 147, 234 n.3
encounters 187
environing 84, 126–7, 140, 199, 201, 204, 221–3, 225
environment 3, 15, 39–40, 126–8, 138, 210, 222, 224
    habits 7–8, 100–1
    human-organism-sociocultural-environmental transactions 40, 44–5, 47
    individuals and 126–7, 202
    moral 201–3

organism-environment interaction 27, 34–5
organism-environment transaction 1–3, 12, 40, 126, 223, 233 n.2
organism-in-environment-as-a-whole 40, 52, 69, 126
organism-sociocultural-environment behavioral transaction 43
person-environment transaction 198–9
physical 7, 94, 111–22
self and 80, 82
social 9
and sustainability education 91, 93, 97
epistemological industry 18, 20
essences 2, 15, 30, 45, 48–9, 196
ethical theory 193–4, 205
value of 199–200
ethnography 5–6
event 49, 88, 95, 126–8, 168
evocation 13, 167, 171–6
existence 2, 5, 13, 15, 19, 21, 27–8, 34–5, 40–1, 45, 48–9, 210
configuring in experience 30–2
in *Okeanos* exploration system 58
poignant aesthetical 15, 207–18
experience 4–5, 9, 12–13, 18–19, 21, 25–8, 33–4, 46, 76, 78, 100, 138–9, 149, 151, 169, 198, 222, 225
aesthetical 15, 169, 179, 181, 184, 208–12, 215
aesthetic consummatory 189–90, 214
"*an* experience" 169, 184, 214
anoetic 181–2
art objects 169
educative 119
existence in, configuring 30–2
as functional coordination 101
habits and 100–1
immediate 4, 22, 150–1, 210
in learning and physical encounters 112–13
learning by 119
modes of 113–14
moral 194, 196–8, 204–5
nonreflective 21–3, 151–2
in phenomenological strain 27
play 76, 78
postulate of immediate 4, 22
principle of continuity 196
pure 5, 150–1, 210

tactile 151–2
Exploration Command Center (ECC) 51, 68
student activities in 66–7
Extinction Rule 58

firm words 26–7, 32
functional coordination 2, 6, 9
learning and physical encounters 116–18
teachers 8, 101–10
functional present 48–50
functional transactions 33
of dive 60–5
functional whole 69, 149
future 45–50
emergence of 45–8

gaps, lingering 187
Global Foundation for Ocean Exploration (GFOE) 56, 58
Greco, J. 18

habits 7–9, 14–16, 22, 32, 40, 77–8, 83, 100–1, 180, 213, 221–3, 231
anoetic experience and 181–2
as bodily aesthetical experience 208–12
functional aspects of 118
learning and physical encounters 113–16, 121
moral 14–15, 193, 195–9, 203
teaching 99–110
walking 224
Hajer, M. 124–5
handicraft education. *See* sensing together
health 223
hedges 26–7
transaction without 29–34
Henricks, T. S. 76, 80–1
Hickman, L. 11, 150–1, 200
Hodkinson, P. 120
how/what continuity 35–6
Huizinga, J. 80–1, 234 n.5
Homo ludens 80, 234 n.5
human-organism-sociocultural-environmental transactions 40, 44–5, 47
Hume, D. 19–20, 23

imaginary oppositions 68–70

imagination 6–7, 70, 198, 213
  and play in democratic education 83–5
immediate experience 4, 150–1, 210
  postulate of 22
inference 27, 34, 48
  containment within 24
  and ontology 20–1
inference paradigm 4, 17, 20–1, 24, 33–5
  existence in 30
Ingold, T. 138–9, 146
inquiry 4–6, 14–15, 22–3, 26, 35, 43, 48–9, 70, 101–3, 128–9, 150–1, 180, 201–2
  artistic 180, 184–6, 189, 191
  circuit of 6, 15, 17, 21–4, 26, 76, 83
  creative 180, 185–6, 189
  instrumental 185
  learning and physical encounters 118–19
  in learning trajectory 180–4, 213–14
  moral 198, 201–3
  objectives of 35
  problematic situation into 183–4
  theory of 149–50
instruction 12, 16, 85–6, 152–3, 156, 167
integration 2, 10
intelligent observation 78–9
intensity 210, 212
intentionality 28–9
interaction 2–3, 25–9, 34–5, 47, 123–5, 138, 221
interactional analysis (IA) 69–70
interactional pragmatism 27–9
  existence and experience relationship in 30
interpretant 32–4
interview 94–5, 101–3, 105–8, 110, 130, 204

James, D. 120
James, W. 11, 46, 212
  pure experience 5, 150–1, 210
joint attention 43–4
joint-transactional process 140–1

knowledge 4, 18, 21, 28, 78, 87–8, 91–2, 94–5, 97, 102, 113, 129, 149, 168–9
  museums and 168–9
  tacit 149
  transactional theory of 150–1

language 5, 10, 12, 26, 48, 89, 139, 161, 163, 187
  acquisition 40–3
  games 87–9
Latour, B. 139, 141
learning 4, 7–9, 14–15, 68, 84, 87–8
  argumentation 91–2
  complexity of 91–3
  critical moments in 93–4
  didactical research problems 90–8
  embodied 120–1
  encounter 90
  by experience 119
  facilitators 235 n.3
  gap 90
  moral concern 215–17
  Okeanos exploration system for 67–8
  PEA 89–90
  political concern 217–18
  privileging process 127
  relation 90
  sloyd 151
  social environment and 111
  stand fast 90
  teachers' and students' actions 94–6
  transactant in 142–6
  transactional methodological framework 88–9
learning and physical encounters 112–13
  continuity, principle of 115
  experience, modes of 112–13
  functional coordination 116–18
  habits 113–14
  inquiry process 118–19
  resistance and 116
learning, DA of facilitation of 10, 124–5
  coordinative function 128
  didactical timing 128–9
  explorative function 128
  facilitators' work 127–8
  generalizing move 133
  performance 125, 130–3
  preparatory work 125, 130
  privileging process 127
  reorienting move 132
  scripting 125, 130
  settings and actions 124–5
  Short Food Supply Chain (SFSC) workshops 129–33

specifying move 133
staging 125, 130
transactional perspective 125–9
learning trajectory 180–1, 208
   anoetic experience 181–2
   bodily aesthetical experience 208–12
   closure of inquiry 184
   inquiry 183–4, 213–14
   problematic situation 182–3, 212–13
literary work 166–8, 177
living-through approach 166–7, 170
logic(s)
   of critical explanation 93
   essence 30, 45, 49
   inquiry 21, 26
   judgment 48
López, F. 200
Lovejoy, A. O. 20, 28–30

Mars Exploration Rover 51, 55
McCuaig, L. 223
Mead, G. H. 5, 32, 39, 44–5, 47–8, 50
   Mind, Self, and Society 46
   Philosophy of the Present, The 44, 46
meaning 31–3, 88, 129, 138, 146
   acquisition of 40–3
   linguistic 30, 40–2, 47
   of text 13, 165, 167, 176
meaning-making 10, 13, 88–9, 93–4,
   99–100, 109, 113, 124–7, 132, 134,
   176
mental functioning 43
mind 5, 17–21, 23, 44, 75, 89, 104–7, 195
   acquisition of 40–3
   realm of 5, 41
mind-dependence 19–20, 29
mind-independence 18–19, 23
mind-object relation 23
moral
   beliefs 197
   deliberation 197, 201
   dilemma 198
   doubt-belief 200–2
   environment 201
   experience 194, 196–8
   problem 197–8
morality 14–15, 193–5
   reflective 194–6
   transactional perspective 202–4
Morris, C. W. 32–3

museum 12–13
   education 165, 169–71, 173, 176
   efferent aesthetic continuum in 168–70
   evocation 13, 171–6
   as exploration 165–77
   function of 168
   new museology movement 169
   Nobel Prize MLK exhibition 170–1
   objects 169–71, 176–7
   object work 13, 171, 177
   Rosenblatt's reader/text/literary work
      relationship and 170–6
   triadic relationship of visitor/exhibition
      object/object work 171–6
   visitor experience and exhibition
      168–70

National Oceanographic and Atmospheric
   Administration (NOAA) 51–2, 58,
   68. *See also Okeanos Explorer (OE)/*
   exploration system
national tests 8, 101–10
the new materialism 11
new museology movement 169
Nobel Prize MLK exhibition 170–1
   triadic relationship of visitor/exhibition
      object/object work 171–6
nonreflective experience 21–3, 151–2
Nussbaum, M. C. 84–5

objectivity 21–4, 30, 34–6, 47
objects 4, 32–3, 35, 49, 80, 138–41, 150–1,
   161–2, 168–71, 176–7, 182–3
Office of Ocean Exploration and Research
   (OER) 58, 70–1
Okeanos Explorer (OE)/exploration system
   6, 51
   activities of subsystems 59
   American Samoa expedition 56
   augmentators 56
   chat room 63–4, 67
   collaboration in activity 63, 65
   communication lines 62
   communication tools 63
   control center onboard 55
   control room 61–2
   dependent hierarchy 57–60, 68–72
   dive 54, 60–5
   durational-extensional transactions
      59–60

ECCs 53, 66–8
  existence in 58
  expedition 56, 58
  functional trans-actions 54, 60–5
  hierarchical command structure 58–9
  imaginary oppositions 68–70
  interactional analysis 59, 69–70
  for learning 67–8
  NOAA bridge deck officer 61
  overview 52–4
  public views 54–5
  purpose of 58
  remote scientists 61–2
  robotically mediated work system design 64–5
  ROV 52–3, 55, 63
  ROV NAV 62
  Seirios camera 52
  self-action view of 59
  shared goals in activities 65
  student activities in ECC 66–7
  transactional perspective of subsystems 57–60, 69–70
  traverse plan 54, 57
ontology, inference and 20–1
organism-environment interaction 27, 34–5
organism-environment transaction 1–3, 12, 40, 126, 223, 233 n.2
organism-in-environment-as-a-whole 40, 52, 69, 126
organism-sociocultural-environment behavioral transaction 43

pandemics 221
  educational setting 225–6
  public narratives and 222, 224–30
  transactional perspective on politics/people and 222–5
Pappas, G. 194, 197
past 48–50
  emergence of 45–8
PEA. *See* practical epistemology analysis (PEA)
Peirce, C. S. 21, 32, 198
  circle of doubt-belief 200–2
person-environment transaction 198–9
phenomenology 21
philosophical system
  containment paradigm 18–20
  cultivated naïve realism 23–4
  objectivity, phenomenology of 21–3
  paradigm 20–1
play
  aesthetic value 78–9, 84
  in Aristotle, and politics 79–80
  artistic value 78–9
  communal 81
  and democracy 82–3
  in democratic education 82–6
  and Dewey's pedagogy 75–6
  dramatic rehearsal 85
  as educational activity/category 79
  education and 78–80, 83, 85
  emotion for 76, 78–9, 83–5
  experience 76, 78
  experimental nature of 77
  Henricks's view 80–1
  Huizinga on 80
  imagination role in democratic education 83–5
  mutually integrated elements 77
  participation 85
  rules 80
  social intelligence and 83
  and social-political life 79–82
  sound 77–8
  and transaction 75–86
  as transactional activity/category 76–9, 81, 83, 85–6
  work and 76
play-communitas combinations 81
playful communitas 81
poem 13
poignant aesthetical experience 15, 207–18
policy reform 7, 14, 99
  teachers' functional coordination and habits 99–110
politics 16, 47, 71, 84, 200
  learning, concern for 217–18
  play and 79–82, 85
  transactional perspective on pandemics/people and 222–5
Pollard, V. 198
Pomponi, S. 51, 66, 73
postulate of immediate experience 22
practical epistemology analysis (PEA) 14, 89–90, 93, 95, 97, 129, 180, 187
  of aesthetic experiences 187–91

pragmatism 17, 21, 27–31, 33, 149–50, 200, 208–9
present 50
  emergence of 45–8
  functional 48–9
  specious 48–9
principle of continuity 115, 127, 196
problematic situation 8, 14, 22, 101–6, 121, 180–1, 189, 208–10, 213, 216–17
  awareness of 212–13
  fulfillment of 184
  into inquiry 183–4
  moral 193–4, 196–7, 205
  quality of 182–3
programming 13–14
project 138
public narrative 15, 221–2, 224, 226
  pandemics and 226–30
pure experience 5, 150–1, 210

qualitativeness 15, 181–3, 210, 214
quality 14, 41, 131–2, 162, 182, 210–12, 217
  durational-extensional 211
  of experience 75, 77–8
  immediate anoetic 5, 48, 210
  moral 196
  of problematic situation 182–3
  temporal 45–6, 48–9
quasi-object/subject 141
Quennerstedt, M. 223

radical empiricism 149, 151
reader 12–13, 165–6
  and text/literary work relationship 166–8
reading
  aesthetic 168, 171, 176
  efferent 167–8, 176
  literature 166
realism 4, 17, 28, 39
  cultivated naïve 23–4, 30
reality 4–5, 18, 21–4, 26–30, 35
realm of mind 5, 41
reflective inquiry 43
reflective morality 194–6
relations 187
remake activities 137, 142–5
Right to Freedom-Martin Luther King Jr, A 170
Rogoff, B. 89

Rømer, T. A. 83–4
Rosenblatt, L. M. 12–13, 165–6, 176
  evocation 167
  Literature as Exploration 165–6
  reader/text/literary work relationship 166–8
  on reading processes 166–8
  text 165–7, 176–7
  on writing processes 167
Rosen, M. 85
Rosenthal, S. 28–9

salutogenic approach 16, 221–3
science education 94–7, 101–3
seeing together 11, 17, 29, 35, 69, 138–9, 149–50
selective teaching traditions 96–8
self 8, 14, 47, 68, 75, 84, 195
self-action 2, 25, 59, 76
sense of coherence (SOC) construct 224
sensing together 11–12, 17, 150–2
  analysis of 153–61
  aspects of 151–2
  body-material-tool transactions 153, 156
  method 152–3
  objective creation 152, 156, 160–1
  pure experience 5, 150
  reaching out 151, 156–60
  taking data 151–2, 156–60
  Teaching and Learning Practical Embodied Knowledge 152
  "what to do next" question 156
Serres, M. 140–1, 146
signs 32–3, 35, 42–3
skepticism 18–20
skilled craftsmanship 185
Sleeper, R. 28–9
sloyd 11, 137, 149
  sensing together in (*see* sensing together)
social perspectives 43–5
stimulus-response 2
subjective minds 18, 23
surroundings 126, 199, 201, 224

tacit knowledge 149
tactile experience 151–2
Taylor, D. M. 227
teachers 7–9, 100–1
  beliefs 99–100

creation of new 101
functional coordination 101–10
intelligent/artistic habit 101
meaning-making 100
moves model 95–6
and national tests in science education 101–10
policy reforms and functional coordination of 101–10
re-learning transactions 8–9
sensing together technique (*see* sensing together)
teaching 87–8
   didactical research problems 90–8
   functional coordination in 101
   literature 166, 168
   PEA of 89–90
   selective teaching traditions 96–8
   self 8
   transactional methodological framework 88–9
telepresence-enabled ocean exploration 52
temporal quality 46, 49
temporal sequence 46, 48–50
text 165–6, 176
   evocation of 167
   and reader/literary work relationship 166–8
theory of inquiry 149–50
Tiles, J. E. 28–9
toddlers 9, 94, 112, 114–16, 120–1
Tomasello, M. 5, 43–4
Toulmin, S. 10
   argumentation 91–2
transactant 11, 137–40
   in educational research 146–8
   in learning activities 142–6
   remake activities 137, 142–5
transaction 2, 4, 6, 10–11, 13, 39–50, 69–70, 111
   crafting activity as 138–9
   definition 2–3, 12, 138
   on ethics and morals 193–205
   existence and experience relationship in 30
   in handicraft education 149–63
   human-organism-sociocultural-environmental 40, 44–5, 47
   imagination and 83–4

integration 10
interaction and 25–9
learning analysis in computer programming 179–92
learning and physical encounters 112–22
learning, DA of facilitation of 125–9
meaning 88
morality 195–6, 200–4
museum as exploration 165–77
museum visitor/exhibition object/object work 171–6
Okeanos exploration system 57–60, 69–70
organism-environment 1–3, 12, 40, 126, 223, 233 n.2
organism-sociocultural-environment behavioral 43
on pandemic, politics, and people 222–5
person-environment 198–9
in philosophy and life 17–37
play and 75–86
reader/text/literary work relationship 166–8
self-action *vs.* 25
teaching/learning processes, methodologies and 87–98
theory of knowledge 150–1
without hedges 29–34
trans-actor 11

undergoing 12, 117, 126, 128, 179–80
Usborne, E. 227

video observation 149, 151

walking rhythm 223–4
weltanschauung 26
what/how continuity 35–6
Wilden, A. 57–8, 60
   dependent hierarchy 57–60, 68–70
   Extinction Rule 58
   imaginary oppositions 68–70
   System and Structure 60
Wittgenstein, L. 10, 41–3, 87–9, 129, 187, 191
work and play 76
Working on Mars (Clancey) 5, 51

www.ingramcontent.com/pod-product-compliance
Lightning Source LLC
Chambersburg PA
CBHW062126300426
44115CB00012BA/1828